THE HOUSE-HACKING STRATEGY

THE
HOUSE
HACKING
STRATEGY

*How to Use Your Home
to Achieve Financial Freedom*

CRAIG CURELOP

BiggerPockets®
PUBLISHING

DENVER, COLORADO

Praise for
THE HOUSE-HACKING STRATEGY

"House hacking is a real estate strategy that every investor should know, especially those who want to become financially free as early as possible. If I had known about house hacking when I was getting started, I could have jump started my financial trajectory faster."

—Joe Fairless, Co-founder of Ashcroft Capital and co-host of *The Best Real Estate Investing Advice Ever* Podcast

"House hacking has the power to forever change your financial position in life, and this book is your roadmap to getting there."

—Brandon Turner, #1 bestselling author of *The Book on Rental Property Investing*

"House hacking is simply the best tool available to middle-class Americans that want to drastically improve their financial futures. Craig just wrote THE book on this subject. If you purchase a house-hack by applying this book's principles, you have an extraordinary probability of becoming a millionaire within the next ten years. Maybe five."

—Scott Trench, CEO of BiggerPockets.com and bestselling author of *Set for Life*

"There are many ways to make money in real estate, but one of the most simple and most profitable is often overlooked. Whether you're someone who wants nothing to do with real estate, someone who has been investing for decades, or are anywhere in between, house hacking is an opportunity for you to get paid to own your home! In *The House-Hacking Strategy*, Craig guides you through the journey of your first (or next) house hack in a way that anyone can understand and profitably put into practice. If you're wondering if this book is for you, it is."

—J Scott, Co-host of *The BiggerPockets Business Podcast* and bestselling author of *The Book on Flipping Houses*

"House hacking is the perfect first leap toward real estate success, and this book is the one-stop guide to all things house hacking. With pages of practical tips and actionable advice, Craig makes it easy to learn how to eliminate that pesky housing expense and use those savings to thrive early in life."

—Mindy Jensen, co-host of *The BiggerPockets Money Podcast* and author of *How to Sell Your Home*

The House-Hacking Strategy:
How to Use Your Home to Achieve Financial Freedom
Craig Curelop

Published by BiggerPockets Publishing LLC, Denver, CO
Copyright © 2019 by Craig Curelop
All Rights Reserved.

Publisher's Cataloging-in-Publication Data
Names: Curelop, Craig, author.
Title: The House-hacking strategy : how to use your home to achieve financial freedom / by Craig Curelop.
Description: Denver, CO: BiggerPockets Publishing, 2019.
Identifiers: LCCN 2019942884 | 978-1-947200-30-2 (Hardcover) | 978-1-947200-15-9 (pbk.) | 978-1-947200-16-6 (ebook)
Subjects: LCSH Real estate investment. | Home ownership. | Rental housing. | House buying. | Personal finance. | BISAC BUSINESS & ECONOMICS / Real Estate / General
Classification: LCC HD1382.5 .C88 2019 | DDC 332.63/24--dc23

Published in the United States of America
Printed on recycled paper
10 9 8 7 6 5 4 3 2 1

MIX
Paper from
responsible sources
FSC   FSC® C008955
www.fsc.org

Dedication

Nine years prior to writing this book, my grandfather passed away. I gave a eulogy at his funeral, which was my first public-speaking endeavor at age eighteen. After the speech, my grandmother, with her 4'1" stature and Armenian accent, thought it was so good that she repeatedly told me that I should become a writer. At the time, many of us laughed at this disillusioned woman. If you had known my writing abilities at that time, you would have laughed too.

I dedicate this book to the woman who helped raise me, to the woman who saw something in me that no one else did, to my Grammy Silvia (Silvia Ohanesian). I love you!

TABLE OF CONTENTS

Foreword..12

Introduction..16
    Why Am I Writing This Book?.....................16
    What Is House Hacking? 17
    Meet the Author: Craig Curelop 18
    What to Expect from This Book 21

CHAPTER 1 | THE POWER OF HOUSE HACKING 23
    America's Biggest Misconception 23
    Why Is House Hacking Powerful?................25
    The Drawbacks of House Hacking...............33
    Should You House Hack?.......................38
    Case Study | Ashley Massis 39

CHAPTER 2 | THE BASICS 42
    Starting the Journey 42
    Getting Your Spouse on Board.................48
    Renting vs. Home Buying vs. House Hacking.....49
    Typical House-Hacking Returns 53
    House-Hacking Strategies.....................56
    Case Study | Jeff White 59

CHAPTER 3 | WHERE TO HOUSE HACK 63
    Property Types 64
    Pick a Neighborhood 68
    Making the Decision..........................77
    Case Study | Zach Gwin.....................79

CHAPTER 4 | ASSEMBLING YOUR TEAM 82
Myth of Team Assembly..83
Lender...86
Finding Your Lender 94
Real Estate Agent 97
Finding an Agent 98
Contractors 101
Case Study | Laura Hines 104

CHAPTER 5 | FINANCING 107
Conventional Loan 108
FHA Loan 108
203k Loan...110
United States Department of Agriculture (USDA) Loan............111
Veterans Affairs (VA) Loan......................................113
HomeReady 114
Home Possible...115
Home Equity Line of Credit (HELOC)............................117
Private Capital 118
Hard Money Loans 118
Portfolio Lending 119
Seller Financing...120
Partnering 120
Case Study | Joe Sadusky 122

CHAPTER 6 | HOW TO FIND DEALS 125
The Multiple Listing Service (MLS)..............................126
Driving for Dollars 128
Direct Mail Marketing 129
BiggerPockets Marketplace 131
Craigslist...131
Wholesalers...132
Friends and Family 133
Case Study | Travis Wylie 134

CHAPTER 7 | ANALYZING DEALS 138
Deal Metrics...139
Tiers of House Hacking 149
Analysis for When You Move Out..........................151
Case Study | Zac Burk 152

CHAPTER 8 | MAKING THE OFFER AND GOING UNDER CONTRACT 155
Purchase Price..156
Closing Date..157
Earnest Money 157
Contingency...158
Closing Costs...159
Fixtures/Appliances 159
Other Items 160
First Actions...161
Due Diligence...161
Inspection 162
Appraisal...163
Case Study | Tyler Blackwell 164

CHAPTER 9 | MARKETING THE PROPERTY 168
Fair Housing Laws.......................................168
Advertising the Property................................172
Marketing Long-Term Rentals.............................172
Where to Advertise Long-Term Rentals 178
Where to Advertise Short-Term Rentals...................182
Tracking Your Results...................................184
Short-Term Rentals: What to Advertise...................184
Creating the Short-Term Rental Listing..................184
Case Study | Rick Albert 190

CHAPTER 10 | SCREENING TENANTS/ROOMMATES 193
Characteristics of a Great Tenant 194
What Is Tenant Screening? 197
Pre-screening 198
Showing the Property 210
10 Most Commonly Asked Questions by Tenants 214
What if You Can't Answer the Question? 218
Case Study | Brett Fink 219

CHAPTER 11 | TENANT DUE DILIGENCE.................. 223
Other Ways to Screen Tenants................................ 234
Denying a Tenant 235
Accepting a Tenant and Next Steps........................... 236
Case Study | Alexandra Hughes 238

CHAPTER 12 | MANAGING THE HOUSE HACK 241
Being a Landlord... 242
Being a Roommate/Neighbor................................ 245
Managing Finances....................................... 246
Case Study | Matt Drouin 252

CHAPTER 13 | FREQUENTLY ASKED QUESTIONS 256
Case Study | David Thompson................................ 263

CHAPTER 14 | CONCLUSION: DO IT AGAIN 267

Acknowledgements 280

FOREWORD

One moment can completely change the course of history.

Penicillin was discovered because a scientist accidentally left out a Petri dish infected with bacteria, and then discovered that the mold that grew seemed to fight the bacteria.

World War I started because of an assassination attempt that only succeeded because the driver of the target's caravan took a wrong turn.

The microwave was invented after an engineer melted a chocolate bar in his pocket while standing too close to radar equipment.

But moments are not only important for the fate of health, wars, and popcorn; one moment can forever alter the direction of a person's life.

Life typically continues along a fairly straightforward path, until one moment causes everything to change. Maybe it's internal, or perhaps external, but these moments exist for each and every person. It's a ripple effect that spreads rapidly, and influences every action and reaction that proceeds that moment. That positive result on the pregnancy test. That pink slip delivered by the boss. That phone call from your doctor with the test results. That acceptance letter into a top college. Moments rock your world, and they redirect your path. Some positive, some negative. Some obvious, some subtle. Some cause a 180-degree turn and others just a one-degree alteration. In short, our lives can be transformed in moments.

In September 2008, I had one of those moments when I was handed $650 in crumpled small bills.

I stared down at the money and something clicked in my head. Something that changed how I thought about money, wealth, real estate, freedom, and my family's future. Something that eventually led to the very moment you find yourself in now, reading this book.

Just a few months prior to that moment, I was, for lack of a better term, homeless. Not in the true sense of the word, but in the "22-year-old-just-sold-my-first-house-and-now-I'm-living-with-my-in-laws" sense. I preferred to no longer share space with my in-laws, so I set out to find my next home. After several months of searching, my wife and I found a house . . . err, more accurately, we found TWO houses.

The property consisted of two single-family homes crammed tightly onto one small lot in a small town's blue collar neighborhood in Washington. The house on the front half of the lot had two small bedrooms, a kitchen without a single appliance, and a bathroom that looked like it had been designed by the mind of Stephen King. The house on the back of the property was the worse of the two houses, with just one bedroom, one bathroom, and no shower. Not afraid to get our hands a little dirty, we made the decision to purchase this duplex and move into that small, 450-square-foot home on the back of the property. After we made a small down payment and spent three weeks painting and making other cosmetic repairs, we moved into the larger home where we spent a few more weeks completing the repairs. Then, with next to zero knowledge about how to be a landlord, we rented out the front house to two college students.

That was when the *moment* happened to me that would forever change my direction.

You see, that was the day those tenants moved in and walked over to hand me that crumpled envelope with $650 nestled inside. It was at that moment when I realized my entire loan payment on the property (including taxes and insurance) was only $620, per month.

$650 in rent. $620 to live there.

Something clicked.

I realized the startling truth: I was getting paid to live for free.

Sure, I still had to pay the electricity, water, and garbage bills. I might need to fix a few things when they break. I had to be a landlord. But this moment forever changed my life because it was when I realized the power of cash flow. The power of living for free. The power of no longer living paycheck to paycheck. I realized that as long as I could effectively manage the tenant in this home, I could live cheaper than all of my friends, enabling me to take some risks while creating my own destiny. I realized the power of freedom, hope, and opportunity.

I immediately quit my job and began flipping houses—a career I never could have started if I had been strapped for cash. However, I was able to do what I loved, verses what I needed to do. I could be intentional about my life.

I began telling others about my purchase (both online and in the real world), and I realized other people were doing the same thing. Individuals and families; rich and poor; and young and old were all using this same strategy to live cheaper, better lives across the world. They were building a foundation for financial independence. Some, like me, bought small multifamily properties and rented out the other units. Some bought single-family houses and rented out extra bedrooms. Some rented their extra space out short term like a hotel through websites such as www.Airbnb.com. But what all these people had in common was their ability to combine the wealth-building power of real estate investing with the need (and desire) of home ownership.

I realized that this strategy might be the best way to build a foundation for financial freedom. I labeled this strategy "house hacking" and I began to preach its merits to anyone who would listen. I spoke about house hacking on podcasts, on webinars, in books, in blog posts, and on stages across the country. And one of those who heard me was Craig Curelop.

Craig was a young and eager financial whiz living in San Francisco who listened religiously to *The BiggerPockets Podcast* that I host weekly. When a position became available for a financial analyst at BiggerPockets headquarters in Denver, Craig jumped at the opportunity. I immediately knew there was something different about Craig. Outside of his obvious intelligence with all things financial, he also had the fire in his belly that marks those destined for greatness. We couldn't hire Craig fast enough; and he was soon packing his bags and moving to Denver—helping to grow what would become the largest real estate investing platform on the planet, BiggerPockets. Craig quickly proved himself as more than just a financial analyst, but as someone we could rely on in many aspects of the business.

Most impressively, Craig didn't just learn . . . he did. Michael Jordan said, "Some people want it to happen. Some wish it would happen. And others make it happen." In the world of financial independence and wealth creation, there are, sadly, many in the first two groups, but very few in that third group. Craig is one of these few individuals who is always raising the standard. Craig immediately used the power of house hacking to buy a home and reduce his own expenses dramatically while living in one of the more expensive cities in America. In turn, he gained extra money to pay off debt, enjoy evenings with friends, and save for future investments. In other words, Craig didn't just listen to good advice, he followed it—and began to reap the rewards. He built a solid foundation, and he inspired many more to do the same. Since then, Craig has become a trusted colleague, real estate investor, friend, and advisor to me and many others. He is the real deal, and I'm excited for the impact that he is about to make on the world with the release of this book.

This book is filled with detailed instruction, passionate lessons, money-saving tips, little-known strategies, advice on mistakes to avoid, and concrete information that could revolutionize your life. You will learn not only the power of house hacking, but exactly how to pull it off—no matter what situation you find yourself in today. I have come a long way since I was that 22-year-old kid with his decrepit duplex. But surprising to many, I still house hack today, enabling me to live in a luxury multi-million-dollar home on the island Maui. (Yes, you can house hack anywhere, with any price range, and at any stage of life!) To put it simply, house hacking can work for you.

House hacking has the power to forever change your financial position in life, and this book is your road map to getting there.

Enjoy the ride!

Your friend,
Brandon Turner

INTRODUCTION

Why Am I Writing This Book?

Let's talk about the largest investment that the average middle-class American makes during their lifetime. Their house. Whether it be the first, second, or third home purchase, the down payments for these properties will be some of the largest cash outlays that they will experience. The typical strategy is to go to the bank, see what you can afford, purchase the largest possible house and live there for thirty or more years. The problem with this is that by buying the most expensive home, they are disposing of most of their investable cash in a down payment and then losing much of their monthly cash flow in mortgage payments. This limits their ability to save, and they get trapped. Trapped in the rat race. Trapped in a job that they hate for eight hours a day, five days a week, fifty weeks of the year to afford the house that they don't have the time to enjoy.

Why do people do this? It's not intentional. It's just "the way life works." Or at least that is what society tells us. What if there was another way? What if you could live in that same house, but instead of paying thousands of dollars a month, you *make* thousands of dollars a month? What if instead of working for forty years, you build enough wealth to escape the rat race and retire in five or ten years? You can enjoy your best years rather than give them away to a fat cat you don't even like working for. You can do what you want, where you want, when you want, and with whom you want.

That is why I am writing this book. I want to persuade you to abandon the long-held belief that buying a nice home in a nice neighborhood that maximizes the limits of your purchasing power is a smart investment. Instead, I will aim to convince you to turn your home into an investment that substantially reduces your living expenses, puts cash into your pocket on a monthly basis, and gives you the opportunity to escape the rat race in five to ten years rather than thirty to forty years. This book is designed for the American worker with a full-time job as his/her main source of income while starting to invest their extra money on the side. Through this strategy, you will have the ability to build massive amounts of wealth, attain financial independence, and live the life of your dreams. You do not need to worry about showing up to an office, arbitrary deadlines, or sitting in traffic to and from work.

Not only will this strategy allow you to build wealth at an outstanding rate, but it will also give you the confidence to advance much further as a real estate investor. You need a lot of money and experience with traditional real estate investing, making the barriers extremely high for newcomers. However, my strategy is different. Anyone can do it. You do not need absurd amounts of money (though you do need some), and zero experience is required.

So, what is this strategy? What is it that allows you to build hundreds of thousands of dollars of wealth, grow your confidence as a real estate investor, and gives you the opportunity to retire from wage work in just a few years?

If you read the title, you have probably already guessed it: house hacking! This book is going to show you the power of house hacking. It will challenge you to live on the upper limits of your comfort zone, and it gives you all the tools you need to go out and execute a house hack with the highest probability of success.

I wrote this book so that you have a full understanding of how you can take the first (or next) large step to take control of your life, break free from the norm, and live the life you were meant to live. Before we get into all the details though, let's define house hacking.

What Is House Hacking?

What the heck is house hacking anyway? In short, house hacking is the single most powerful way to build wealth. There is little luck involved and anyone can do it. The idea is that you buy a piece of residential real estate (one to four units), and you live in one unit while renting out the remaining unit(s). The rental income partially (or fully) covers your mortgage so you can live cheaply (or for free) while building equity in the property as the loan gets paid down, and the property value appreciates over time.

You will likely be obtaining an owner-occupied loan with a house hack. This means that you will be required to live in the home for a year. However, you will likely have saved enough money from your first house hack investment to do another hack after you complete your year requirement. Watch the snowball begin to form now that you have an investment property and your second house hack in the works. Repeat this process for three to four years and you have a high probability of achieving financial freedom in five to ten years.

Throughout this book, you will be able to see how you can build hundreds of thousands of dollars of wealth over the course of five to ten years as you gain experience with real estate investing, all with less time expensed than your regular wage-paying job.

Anyone can successfully execute this house-hacking strategy, but this book is not for everyone. It is for those who are willing to read with an open mind and slightly change the way they live to amass significant amounts of wealth. As I describe later, there is a spectrum on just how aggressively you can pursue a house hack. On one end, there is a strategy where your living situation changes minimally, but the financial benefits will also be minimal when comparing with the more aggressive end of the spectrum. My goal is to push you further along the spectrum so that you can experience the best possible financial outcome while still living a comfortable life.

Meet the Author: Craig Curelop

I graduated from Northeastern University in Boston, Massachusetts with a finance degree in 2015. I pursued my dreams of being a Silicon Valley venture capitalist and was "living the dream." I had a nice apartment just a few blocks from Oracle Park (formerly known as AT&T Park) where the San Francisco Giants play and worked in downtown Palo Alto, California.

After about twelve months into my stint as a venture capitalist, I concluded that I absolutely hated it. There was no way I could spend the next forty years or more doing this job. I looked at the people around me, and they seemed content with their day jobs. Did I want to be like them, living the same life that I was then, but just a few feet down the hall? Surely, not! There had to be a better way.

Enter the concept of financial independence, real estate investing, and BiggerPockets. The concept of financial independence can be lost on some people. Growing up in a middle-class family, it was lost on me. That was until I read *Rich Dad Poor Dad* by Robert Kiyosaki and Sharon Lechter. In that book, I learned the secret that separates the rich from the middle class: The middle class tend to exchange time for money by working salaried jobs and spending almost everything they make on their living expenses. The rich, on the other hand, focus on building wealth. They save and invest their money in assets that provide a passive stream of income. Once the income stream from these assets cover their expenses, they can quit wage work and do whatever it is they want with their lives. This is financial independence!

Let me give you an example of what this looks like. Oscar has been working a salaried job for ten years now. By saving and investing much of his extra income into real estate, he now has ten properties that pay him a total of $5,000 per month or $60,000 per year. Oscar is confident that he can spend less than $60,000 per year and is now able to quit his salaried job and do whatever he likes: travel, spend more time with family and friends, start a business, volunteer, or anything else he desires.

Real estate is not the only asset that can provide you with passive income. Stocks, bonds, index funds, and businesses are a few others. My favorite—as you might have guessed—is real estate investing. The idea of owning a tangible piece of property that gives me a monthly paycheck, appreciates overtime, and allows me to have total control fascinates me.

Though I knew I wanted to invest in real estate, I had no idea how to begin. Similar to almost anything else, the first step is the educational phase. I read books on real estate, listened to podcasts, watched webinars, and soaked up as much information as possible. That was when I discovered what the most logical first step to real estate investing was—what this book is all about—house hacking.

I thought of the quote by well-known businessman Jim Rohn: "You are the average of the five people you spend the most time with." I realized that I was in the wrong place and needed to get out. After six months of intense learning, I saw a job posting for a financial analyst at BiggerPockets. On a whim, I applied for the job and was lucky enough to receive an offer.

In April 2017, I made the move. I quit my job in Silicon Valley and moved to Denver, Colorado. I was ready to get started and buy my first house hack. I had a laundry list of things to do when I arrived in Denver: Start a new job, buy a car (to Uber), find a lender, find a real estate agent, and finally find a house-hack property.

I closed on my first house hack only a few months later, a newly renovated duplex just north of City Park, Denver's largest park. The duplex had two units, each with one bedroom/one bathroom. The selling price was $385,000 and I purchased it with a 3.5 percent FHA loan and $17,000 down. I lived in the first floor unit and rented out the top unit. Despite living in the less desirable unit, I was still unable to live for free with cash flow from my rental unit. Real estate prices in Denver were just too high!

So, what did I do? I took what I could get, grabbed a box of Twinkies, and started watching *Friends* reruns.

Just kidding! Of course, that's not what I did. I would not be writing this book if that's what I had done. I started thinking to myself, "How can I make this property work? How can I live for free?"

I had an answer. I decided to list my bedroom on Airbnb (and throughout this book I will reference Airbnb because that's what I have used, but you can research and utilize any of the home sharing/vacation rental websites out there). Since I would no longer be able to sleep in my room, I converted my living room into a quasi-bedroom by putting up a cardboard room divider and a curtain. I put a futon behind the curtain and that is where I lived for a year. Sounds horrible, right?

Surprisingly, I enjoyed it. Not only was I able to make an extra $500-$700 per month while also living for free, but I was also able to satisfy my travel bug by meeting people from all around the world. I had guests from Australia, Poland, Portugal, Brazil, and a number of destinations throughout the United States. In fact, I am still in touch with a few of my guests today (including one that I kind of dated for a few months).

After a year of living behind the curtain, I decided that enough was enough. I had saved enough money to purchase my second house hack. This time, it was a five-bedroom/two-bathroom single-family residence in Thornton, Colorado, just ten miles north of my office in Denver. I live in one bedroom (an actual bedroom with real walls, windows, a door, and a closet) while renting out the other four bedrooms. The rent from the four bedrooms exceeds my mortgage payment by over $1,000, and I still live for free.

I now have two properties: the duplex that is rented out and makes $500–$700 per month after expenses, and the single-family residence that I currently live in that makes $700–$1,000 a month. Given that my living expenses are so low, I am almost financially independent. To clarify:

Property 1: $700 per month

Property 2: $1,000 per month

Total monthly real estate income:
$700 + $1,000 = $1,700 per month

What do I do for fun? I am a lot like any other twenty-something in Colorado. I hang out with friends, play basketball, snowboard, rock climb, exercise, bike, and of course learn about real estate and personal finance.

What to Expect from This Book

Now that you know more about me, let me tell you more about this book. Or better yet, let me tell you what this book is not about. This book is not going to give you financial independence. It is not going to contact real estate agents and lenders, or analyze properties for you. And it is certainly not going to provide offers, find tenants, and manage the house hack for you.

What it will do is tell you exactly *how* to do all these things. It will show you the way, but it will not force you to act: That is on you! You can lead a horse to water, but you can't make it drink.

This book is a one-stop shop for everything you need to know about house hacking. Little of this content is brand new information, as much of it can be found on the BiggerPockets forums, blogs, podcasts, and webinars. But who has that much time? I understand that you probably don't have the time, but I do. I have taken all of that information and rolled it up into one place so that you don't have to search endlessly for house-hacking tips.

I am a perpetual student of house hacking and real estate investing. I frequently meet with fellow house hackers and learn from their experiences. And you already know that I walk the walk and house hack myself. This book distills all of the information that I have garnered, and it puts it into just a couple of hours of reading.

I will crunch some numbers and show you the power behind house hacking. I will introduce a new concept called net worth return on investment (NWROI), a percentage that represents your total net worth in relation to your initial investment. I will show you the multitude of ways that you can house hack. You will learn how to find and analyze properties that you can house hack. How to assemble the best possible team. How to get over the common obstacles and roadblocks. How to manage the property. How to know what work you should do yourself versus what should be hired out. I will teach you all of these, and much more!

Do you remember in high school or college when the instructor presented a problem that COULD only be solved in one way? That is one of academia's biggest problems. In reality, problems can rarely only be solved one way. There are multitudes of ways to solve a problem, and at the end of each chapter in this book, I will have a case study of a fellow house hacker, which will show different methods used to solve house-hacking problems. I hope that you can take the information from the chapters and see how it applies in real life scenarios.

By the end of the book, you should have all the knowledge required to house hack. The only thing that will be standing between you and your first house hack is action. Starting something is often the hardest part, especially when you know nothing about that subject. That is where I come in with this book designed to give you the tools you need to feel confident about taking on your first house hack.

I will give you actionable steps at the end of each chapter so that no matter where you are in your house-hacking journey, you can find your place in this book and you can look at the next actionable step you can take to continue moving forward. The actionable step of this chapter? Turn the page!

CHAPTER 1

THE POWER OF HOUSE HACKING

America's Biggest Misconception

What is your largest expense? The majority of the United States population would not hesitate to reply with "housing." Whether you are paying rent or paying down a mortgage alongside with taxes, insurance, maintenance, and all the other expenses associated with owning a home, your house is likely what you spend most of your money on each month.

If you ask these same people what they feel is their largest "asset," I would bet that you would get the same answer, "my house." If you have read *Rich Dad Poor Dad,* you know that our definition of "asset" is much different than the conventional definition. The conventional definition is something like "property owned by a person or company, regarded as having value and available to meet debts, commitments, or legacies."

My definition, taken from Robert Kiyosaki and Sharon Lechter's, *Rich Dad Poor Dad,* is much simpler. An asset is something that puts money in your pocket every month. A liability takes money from you every month. For example, when you own a rental property, stocks, or bonds you will get paid rental income, a dividend, or interest each month. These are assets because you receive income from owning them. Buying a car, on the other hand, is a great example of a liability. You are making monthly payments on a vehicle that depreciates over time and costs money in terms of gas, insurance, and maintenance.

Arguably, the biggest misconception that most Americans have is that their home is their largest asset. When, in fact, it is their largest liability. However, there are some exceptions. A few of them are exemplified at the conclusion of each chapter. You will read fellow house hackers' stories in this book who have used strategies outlined here to turn what could be their largest liability into their largest asset.

They strategically designed their lifestyle so housing is not their largest expense. As a matter of fact, through the strategies I talk about in this book, they have completely eliminated housing as an expense and they make money from their living situations every single month. And yes, their lives look just like yours. From the outside, you would not think that they are any different because they have day jobs, errands to run, and families to care for.

Rather than talk about these people as a mysterious cult, let's get into an example. Meet my imaginary friend Steve. Sick of paying $800 a month in rent to some mystical landlord, Steve decided to take action. He read *Set for Life: Dominate Life, Money, and the American Dream* by Scott Trench, and he found strategic ways to pinch his pennies until he could save enough money for a down payment on a duplex. After 18 months, he had saved $20,000! He found a duplex in an up-and-coming area of a major U.S. city for $350,000. The duplex was side-by-side units, each with two bedrooms and one bathroom.

With the money he saved, he put down a 3.5 percent or $12,250; he found a tenant to occupy the second unit, and a friend to occupy the second bedroom. His monthly payment to the bank was $2,000 and he was collecting $3,000 in total rent. The total rent fully satisfied his mortgage, and he was still making $1,000 over the mortgage. Now, not only has he eliminated his living expense, he is *making* money every single month on his living situation. How many people can say that?

In case you're like me and got lost in all of those numbers, here is a recap:

Purchase price: $350,000

Down payment: $12,250

Monthly rent: $3,000

Monthly mortgage payment: $2,000

Money in Steve's pocket every month: $1,000

Money saved from not paying rent: $800

Total money in Steve's pocket every month: $1,800

This is all happening while the property is appreciating and he is paying down his mortgage. This strategy is what BiggerPockets has coined house hacking. Sound familiar from the introduction? House hacking comes in all shapes and sizes. You can take Steve's strategy, which is the most popular, by purchasing a duplex while occupying one unit and renting out the other one. You could also purchase a property with a mother-in-law suite and rent that out as a short-term rental—whatever is best for your situation.

House hacking is certainly the easiest for young, single individuals who do not have families, are flexible, and can move easily. However, this is not to say that middle-aged or older people with a family can't house hack. They absolutely can! It's just that they may find it more difficult, and will likely be restrained to the "short-term rental" strategy if they do not want to significantly change their lifestyles. I'll get into more details on the different strategies later. Just trust me when I say that anyone can do it!

So now you should be clear on the concept of house hacking. To summarize, it is when you purchase a one- to four-unit property, live in one part, and rent out the others so that the rent from your tenants is fully covering your mortgage. Your largest expense (housing) is likely eliminated or drastically reduced, allowing you to save more money and propel yourself toward financial independence.

Why Is House Hacking Powerful?

Are you excited about the idea of building extreme amounts of wealth; and about not having to spend five days a week, fifty weeks a year, for thirty to forty years stuck inside a cubicle? Rather than waiting for the weekend or your next vacation, your entire life will feel like a weekend or vacation. Once you escape that 9–5 grind, your life opens up. You can travel, spend time with family, start a business, volunteer . . . the possibilities are endless! We call this escaping from the rat race.

If you are excited about breaking free from the rat race, house hacking is the most powerful way to make this a reality. I have yet to hear of a strategy that provides better returns without the help of winning the lotto, receiving an inheritance, or of course the usual 9–5 grind. If you can challenge this assertion after you have fully read this book, please email me at craig@biggerpockets.com.

One of the biggest benefits of real estate is the ability to use leverage otherwise known as debt. Let me explain. Let's say that you are trying to move a 2,000-pound boulder to reach a pot of gold. You can try to push, pull, and jerk that boulder with your hands, but unless you are Hercules, that boulder is not going to budge. You need help. So, you get this long metal, crow-bar looking tool called a "lever." You shove the lever underneath the boulder. You push (or pull) on one end of the lever, which will help you move the boulder. The longer the lever, the more "leverage" you can gain, and the easier it will be to move the boulder and obtain your pot of gold.

Think of this "lever" as your mortgage, and your strength as your down payment. The longer the lever, the less energy you need to move that same boulder. The larger the mortgage (less of a down payment), the less money you will need to purchase that property.

Good riddance to the days where you can purchase a property with no down payment. We do not need another 2008 crash. From all of the networking that I have done over the years, the largest hurdle for most people who want to purchase a property is coming up with the 20 percent down payment.

What many people don't know is that the government likes to reward people who are buying homes where they intend to reside. How? Fannie Mae and Freddie Mac. These two government-owned operations purchase mortgages from banks, accept lower priced mortgages and require a smaller down payment from people who purchase a property with the intention of living there for at least one year.

As of this writing in 2019, there are several different loan products that adhere to these terms ranging from 1–10 percent down payments. The most common amongst house hackers seems to be the 3.5 percent Federal Housing Administration (FHA) loan. I will go into depth later about financing. For now, just know that rather than putting $50,000 down on a $250,000 property, you can put less than $10,000 down for that same property when you house hack. You are using a longer lever to move that boulder.

Not only does that lower down payment give you higher purchasing power, but it exponentially increases your return. With such a low initial investment, your return on that investment is much higher. I'll go into depth about the numbers and the returns you will receive later.

Cash Flow & Loan Paydown

Let's talk briefly on how mortgages work. A mortgage is just a fancy word for "loan on a property." An owner-occupied mortgage is that same loan, but requires you to live there for a more favorable price or terms. With house hacking, you are likely going to obtain an owner-occupied loan. For the purposes of this discussion, let's say that you are getting a 3.5 percent FHA loan.

If you purchase a property for $100,000, you will be responsible for putting $3,500 down in exchange for a $96,500 loan to be paid back monthly over the next thirty years. Assuming a 5.25 percent interest rate, the monthly payments would be $532.88 per month. Each monthly payment will be a combination of principal and interest. The principal is the actual balance of the loan the bank gives you—in this case $96,500. The interest payment is the amount that you are paying the bank for lending you money.

In the first month, the concentration of interest payment will be highest, and as you continue to pay down the mortgage every month, an increasing amount of that $532.88 payment will be applied toward the principal. Take a look at the amortization schedule below to see how each payment over the next twelve months is comprised.

Month	Beginning Principal	Payment	Principal Portion	Interest Portion	Ending Principal
1	$96,500.00	$532.88	$110.69	$422.19	$95,967.12
2	$95,967.12	$532.88	$111.17	$421.71	$95,855.95
3	$95,855.95	$532.88	$111.66	$421.22	$95,744.29
4	$95,744.29	$532.88	$112.15	$420.73	$95,632.14
5	$95,632.14	$532.88	$112.64	$420.24	$95,519.50
6	$95,519.50	$532.88	$113.13	$419.75	$95,406.37
7	$95,406.37	$532.88	$113.63	$419.25	$95,292.74
8	$95,292.74	$532.88	$114.12	$418.76	$95,178.62
9	$95,178.62	$532.88	$114.62	$418.26	$95,064.00
10	$95,064.00	$532.88	$115.12	$417.76	$94,948.88
11	$94,948.88	$532.88	$115.63	$417.25	$94,833.25
12	$94,833.25	$532.88	$116.13	$416.75	$94,717.12

Do you see how the interest portion of the payment decreased over time, but the amount applied to the principal increases? When you are paying down your principal, you are building equity in the property by paying back the balance of the loan.

The best part about house hacking is that you are not actually paying the loan: Your tenants are! Not only are you living for free, and maybe even cash flowing, you own more and more of your house each month.

Equity through Appreciation

Fortunately, paying down your loan is not the only way to build equity in your property. You can also do this through appreciation. There is natural appreciation and forced appreciation.

Real estate has essentially been around since the beginning of time. In fact, the word "landlord" comes from medieval times when there was a "lord of the land." Since I started tracking United States real estate values back to the early 1900s, the average growth rate for a property in the U.S. is about 6 percent. The differences are based on the location throughout the country, but we are going to use the U.S. average of 6 percent. By doing absolutely nothing, you are building equity in your property by 6 percent of its purchase price each year. This is natural appreciation.

Forced appreciation is when you do something to the property to improve the value. House flipping is a great example since house flippers buy distressed properties at great values, fix them up, and then sell them for a profit. Let's say a flipper purchases a property for $100,000. They put in $50,000 worth of repairs so the total all-in cost is $150,000. They turn around and sell the home to a buyer for $200,000. That $50,000 beyond the costs that the flipper paid can be seen as forced appreciation. To recap:

Purchase price: $100,000

Rehab: $50,000

Total cost: $150,000

Sales price: $200,000

Forced appreciation: $200,000 - $150,000 = $50,000

When you are house hacking, you do not need to redo the entire property. You can force appreciation by adding a bedroom or a bathroom, redoing the kitchen, or sometimes just changing the cabinets and painting.

Appreciation builds the most wealth through real estate investing. A 6 percent interest rate on a $100,000 property will net you $80,000 in appreciation over ten years whereas the property itself may only cash flow $100 per month or $12,000 over ten years.

Learn to Landlord

One of the caveats of using a low down payment loan is that you need to live in the property for at least one year. While this may seem like a hindrance, it is actually working out in your favor. As a house hacker, you are likely new to the real estate game. What better way to transition from tenant to landlord than to be a landlord that lives amongst your tenants?

By living in the property, you drastically reduce the probability that something will go unfixed for an extended amount of time. Your tenants, who you will either live with, or see frequently, will have no qualms telling you about a leaky faucet or an outlet that may not be working. You can then fix the problem or call someone to have it done for you when you go home rather than having to make a separate trip to your rental property.

Not only will you be one of the first to know if anything goes wrong with the property, you will also end up building a relationship with your tenant(s). If you are a nice person who tends to get along with most people, then this will work to your advantage. Your tenants will start to feel like you are friends, and more likely pay rent on time each and every month.

Tax Benefits

Anyone who talks about taxes who is not a certified public accountant (CPA) will always cover themselves by disclosing that they are not a CPA. I am no different. I am not a CPA, and I am not legally able to give tax advice. What follows is not tax advice; it is simply how I've used the tax code to my advantage when purchasing properties.

Buying a home is considered part of the American dream. Uncle Sam and the United States government love to see people buy property, and they reward them accordingly. When you purchase real estate (including house hacking), you can take full advantage of the tax code in three ways:

1. Tax write-offs
2. Depreciation
3. 1031 exchange or 2-of-the-last-5-year rule

When you are collecting rent on a property, you have started a business that generates income and has expenses. As a business, you are taxed on the bottom line. For example, if you generate $10,000 in rental income and have $8,000 in expenses, you will be taxed on the $2,000 difference. If you are in the 33 percent tax bracket, you will have to pay $660.

Rental income: $10,000

Expenses: $8,000

Net income: $10,000 - $8,000 = $2,000

Taxes paid: $2,000 × 33% = $660

If you are looking to save on taxes, the goal is to look for methods that can increase your expenses so that the bottom line number is reduced. I'm not saying go out and spend money on random things for your business that are not needed. If you earn $1 that is 67 cents after taxes, it is still better than spending the dollar, and having zero dollars in the end.

Instead, it is best to make sure you are recording each expense appropriately. There is an entire book dedicated to saving on taxes for real estate investors called *The Book on Tax Strategies for the Savvy Real Estate Investor* by Amanda Han and Matthew MacFarland. I highly recommend you check it out to see what you are able to write off so that you can reduce your tax liability as much as possible.

Let's talk about depreciation. It sounds bad, right? Who likes something that depreciates? After these next few paragraphs, you surely will!

As of this writing, the IRS requires the real estate investor to spread out the cost to purchase residential real estate over 27.5 years for residential buildings. The fancy word for this is "depreciation."

Depreciation is a non-cash expense, which means that it does not come out of your bank account like your mortgage payments, insurance, maintenance, and repairs. It only shows up when you are displaying your financial statements to your accountant and the IRS at the end of the year.

Yes, you read this correctly though I understand that it can be confusing. Although your property will likely "appreciate" in value over time, the government requires you to take a "depreciation" expense. This means that you have an added expense and a lower taxable number as described above.

Let's get back to our example of buying that $100,000 house. At the end of the year, before our depreciation expense, we have taxable income of $2,000. Now, we must include the depreciation expense. To do this, we remove the estimated value of the land and divide over 27.5 years. We will assume the land is worth $5,000 so dividing $95,000 ($100,000 - $5,000) by 27.5 gives us:

$($100,000 - $5,000) / 27.5 = $3,454$ *depreciation expense*

Now, we subtract this depreciation expense of $3,454 from our taxable income of $2,000.

$$2,000 - $3,454 = -$1,454$$

Whoa, so rather than showing the IRS that we earned money last year, to them, we actually lost money. Luckily, you are not going to be paying taxes on money that you lost. Instead, if you make under $150,000 (in 2018 tax code) in your normal W-2 or 1099 job, you will be able to offset your income by $1,454, which thereby reduces your overall tax liability.

Isn't depreciation a wonderful thing?

Tax write-offs and depreciation are two of the major tax benefits when it comes to buying and holding real estate investments. There are also tax benefits when you sell a property from the 1031 exchange and the 2-of-the-last-5-year rule.

The object of the 1031 exchange is to defer capital gains taxes upon the sale of your property. A capital gains tax is incurred when your property appreciates and you go to sell it. For example, we bought that property for $100,000. Over the course of ten years, let's say it appreciated to $150,000. You will be responsible to pay taxes on the net $50,000. Those taxes are called capital gains taxes.

Section 1031 of the tax code says that a real estate investor is allowed to sell a property, purchase another, larger property, and defer the capital gains taxes that were incurred on the sale until the investor sells the larger property. The caveat to a 1031 exchange is that the investor must identify a larger property within forty-five days and close on that property within 180 days of close. It is not forty-five days plus an additional 180. You have forty-five days to identify the new property, and then an additional 135 days to close, making the entire transaction 180 days.

Notice that I have been saying "defer" capital gains. Unfortunately, you will be responsible for paying these taxes eventually, or will you? If you decide to sell the larger property at any time for cash or any non-real estate investment, you will be responsible to pay the capital gains tax. However, if you continue to do 1031 exchanges or hold the property until your death, the capital gains expense gets wiped away.

There can be an entire book written on 1031 exchanges, but I digress.

Let's talk about the 2-of-the-last-5-year rule. This is another strategy many house hackers and other homeowners use when selling their property.

This part of the tax code says that if you live in a property for two of the last five years, you are able to sell the property without any capital gains tax up to $250,000 if you are single, or up to $500,000 if you are married.

If we purchase that property for $100,000 and decide to house hack, we are already required to live in it for one year. If we just live there for one more year, we could turn around and sell the property and owe no capital gains tax. Don't let the rule mislead you. It does not have to be two consecutive years. You can live in the property for one year, move out, and come back in three or four years to live in it for the last year. You can then sell with no capital gains tax owed. Not a bad deal, huh?

The Drawbacks of House Hacking

I am writing a book about house hacking, so I am going to obviously advocate for it—especially because the house hacks that I have completed have had a significant impact on my life. I want you to experience the same life changes. Like anything in this world, there are common objections to house hacking. I am going to touch on those objections, and explore how I overcame them.

1. More Work

House hacking is essentially a small business. While it is mostly passive, there are times when you need to do some work. For example, filling a vacancy, accommodating a maintenance request, or keeping track of rent, security deposits, etc. are all things that must be done as a landlord.

Not only is it more work on your day to day lives, but your taxes also become that much more difficult to complete. Rather than taking the W-2 you receive in January, you will also have to fill out a Schedule E (Form 1040) and remember to account for all expenses for the maximum tax savings.

Overcoming

Becoming a landlord sounds like a lot of work and stress. Who wants to be answering calls in the middle of the night when a toilet is clogged? Let me tell you something, I have a lot of friends who are landlords and not once have I heard of anyone having to deal with an incident at odd hours.

Most things can wait until the morning.

I am not going to deny that it is more work on you than renting. It absolutely is. Most of this work is up front or during the first few months of buying the property. Once you are settled with tenants renting your unit(s), you might find yourself working an additional three to five hours a month. That's only a small amount of time for a large payoff. The tasks you do for the house hack are hundreds of dollars per hour tasks.

2. Living with (or Next to) Others

There are many ways to house hack. You can purchase a single-family residence and have roommates/tenants. You can live in a duplex, triplex, or fourplex and rent out the other units. You can also purchase a single-family residence with a basement unit or auxiliary dwelling unit that you rent out short term. Either way, if you are living by yourself in a nice, one-bedroom apartment, it is going to be very difficult to go back and start living amongst a bunch of people. Naturally, you will lose some privacy. Even if you are not living in the same unit as your tenants, it is likely that you can no longer throw any large parties without first inviting (or asking) your neighbors.

Living with others can become an issue if you have a family. Do you want a complete stranger living in your house with your kids? I am a firm believer that most people in this world are nice. However, it just takes one jerk to sour the experience of house hacking for you. This might not be a risk you are willing to take.

Overcoming

If you are accustomed to living by yourself, living with others can be difficult. But try to look at this situation in a positive light. Living by yourself can be lonely. Why not make a few more friends? Now you have someone who can help clean. If you are house hacking while using a long-term rental strategy, you need to make sure to properly screen your tenants. You do this to not only confirm they will pay their rent on time, but also to make sure that they will be good roommates.

It makes sense to purchase a place with a basement unit that has a separate entrance, or a property that has an auxiliary dwelling unit if you really value your space. That way, you can rent out this space without ever running into your tenants. Both you and the tenants will appreciate this arrangement.

You can consider nontraditional options if you do decide that you want to pursue a short-term rental strategy, but do not have the ability to be separate from your tenants. I posted my bedroom on Airbnb and met friendly and interesting people. You will have a revolving door of strangers coming and going every few days. Maybe this sounds unappealing to you, but remember, the situation is temporary. A guest who bugs you will be gone in a few days. I really enjoyed having travelers stay with me as I learned about their lives and gave recommendations of what to do in my city.

3. Keeping a Professional Relationship
This tends to be more of a problem when house hacking a single-family home and renting by the room. There is a lot of ambiguity surrounding whether the people you live with are "tenants" or "roommates" when you do this method. In many cases, they start to feel like "roommates," but be careful of this. You do not want to get too close to your tenants because they might begin taking advantage of you. This has not happened to me, but I have heard stories of tenants asking to pay rent late, or not cleaning up around the house.

Overcoming
Remember that when you house hack, your tenants are tenants, and are NOT roommates. You can make them feel like roommates by getting along with them and being cordial, but be careful about getting too close.

My advice is to be friendly to your tenants in passing, but don't hang out with them too frequently outside of the property. This obviously does not apply if your tenants were your friends before you started house hacking. (In which case, you hope that they are good enough friends to always pay their rent.)

4. Live in a Crappy Investment Property
When you house hack, you are doing it primarily for the overall financial impact. For that reason, you will try to buy a relatively inexpensive space that you can charge the highest possible amount for—that is reasonable for the location and condition of the property. If you are buying an inexpensive property, it is likely a bit run down or in a less desirable area. Either way, you will be scaling back your lifestyle. This means moving out of the high-rise downtown and settling into a place that is much more modest.

Overcoming

To maximize your house-hacking cash flow, it is best to purchase a property that needs some work. Purchasing a property in a decent location that needs work is a great value-add opportunity. We call that "forced appreciation." It's forced because you are enhancing the value of the property yourself, verses just relying on market appreciation.

There is no requirement out there that says you need to purchase a dingy property. You can absolutely purchase that newly renovated property downtown, live in one unit, and rent the other. Your cash flow will likely be lower than if you purchased a dingy place, but it still will be significantly higher than if you rented. It's up to you how aggressive you want to be when purchasing the house hack.

5. What If the Market Tanks?

Typically, a house hack will be your first real estate investment. It's not easy parting with almost all of your savings and throwing it into a property. What if we see another Great Recession and the market tanks?

There's not much I can say about this. The market does what it wants. It goes up and down, and you just have to ride it out. If the market plummets the day after you close on your property, that is unfortunate for you. However, it doesn't mean that you cannot overcome these obstacles, which I will talk about shortly.

Overcoming

You need to make sure you will be okay when the tumultuous market goes up, when it goes down, and even when it stays the same. How do you do this? You prepare yourself by running the numbers.

You need to make sure that you can afford your place regardless of whether you are at zero percent or 100 percent vacancy. If not, you need to make sure that your rent (including a vacancy factor) covers your mortgage and lifestyle so that even if rents decline by 10–20 percent, you will be able to stay afloat.

6. A Lot of Money Down

When you compare purchasing a house hack to renting, you are spending a lot more money up front. When you are renting, you are typically responsible for first month's rent, last month's rent, and a security deposit. If you are living in a place where rent is $1,000 then you are spending

$3,000 in upfront costs.

When you house hack, you are going to need to put 3–5 percent down, pay a couple of thousand dollars in closing costs, and then spend even more money to fix up the property. You do want that "forced appreciation," right?

On a $300,000 house, you could be paying $15,000–$20,000 in just purchasing the property. Depending on the size of the rehab required, these costs can climb closer to $30,000. Again, while it's much cheaper than putting 25 percent down on a conventional investment property, it is still more of an up-front cost than renting.

Overcoming

When compared to renting, you still need to come up with a fairly large chunk of money. $20,000 is not pocket change. This is where you need to pinch your pennies to get there. In the end, there really is no better return on your investment than house hacking, without creating a full-time job for yourself.

When you purchase a property for $20,000, there is a high probability that you will be able to make that entire sum back in the first year just through the cash flow, loan paydown, and rent savings. That is a 100 percent return! And we are not even including appreciation, or the tax benefits that come with owning real estate. This is not spending money, this is investing money.

7. What If the Tenants Don't Pay?

This is absolutely a risk. You are relying on someone else to continuously give you money to make your investment work properly. Unfortunately, an individual is more likely to avoid paying you than a company would if you are investing in high dividend yielding stocks.

As a house hacker, these are all noteworthy risks. However, I know that I cannot leave you with such a negative outlook on house hacking.

Overcoming

There will certainly be a time when tenants won't pay their rent. But if you screen them correctly, these missed payments can be drastically reduced. It is a small price to pay given the overall return of house hacking.

To avoid late or missed payments, or having to track everyone down once a month, I highly recommend setting up a service where rent can be deducted automatically from their accounts. I use www.Cozy.co. It's a free service that allows you to post your lease terms on the site and link your tenants' bank accounts; it then automatically withdraws rent each month. Set it and forget it. No need to track down your tenants.

Should You House Hack?

Now you have the good, the bad, and the ugly of house hacking. All that's left is deciding if house hacking is right for you. Do you have what it takes to save for the initial down payment, become a part-time landlord, and scale back your lifestyle in order to increase your net worth by hundreds or thousands of dollars each month? You have to decide if the sacrifices now are worth the financial independence later.

If you decide to embark on this journey of house hacking toward financial independence, know that you will be doing things differently. People will often not understand, and will likely judge you for going against societal norms. What makes it even more awkward is that the people often judging and cautioning you about this lifestyle are not strangers. Instead, they are your best friends, family members, and mentors—people that you love and have been listening to your entire life. You must understand that they have not done the research that you have, they have not read this book, and they have not tested the strategy for themselves. You can hear their advice, but you do not need to listen. The house-hacking strategy has been tested many times, but is still far from mainstream. It might seem risky to your family; or crazy to your friends; but you will see that it all makes sense when you run the numbers. Numbers do not lie.

You are doing something differently, and different scares people. Especially those who care the most about you. The societal norm that much of America has been brainwashed to believe is to put away 10 percent into your retirement accounts, purchase a home with 20 percent down, finance a car, and live this cushy lifestyle that is supported by a 9–5 job they hate. They work this job five days a week, fifty weeks a year, and for forty to fifty years of their lives. Many people are content with this. Since you are reading this book, you are not. Life is too short to be stuck in a cubicle, behind a machine, or traveling to places where you do not want to go.

Rather than saving a paltry 10 percent, by house hacking and eliminating your largest expense, you will be able to save 50, 60, or even 70 percent to shorten your career from fifty years to only five to ten years.

If you want to be like everyone else, this book will have no use to you. However, if you want to live the life of your dreams—doing what you want, when you want, and with who you want—read on.

CASE STUDY
ASHLEY MASSIS

- **House-hacking strategy:** Rent by room and live-in flip
- **Age at first house hack:** 24
- **Location:** Charlotte, North Carolina
- **Net worth return on investment (NWROI):** 1,139%

Ashley Massis lives in Charlotte, North Carolina. She was first introduced to house hacking back in the mid-2000s when her father purchased a property in the town where she went to college. She lived in the house for free by collecting rent from her friends who lived in the house.

After graduating and then attending graduate school for three years, she abandoned the real estate life and moved to New York City. She worked in retail and started a blog called *New York Social Status*, which reviews the tastes, trends, and tunes in NYC.

After surviving the New York hustle for three years, Ashley knew that she wanted to get back into real estate. Ashley moved to Charlotte in 2013, where she purchased her first house hack. At the time of her purchase, she was a bartender while still writing for her blog part time. With her 2012 tax returns, she purchased a three-bedroom, two-bathroom house for $170,000 with a down payment of $9,000. The house was in good condition, but it needed a couple of modern updates. Within the first week of owning the property, and before she could even get started on the rehab, the house was struck by lightning (talk about bad luck). Thanks to that shock (pun intended), she realized that the wires were not grounded. As a result, the water heater was destroyed and much of the house needed to be rewired. Total lightning damages were approximately $6,000.

Moral of the story here? Always be sure to do your due diligence. The inspector that she had hired did not ensure that the wires were grounded. Even the best inspectors miss things. The best way to combat this problem is to fight for a home warranty on the property. A home warranty is when the seller promises to pay for any major repairs to the property during the first year of ownership. What is considered to be a major repair? That is for you to decide. I would recommend saying any repair that costs over $1,500 should be the responsibility of the seller for that first year.

Once the lightning mess was cleaned up, Ashley rented out the other parts of the house. She rented a room to a traveling nurse who was in Charlotte for four to five months, and Ashley also allowed her boyfriend (at the time) to move into the third bedroom. He lived there for about eight months before she kicked him out. During the time of occupancy, Ashley was getting $600 from both her roommate and boyfriend while her total mortgage payment was $1,200. After putting aside $250 per month in reserves, she was paying $250 per month to live in a house that was building equity through loan paydown and appreciation (both forced and natural). Prior to moving into the house hack, she was paying almost $1,300 in rent. That is $1,050 in monthly savings.

After eight months of saving money, living with roommates, and making cosmetic renovations to the house, she decided it was time to kick everyone out and begin the larger renovations. At 24 years old, she rehabbed the master bedroom and the entire kitchen, and took out a wall. She did this mostly by herself with some guidance from her father who was a general contractor in New York State. After about $45,000 of rehab costs (including the lightning damages), she was able to sell the house after two years (for tax purposes) for $305,000. Her net gain from appreciation alone was $135,000. Because she lived there for two of the past five years, she did not have to pay any taxes on the gain!

Let's put it all together. After putting $9,000 down, Ashley benefitted from $12,000 in annual cash flow, $67,500 in annual appreciation over the two years, and loan paydown of $23,000 annually since she made several extra payments with her cash flow.

NWROI: $12,000 + $67,500 + $23,000 = $102,500 / $9,000 = 1,139% return

After factoring in the three main wealth builders of house hacking, Ashley was generating a return of 1,139 percent! With additional tax savings, she was looking at well over a 1,200 percent return. Please tell me another investment that can make a similar return.

With the proceeds from the sale, Ashley was able to rinse and repeat. She purchased another house hack where she turned the garage into a master bedroom. Because of house hacking, she discovered her love for rehabbing homes while building wealth at the same time. Ashley got her general contractor's license and she, alongside her husband, are looking to graduate from house hacking and get into purchasing homes and subdividing the lots where possible.

WHY *"I house hack because I was most concerned with having that safety net. I grew up during the Great Recession and saw lots of people struggling to get by. There is no way I ever wanted to ever be in that position, and house hacking was the means to do so.*

Additionally, my true passion is for writing. I went to school for English, created my own blog, and it is something I really enjoy doing. As many of you know, becoming a writer is very difficult and even more difficult to make a wage doing so. With financial independence through house hacking and real estate investing I'm able to do that."

ACTION STEPS

❏ Read this book!
❏ Sign up for a BiggerPockets account (it's free!)

CHAPTER 2

THE BASICS

What happens to a large house built on a weak foundation? It may stand for a period of time. However, as you continue to build onto the house while it tries to withstand the elements, it crumbles into a state of dilapidation. In this chapter, I am going to lay the foundation for house hacking so you will be able to withstand whatever is thrown your way.

Starting the Journey

The first step toward financial independence through real estate investing is finding ways to earn more and spend less so that you can save up for that first house hack. You will see many of your friends spending close to half of their income on rent, buying (or leasing) new cars every few years, and frequently going out to fancy restaurants. After all, they have been living on a college student's salary for four years. They deserve it, right? Not quite.

On the other hand, you have chosen to look at life from a different perspective. You are used to living like a college student, so you continue to do so. You live a couple of miles from downtown and share an apartment with roommates just like you did in your college days. You avoid the lifestyle creep. You know that it's much more difficult to scale back your lifestyle than it is to scale up.

Your friends and colleagues will have an idea how much you make, and will be confused as to why you are choosing to live like someone who earns half of your salary. You'll try to describe the concept of financial independence. Some will not be able to grasp the idea; others will understand, but not believe it; and the remaining few will actually understand the strategy and your decisions to live like you do.

During the first part of your journey, be prepared to continue living on a college student's salary, while earning a grown-up salary. It will feel weird. It will feel different. Embrace it!

This is easier said than done. This will be the most difficult part in your journey toward financial independence. How do you get through it? First, you will need to find your "Why?" In other words, you will need to find *your* ultimate purpose for seeking financial independence. It can't just be that you want a lot of money. There must be a deeper purpose. Your *why* must be non-monetary, and your purpose for living. Perhaps it's so that you can quit your job so that you can spend time with your (future) kids? Maybe you want to experience what the world has to offer and give back in terms of volunteering or starting a nonprofit? The things you could do once achieving financial independence are unlimited. Do not limit your beliefs. Do not let society limit your beliefs. Close your eyes. Picture your perfect life, and understand that financial independence will help you get there. (Seriously, take a few moments to do this.)

Are you still having trouble determining your *why*? Let me show you how I got to mine. I did this exercise where I had a conversation with my 3-year-old self. I did this in my head, of course. However, rather than ignoring the silly questions that my toddler self was asked, I addressed them. The only catch in this exercise is that your 3-year-old self needs to begin every sentence with the same word. That word is *why*.

Always start this exercise with the 3-year-old you asking, "Why did you get out of bed this morning?" and respond to your 3-year-old self honestly. Your 3-year-old self will then respond with, "Why [insert your previous answer here]?" And you are to repeat this process five to eight times until you get to that gut wrenching, tear-jerking, knife-in-your-heart reason.

This is an important exercise. And I will warn you—you may feel ungrateful once you start answering these questions. You may even feel as though you are offending some of those who are closest to you. Don't worry. The intention here is not to offend anyone, but it does mean that you are getting closer to your *why*.

Here is an example of the conversation I had with my 3-year-old self:

1. Why did you get out of bed this morning?
To go to work.

2. Why did you go to work?
To earn a paycheck and grow my career.

3. Why do you want to earn a paycheck and grow your career?
To increase savings and invest in assets that provide me passive income streams.

4. Why do you want to invest in assets that provide you passive income streams?
To be financially free, travel, spend time with family and friends, volunteer, donate, and not have to worry about a job. Most people stop here! While this can be powerful, it's not powerful enough. It's far too easy to say, "I travel enough," "I love my job," or "insert excuse here" once your motivation wanes.

5. Why do you want to be financially free?
I was always told that the most basic form of success was to make the next generation's life easier. I consider myself tremendously fortunate and eternally grateful that each of the prior generations in my family worked hard to successfully create a better (and easier) life for the next generation to follow. That is no easy feat, and I certainly do *not* want to end that streak.

To help answer this question, I performed an exercise where I reflected on my childhood to see what could have been improved. My parents, grandparents, and great-grandparents made this a very difficult exercise for me. I had everything a kid could ask for: a wonderful family who selflessly worked (and still do work) to give my sister and me unconditional love, support, and guidance.

But after digging deep, I figured it out! Because my parents were working so hard, their time with us was limited. By limited, I do not mean that there was no time spent with us. The time we received was plentiful, but it was certainly not "unlimited." We could never take vacations that lasted more than a week since my parents always had to hurry back to work. The profane "we can't afford it" catch phrase littered our lives, and it restricted us from living up to our fullest potential.

My purpose (my *why*) is to completely free up my time while never having to again utter the words, "we can't afford it." I have the freedom to pursue my true passions. I can spend time with my parents as they grow old, my (future) wife as we grow old, and my (future) kids as they grow up and have kids of their own.

That is why I wake up each morning to go to work and earn a paycheck so that I am able to invest in cash-flowing assets and create financial freedom. This will allow me to provide my family with what they want—which I believe more than anything will be time spent with them.

How do I make this time I spend with my family invaluable and unlimited so that I will rarely need to worry about choosing work over precious moments? I need to create passive income streams that sustain my life's expenses. To simplify, with $10,000 of monthly passive cash flow and zero hours worked, I will be able to sufficiently support my family while making my time invaluable. After all, if I make $10,000 per month at a full-time job working 40 hours per week or 160 hours per month, then my dollar wage is roughly $10,000 / 160 hours or $62.50 per hour. If I can make that same $10,000 with zero hours of work, my dollar wage is $10,000 / 0 (or infinite).

Whatever your *why* may be, I promise you that this will help you push through the first few years of penny pinching and saving aggressively toward that first down payment.

If that motivation of *why* is not helping, and you are still feeling like you have no support from the people in your life, I recommend finding a group of people in your area who are similar to you. Search your area for local ChooseFI groups and BiggerPockets meetups. People in these groups have the same goals of financial independence, and many are already living it. They will keep you motivated, make you feel included, and confirm that you are in fact doing the right thing.

Mid-Journey

You are now a couple of years into your journey. You've been saving. You have purchased your first, second, or maybe even third house hack in the past one to three years. This in itself is going to be different from your peers who will still be trying to save for their first "forever home." You, however, already have a few properties that you are renting out and the snowball is accumulating at an exponential rate.

You are saving 70–80 percent of your income, your net worth climbs into the hundreds of thousands, and liquid cash may be approaching high tens or low hundreds of thousands of dollars. You are now able to pay out $50,000–$100,000 for an investment without it having a material impact on your lifestyle.

That $100 expense that seemed like a big hit only a few years ago now barely moves the needle. Now, the $100 expense feels more like a $10 expense. This is where you need to be careful though because it is still a $100 expense. This is not a time to be frivolous; you still need to practice frugality. You can lighten up a little bit from your first couple of years, but keep your eye on the prize!

As an example, here are a few things that I spend money on that I used to refrain from:

1. Going out to eat/drink socially one to two times per week
2. Traveling to Southeast Asia and visiting friends around the country
3. Learning to snowboard and getting a rock climbing gym membership

These add value to my life so I'm happy to not pump the brakes on every expense. If you go all out the whole time, you will burn out. Remember, spend money on things of value and enjoy the journey.

How can you tell what is of value to you, and what is not? First, you need to get it out of your head that people care what you do. No one cares what car you drive, what clothes you wear, what type of wine you drink, or where you decide to go out to eat. They are too busy worrying about themselves to have the time to worry about you. If you purchase anything to impress someone, you are doing it wrong. Only purchase things that add value to you and your life. If someone is going to like you based on the things you have, they are shallow and you should not want to be friends with them anyway.

During this part of your journey, you will start to see the light at the end of the tunnel. You will see passive income coming in and you may just be a few steps away from having your passive income fully exceed your expenses. Stay the course. Do not let the extra money get to your head. However, do spend money on things that you enjoy now, and will continue to enjoy for the rest of your life.

Post–Financial Independence

Congratulations! You have reached financial independence. You have spent the past five years house hacking, spending money on only the things you absolutely love, and you now have enough passive income to cover all of your life's expenses. It is now time to start reaping the rewards. This does not mean you can start spending lavishly. You can quickly move backwards along this journey if you start spending your money frivolously, and you find that your passive income no longer covers your monthly expenses. It's best to sustain your frugal lifestyle even during these first few years of financial independence.

I know what you are thinking.

What the heck?! I thought the purpose of financial independence was so I don't have to worry about money. Now I'm there, and I still need to worry about money?

Yes, once you have reached financial independence, you are able to sustain your current lifestyle through passive income and do not need to worry about working for your money. You are officially no longer tied down to your salaried job. You don't *have* to quit, but you have the option now. After achieving financial independence, you can confidently walk into your boss's office and ask for a raise, extended time off, to work remotely, or anything else that will make your day-to-day life more enjoyable.

If they say yes to your request, great! If they say no, you have the power to quit and make your passive income become your main source of income. This is what the house-hacking community likes to call FU money.

If you do decide to quit, you can elect to pursue a passion. But again, be careful! You cannot spend money on anything and everything overnight. You do not want to slip backwards and lose your financial independence. If you do want to elevate your lifestyle, continue saving as much money as possible while investing in assets that provide you with passive income. As your passive income grows, you can spend more and more money on the things you may enjoy. If your passive income can sustain that BMW payment, or that boat you've always wanted, or that nice Armani suit you've had your eyes on, then go for it. But I cannot reiterate this enough: only get it once your passive income can sustain it.

Now that you have financial independence, you can do whatever you want with your life. You have very little responsibilities. You can spend your days traveling, spending time with family, volunteering, or growing your own business. The world is your oyster.

No part of this journey toward financial independence is normal. You begin the process by looking much poorer than most of your peers, but you end up being much richer than most of them. You rarely go out and save money any way that you can in order to begin house hacking during the first part of the journey. Then, you are owning property, but still living with roommates in perhaps not the most ideal situation. But by eliminating your largest expense (housing) and continuing to be frugal in other aspects of your life, you will save 70–80 percent of your income while your bank account grows exponentially. It's much better to *be rich* than to *look rich*. Finally, you hit the point where you reach financial independence, and while your peers are stuck in a cubicle for the better half of their lives, you can be scuba diving in the Galapagos, catching your son's little league game, or volunteering with your favorite charities.

Does this sound normal to you? Of course not! But who wants to live a normal life? I want your life to be extraordinary, but you need to do things differently than everyone else to obtain this lifestyle. Dave Ramsey, a businessman and creator of Financial Peace University, says: "Live like no one else *so you can live like no one else*." House hacking is the first and largest step you can take to live like no one else now, but live like they dream later.

Getting Your Spouse on Board

Assuming that you are okay with these first few years of sacrifices, the hardest part for many people in serious relationships seems to be getting their significant other on board. I'm not a relationship expert or psychologist of any kind. However, what I have found to be most effective is first realizing that your significant other's goals may be different than your own. They may think differently than you, have different goals than you, or have different motivations. If you picked up this book, you have likely already been convinced. The point that convinced you may not be the same point that convinces your significant other. What motivates your spouse?

At the time of this writing, I do not have a significant other. However, let me tell you about a friend and fellow house hacker, Scott Trench. Unlike me, Scott does not care much about traveling. I'll compare our motivations, and you will see some differences. While we are both fully invested in house hacking and pursuing financial independence, we do it for different reasons.

Scott is a hardworking businessman. He loves to take small companies, create and improve upon systems, and then watch these systems grow and thrive over time. Similar to what he is doing with BiggerPockets, he enjoys scaling businesses. He enjoys creating systems and finding the best possible people to hire and improve these systems so that he can step away and work on the things that he does best, which is scaling the business and creating systems.

Because Scott is financially independent, he can continue to do this in perpetuity. As Scott always says, he is now in a position where he can "play to win" rather than "play not to lose." Unlike Scott, many Americans would not be able to survive for more than three to six months if they lost their jobs. Scott, on the other hand, can survive forever. In the future, this will allow him to take executive positions in nascent companies that cannot afford to pay an executive's salary. Instead of receiving a normal six-figure salary, Scott can opt for an equity stake in the company. When Scott performs, he now has the ability to create multiples of that six-figure salary, a risk that I am sure he would be willing to take.

On the other hand, I'm not motivated by growing businesses. I don't care about becoming the executive of a startup that makes it big. What fulfills me is freeing up my time so that I can do what I want, when I want, where I want, with whom I want. I want to travel the world and experience all that it has to offer. When it comes time to start a family, I want to be there 100 percent of the time for my kids. That means never missing a single Little League game, recital, or concert; and maybe even chaperoning a few field trips along the way.

The point here is that there is no right or wrong answer. If you were to try to convince Scott to house hack so that he can travel the world, he would probably scoff at you. That's not his interest right now—and maybe never will be. He is much more of a homebody who loves to help people achieve financial independence on a massive scale in Denver. On the other hand, if you were to convince me to pursue financial independence to grow a business, I would likely look the other way.

This situation is no different when it comes to what motivates your significant other. Find a way that house hacking and financial independence can help you achieve these dreams together.

Renting vs. Home Buying vs. House Hacking

Okay, enough of the sappy stuff. Let's get into some of the differences between house hacking vs. renting vs. purchasing a home the conventional way. We will run through several examples with Joe (renter), Mary (conventional buyer), and Sally (house hacker). To illustrate my point, I need to lay down a few basic assumptions.

- Each individual has the ability to purchase a $300,000 house with 3.5 percent down.
- Each person has $10,500 in savings.
- Each person can pay their mortgage payments/rent through their income without going into their savings.
- Rent and property value increases at 3.4 percent per year.

We understand that everyone's situation is different. However, most of the variables will be the same to isolate the different strategies so you can see the financial impact on each with this example.

Renting

Meet Joe. He is a great guy with a banking job in downtown Metropolis. He makes great money and receives excellent benefits; and to be closer to work, he lives in a large apartment complex close to the office. He has $10,500 saved up and is paying $1,500 in rent with utilities included. This includes a gym, outdoor pool, and a nice lounge area where he and his friends can hang out.

Joe enjoys renting because he did not have to pay a significant sum of money for a down payment—just $3,000 for a security deposit and the first month's rent. However, what Joe may not realize is that during his first year, he will pay $18,000 in rent while building little wealth in the process. Assuming a 3.4 percent increase in rent each year, he will continue to fail building wealth through his housing. Instead, he is paying down his landlord's mortgage. Over a thirty-year period, Joe will pay about $915,000 in rent while paying $0 equity to himself. He began with $10,500 that he invested in the stock market, which is now worth just under $265,000. By renting and investing that $10,500 in the stock market, instead of using it for a down payment, it has resulted in a -$650,000 net worth impact.

While Joe is living a fine life now, he is not establishing himself for financial success in the future. Joe's recap:

- Renting an apartment downtown
- Paying $1,500 in monthly rent until he moves, or landlord raises rent
- Beginning with $10,500 in savings that he decides to invest in the stock market
- Thirty-year net worth impact on living situation: -$650,000

Home Buying

Let's visit our friend Mary. She has been renting for years now and has had enough. She is sick of giving one-third of her paycheck to her landlord every single month. She has $10,500 in savings and decides to use that as a down payment on a property of her own. She understands that she will need to move out to the suburbs. However, it's much quieter there, she has more space, and the house is large enough for a family. She plans to be here for a while.

The purchase price on the house is $300,000. Because Mary is going to live there, she takes out an FHA loan so she only needs to put down 3.5 percent or $10,500. Mary is aware of all of the added expenses that come with owning a home. Outside of the mortgage, which includes principal, interest, taxes, and insurance (PITI); she understands that she also needs to budget for repairs, maintenance, and other homeowner expenses. After all expenses, Mary ends up paying $2,400 per month for her and her family to live in this new home.

While Mary is building equity in her home from paying down the loan and appreciation, the equity built does not quite exceed the expenses she is paying to live there. While still much better than Joe's situation during a thirty-year period, Mary's net worth impact will be -$285,000. Mary's recap:

- Purchases a "forever home" in the suburbs
- Makes monthly mortgage payments of $2,400 for thirty years (or until a refinance)
- Benefits from loan paydown and appreciation
- Thirty-year net worth impact on living situation: -$285,000

House Hacking

The third stop on our journey is to our friend Sally's house. After months of renting and paying off someone else's mortgage, she concludes that she is fed up with paying for any housing costs whatsoever. She does not want to pay rent. She does not want to pay a mortgage. She wants to live for free!

Sally is a working adult though. She cannot just start living in her parent's basement. Nor does she want to live under a bridge. They said that it's impossible to live for free. If she decided to listen to everyone else, she would be more like Joe and Mary who are losing hundreds of thousands of dollars on their living situation over the course of thirty years.

Fortunately, Sally ignored the naysayers. Rather than accepting the common notion that she cannot live for free, she looked for ways to make this a reality. Sally discovered that she could purchase a one- to four-unit property with only 3.5 percent down. In her area, these properties ranged from $250,000 to $400,000. With an average of $15,000 down, she could have her own property.

To remain conservative, Sally purchased a five-bedroom, three-bathroom single-family home for $300,000. She put 3.5 percent down so her down payment was only $10,500. Her full mortgage payment (including PITI, a mortgage payment that is the sum of monthly principal, interest, taxes, insurance, and private mortgage insurance) was about $2,000. Rather than pay the mortgage herself, Sally decided to rent out the other four bedrooms to friends. They each paid her $750 a month for a total of $3,000. She was then living for free while making $1,000 over the mortgage. She set $400 per month aside for "reserves" and went on to reinvest the remaining $600. Sally completely eliminated her living expense and is now making $600 per month on her living situation.

So how does this look over the course of thirty years?

Like Mary, Sally is building equity in her home through appreciation and paying down the loan. However, as we discussed in the previous chapter, she also benefits from the cash-flow savings and tax benefits. The tax benefits portion of this example is outside the scope of this book, so I highly recommend that you pick up *The Book on Tax Strategies for the Savvy Real Estate Investor* by Amanda Han and Matthew MacFarland to learn what you can or can't deduct and how to handle depreciation and other expenses so that you pay the least amount possible in taxes.

In the first year, Sally will make $7,200 above all of her expenses, not including her rent savings. If we assume Sally pays $650 in rent ($7,800 per year) prior to purchasing this property, her cash flow or the amount she could save would be $15,000 in her first year, and that would increase as her rent would have been raised, but her mortgage payment stays the same.

When factoring in all of the wealth builders of house hacking—cash flow, loan paydown, and appreciation—Sally's total net worth impact will be $2.6 million over the course of thirty years. In case you skimmed that, let me repeat that figure: $2.6 million! That is more than what most people save in an entire lifetime and, even if they do, they would have had to work forty years to accumulate that amount. This is just purchasing a property, saving on living expenses, and watching it appreciate over time.

In this example, we assume that Sally lives in this house hack for the entire thirty years. Of course, this is not realistic. Sally is required to live in the house hack for one year. However, after that year, she will have saved enough whereby she can rent out her first house hack fully (more cash flow) and do it again. And again. And again. The snowball accumulates. If she house hacks three or four times in three or four years, she will be setting herself up to be a multi-millionaire in the next ten years. Sally's recap:

- Purchases a three-bedroom, two-bathroom home similar to Mary's
- Rents out the rooms instead of living there by herself
- Makes $1,000 per month above her mortgage and $600 after setting aside reserves
- Benefits from cash flow, appreciation, and loan paydown
- Thirty-year net worth impact on living situation: +$2.6 million over thirty years

Typical House-Hacking Returns

Through these three examples, I hope you can see the power of house hacking. I truly believe that it is the best type of real estate investment. Let's dive a little bit deeper and talk about returns. There are tons of ways people look at returns in real estate. For this scenario, we are going to look at total net worth return on investment. This is a percentage that I made up, and the idea is to see how much we can increase our net worth based on our initial investment over the course of one year. This can be calculated over many years as well, but to keep everything consistent (and easy to understand) without worrying about the time value of money, I am going to show the net worth change over the course of one year throughout this book.

A quick example would be the following: You put $10,000 down on a property that increases your net worth by $5,000 over the course of one year. Your net worth return on investment would be $5,000 increased net worth divided by $10,000 initial investment for a 50 percent net worth return on investment.

$5,000 earnings / $10,000 initial investment = 50% net worth return on investment

I hope that I have already convinced you that house hacking can have a powerful impact on your financial position when compared with renting or purchasing a home traditionally. Now, let's look at how it compares with other investment types that are relatively passive.

In the next couple of paragraphs, we will compare the returns you get house hacking with what you get on a traditional buy-and-hold property, stock market investing, and note investing.

Let's revisit Sally's house hack from the previous example. She put $10,500 down on the property. Over the course of the year she has an effective cash flow of $15,000 per year. She is cash flowing $600 each month and not paying rent. She had been paying $650 per month in rent so that is a total monthly savings of $1,250 per month, or $15,000 per year. Assuming a 6 percent appreciation rate, the value of the home will have increased by $18,000 and would have paid her loan down by about $5,600.

Without even including the tax benefits, you will notice Sally's net worth return on investment in the first year will be:

$18,000 + $10,200 + $5,600 = $38,600 total net worth gained

$38,600 / $10,500 = 367% net worth return on investment

Do you see that? By investing $10,500 in a house hack, Sally is able to increase her net worth by 367 percent of that $10,500 in just the first year. In other words, for every dollar that Sally puts into this strategy, she will receive $3.67 in return after one year. Is that a deal that you would do? I sure would!

As you can see, the dollar value of the cash flow, appreciation, and loan paydown are like that of a traditional buy and hold. What really powers the returns of house hacking is the low down payment. By investing $10,500 in a house hack compared with $60,000 in a conventional purchase, your net worth return on investment goes from 56 percent to 367 percent.

$38,600 / $60,000 = 64.3% net worth return on investment

Don't get us wrong, a traditional buy and hold is still a great investment. But would you rather have 64.3 percent or 367 percent? I understand that I am making you pick the better of two angles, which is why I love real estate.

Now to compare this strategy with the stock market.

I am writing this book for the average individual. This does not apply to the Warren Buffetts of the world. Either way, there is only one Warren Buffett. He did not just passively invest in the market either, he spent the majority of his time researching companies to make educated decisions on where he would invest his money. In fact, I do not think anyone has spent more time researching these companies before investing.

I think it is a fair assumption that you are not spending as much time on investing in particular stocks as Warren Buffett. Given that you do not have the amount of hours in a day to become an expert at stock investing, I am going to assume that you will achieve the returns that the stock market averages. Over the course of the past 100 years, the market increases 7 percent per year. Of course, some years are much better and others are much worse. For this example, I am using the average.

If you take that same $10,500 and invest it in the stock market at a 7 percent return, it will be $11,235. Over the course of the year, you would have a $1,235 increase to your net worth. Compare that to a $38,600 increase. It's laughable! The odds that you are going to achieve returns equal to (or greater than) a house hack in the stock market are slim to none.

Let's compare this with another type of semi-passive real estate investing, note investing. Note investing sounds scary, but a note is just a fancy word for a loan. Your mortgage is a "note." When you invest in notes, you are the bank. Someone who would come to you for a note would be an individual who cannot obtain a loan at a traditional bank. Either they have bad credit, not enough income, or they need the loan fast.

For this reason, your interest rates are much higher than a bank would charge. While a bank may charge 5 percent interest, you can charge closer to 10-12 percent, and even tack on some added fees. The borrower of the note is required to pay you back over a predetermined period of time. If they do not make their payments, then you are able to proceed with foreclosure and obtain the property for pennies on the dollar.

This can be a great way to invest and obtain a property for a cheap price. However, you need hundreds of thousands of dollars to invest in notes. I assume you do not have that amount of money available if you are reading a book about house hacking. Secondly, in order to see these great returns, you will need to foreclose on someone's property. How do you think that would make you feel?

Truthfully, I have not found returns from any type of investment that are better than house hacking. Sure, you can see great returns on some individual deals if you are flipping, wholesaling, or land investing. But these are very active ways to invest. I am not trying to create a second job for you; I want you to excel at your day job while your investments effortlessly make you money while you sleep (in your house hack).

House-Hacking Strategies

If you are reading this with kids in the next room, or if it seems impossible to do what our friend Sally does, don't worry! There are many different forms of house hacking, and I am sure that one will work for you. Each of these strategies are a form of house hacking, and they fall on a spectrum of least to most profitable, which correlates almost exactly with the least to most work or lifestyle change.

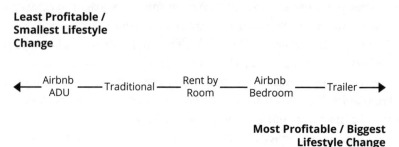

1. Renting Out an Additional Dwelling Unit

Ben Leybovich, an active user on BiggerPockets and a friend of Brandon Turner, calls this "luxurious house hacking." You either purchase a property with an additional dwelling unit, or you build one yourself. It's helpful if the unit can have at least a small kitchenette, an operative bathroom, and a comfortable bed to sleep in.

Then, you guessed it—rent it out! You could rent it full time or on Airbnb. Municipalities are becoming more and more strict with their short-term rental laws, so do your homework and look at your city's short-term rental laws before purchasing a property, or putting your own property up for a short-term rental.

If short-term rentals are okay in your city, you can put it up for rent. This way, you and your family enjoy your own personal space in the main house while your guests enjoy their own space in the guesthouse.

Since you are still occupying the vast majority of your house, it is considered the least profitable (and aggressive) way to house hack, but it can still significantly offset your mortgage while you and your family enjoy the main house.

2. The Traditional House Hack

The most popular is still the traditional house hack. This is when you purchase a two- to four-unit property with a low down payment residential loan. The 3.5 percent down FHA is popular in Denver, but there are others, especially if you are a first-time homebuyer.

You live in one unit (perhaps with a roommate) and rent out the other unit(s). The rent from your roommate, plus your other units, should either cover the mortgage or come close to covering the mortgage. When you move out and rent the unit that you used to live in, the property cash flows nicely.

This strategy works in most lower-priced markets, but it is almost impossible to find a deal where you will fully cover your mortgage in the higher-priced markets. However, you do not need to totally offset your mortgage to still reap a lot of the wealth-generating benefits of house hacking. Even offsetting your $3,000 mortgage by $1,000 a month is still $1,000 a month in savings.

3. Renting by Room

This is a strategy that one of my good friends has deployed, and it is working magnificently. The idea is to purchase a large single-family home that has at least four bedrooms and two bathrooms; and then live in one bedroom while renting out the others. You can typically get significantly more income when you rent by the room.

Purchasing a single-family home (especially as a first-time home-buyer) opens up potential financing options. At the time of writing this, I know they have 1, 3, 3.5, and 5 percent down loan options on single-family homes. The low down payment with the increased rental amounts really boosts your cash-on-cash returns.

We have not even approached appreciation yet. Single-family homes are known to appreciate more quickly than multifamily homes. This is the case because both investors and non-investors are interested. With more demand comes higher prices, not to mention that non-investors will typically pay a premium given that they are looking for a home, not a deal.

4. Calling the Living Room Home & Renting Out the Rest (Seriously)

They call it a "living" room for a reason, right? This is my current strategy. As someone who lives in a city where price points are relatively high, it is increasingly difficult to find a property ideal for a traditional house hack. This means I had to get creative.

With this strategy, I rent out the upstairs unit like a traditional rental. However, this was not enough to fully cover my mortgage. I decided I would put up a room divider and a curtain to section off a portion of the living room and call it my bedroom. That's where I rest my head, and I am happy with the situation most of the time.

Since I am not occupying my bedroom, I can now rent it out on Airbnb. Though this might not work for everyone, it works for me. It allows me to cash flow anywhere between $250 and $750 per month (after reserves), depending on the seasonality of Airbnb.

5. *Living in a Trailer/RV & Renting Out Your Primary Residence*

My friend, neighbor, and colleague has taken house hacking to the next level! He purchased a stationary RV for $1,500. He places the RV in his parking space where he resides while fully renting out his one-bedroom apartment on Airbnb. This strategy is for the hustler who is clearly willing to do what it takes to achieve early financial independence. This makes a lot of sense for the young and single individuals looking to eliminate their housing expense.

6. *Live-in Flip*

Bonus strategy! The live-in flip is a strategy that infamous Mindy Jensen, co-host of the *BiggerPockets Money Podcast,* is famous for promoting. This is when you purchase a property with that same owner-occupied loan with the intention of living there for at least two years, fixing it up, and then selling it.

Notice that you need to live in the house for two years for this strategy. This reverts back to that section of the tax code we discussed that says if you live in a property for two of the last five years, you can then sell it without paying capital gains tax on the first $250,000 of capital gains ($500,000 if you are married). This is a huge benefit to real estate investors.

Let's run through a quick example. Hayley purchased a property for $200,000. The property was livable but needed some cosmetic updates. Over the course of two years, she replaced the floors, bathrooms, and kitchen; as well as repainted all of the walls to give it a new look. Along with natural appreciation, Hayley increased the value of her home from $200,000 to $300,000 in two years. She can now sell her property for a net gain of $100,000 and pay zero taxes on the gains.

This strategy works great for those who are handy, and not afraid to put some sweat equity into the property. Also note that it can be used alongside any of the aforementioned house-hacking strategies. While you are renovating the property, you can rent out the space that is not being renovated so you are still living for free.

That brings us to the end of this chapter. The foundation has been laid. Next, we are going to start building on that foundation with everything you need to know about house hacking. But first, let me introduce you to my friend Jeff White who has gone from living a life of luxury to slowly scaling back and living a life of frugality through house hacking.

CASE STUDY
JEFF WHITE

- **House-hacking strategy:** Traditional and Airbnb
- **Age at first house hack:** 33
- **Location:** Denver, Colorado
- **NWROI:** 151%

Jeff White is not only a hardcore house hacker on BiggerPockets, but he is a good friend. I know his story well, and could not wait to share it with all of you. Let's start from the beginning. The year was 2014 and Jeff was living the high life. He had just purchased this beautiful condominium in one of the nicest parts of Denver for $150,000. It was a two-bedroom, one-bathroom loft-style condo with 1,030 square feet that featured a great spiral staircase all to himself with no roommates. Everything was newly remodeled, and his place looked like it could have been the featured residence in a luxury high-rise condo advertisement. He was living his best life, right? Wrong!

While the place was incredibly nice, after the Home Owner's Association (HOA) fees and other expenses, he was paying over $1,200 a month to live there. This is quite expensive for Denver in 2014.

A couple of years later, his girlfriend, Suly, alerted him that her sister was selling a duplex in a suburban town south of Denver. She wanted out, and she was willing to sell to a family or friend at an extreme discount. At the time, Jeff respectfully declined the offer since he had just purchased a beautiful place in the heart of Denver. Why would he want to purchase this slightly outdated duplex and live farther from work, friends, and the city he called home?

Shortly after declining the offer, the duplex was sold to an investor. Jeff quickly realized the huge mistake he had made in not accepting the offer from Suly's sister. Although he missed out on a good deal, this situation piqued Jeff's interest in real estate. He picked up Mark Ferguson's book, *Build a Rental Property Empire,* in October 2016. In that book, Mark briefly describes the concept of house hacking and the concept of purchasing a two- to four-unit property, living in one unit, and renting out the others. Jeff started scouring the internet, looking for more information on the subject. That is when he found BiggerPockets.

After reading articles, listening to podcasts, and reading books, he felt confident enough to start looking for his first house hack in January 2017. Shortly after beginning the process, Jeff found a prospect. It was a side-by-side duplex in an up-and-coming part of Denver. Each side was 620 square feet, which had been converted from one-bedroom and one-bathroom units into two-bedroom and one-bathroom units. Jeff was eager to start his journey, so he submitted an offer for $385,000, and went under contract.

After going under contract, due diligence began. He went through the FHA process, completed the inspection, and everything seemed to check out fine. It needed some work, but he wanted to improve the property to increase the value. Just before the inspection deadline, he got a call and found out both sets of tenants wanted to meet him in person. When arriving at the property, the tenants warned him about purchasing it. They said that the prior landlord (the seller) was a slumlord. Apart from the noticeable things that Jeff thought he could fix, the tenants warned him that the water heater was leaking carbon dioxide into the unit, and had been doing so for quite some time. There were no smoke or carbon monoxide detectors, and the prior landlord still charged over $1,300 per unit. The tenants could barely afford the current rent so they were concerned that Jeff would be raising their rents once he purchased the property.

Soon after entering the property, Jeff's girlfriend told him that there was no way they were living in this property. Before leaving, Jeff asked the tenants if there was anything else he should know about the units. One of them dropped their head and whispered, "bed bugs." After further inspection, it turned out that the property was infested with bed bugs—one of the worst cases that the exterminator had ever seen. In light of this new discovery, Jeff exercised his right to get out of the contract before the inspection deadline. It was back to the drawing board.

After a few more months of looking, they found a fourplex in an up-and-coming area in the southern part of Denver that needed some work for $630,000. The inspection came back with mold, minor electrical issues, and door jams that were not functional. Easy fixes, but all of these issues needed to be cleared before they could move in.

Jeff ended up putting 6 percent down using the FHA loan, which made his down payment and closing costs about $40,000. After closing on the deal, he invested an additional $30,000 for mostly cosmetic refurbishments: floors, countertops, cabinets, tiling, paint, new appliances, doors, and washer/dryer hookups in each unit that increased the value of his property to $700,000. As he was doing the work, Jeff had to evict the tenants in one of the lower units. There were eight people living in a two-bedroom apartment. None of them were on the lease and Jeff did not realize this until after he closed. Luckily for Jeff, the eviction process was an uncommonly easy one. He asked them to leave and they did. This could have been much worse. If you are buying a place with inherited tenants, be sure to do your due diligence on those tenants to know all the details from the beginning.

After 60 days of rehabbing the property, Jeff and Suly moved into one of the units and rented out the other three. They were receiving $4,800 in rent, and their mortgage payment (PITI) was $3,600. Jeff and Suly were living for free and making $1,200 over the mortgage. They did not stop there though. After a few months of living in the property, they decided to Airbnb one of the empty bedrooms in their unit. The property was now cash flowing even more! They were receiving about $5,300 in rent on the same $3,600 mortgage, while also putting away $300 per month in reserves.

After all of the savings, Jeff and Suly were able to do it again a year later. This time they purchased a single-family home in a suburb north of Denver with a mother-in-law suite. They took the mother-in-law suite and rented out the main house to a family. Jeff and Suly continue to live for free while building tremendous amounts of wealth from their properties.

WHY

"I house hack because I want to quit my salaried job and pursue my passions. I'm a painter and love art so I would love to go to Florence to learn about art for a few months without having to worry about a paycheck. There may or may not be kids in our future. If there are, I'm going to want to spend time with them. Like almost anyone else pursuing this strategy, it's not about the money or building up a high net worth number. It's about escaping the rat race and living the best life that I am meant to live."

ACTION STEPS

❏ Figure out your *why*. Take a day to yourself and go on a hike or something out in nature. Ditch the technology and just think about what you truly want out of life. What is your life's purpose? Once you figure this out, living differently is easy.

❏ Continue educating yourself on the *BiggerPockets Real Estate* and *Money* podcasts. Other great podcasts include Hal Elrod's *Achieve Your Goals* as well as Brad Barrett's and Jonathan Mendonsa's *ChooseFI*.

CHAPTER 3

WHERE TO HOUSE HACK

My family and I were at the Cheesecake Factory the other day. We love almost everything on the menu, but we always run into the same problem: an overabundance of choices! We peruse the menu and debate whether to get chicken, steak, a burrito, or perhaps a salad—the options are endless. Eventually, we end up picking the same meal we ordered the last time because we understood the description and we knew we liked it the last time. Instead of just choosing the item that we liked, we wasted twenty minutes trying to figure out if we were daring enough to try something new. I have talked to many people who frequent the Cheesecake Factory and they feel the same way, so we are not alone.

Cool story, yeah? What does this have to do with real estate investing and house hacking? Picking a real estate market to invest in is just like ordering a meal at the Cheesecake Factory. There are nearly endless options and things to consider, but at the end of the day, you will most likely go with what you know, and what makes you comfortable. This market is usually where you previously invested.

House hacking, on the other hand, limits your options. It's the equivalent of going to your family diner with a one-page menu. There are only a handful of options: property type, neighborhood, and location within that neighborhood. But with fewer options comes the ability to evaluate all of them and make better decisions. You are also required to live in the property for at least one year when house hacking. This means that you can invest anywhere in the country, but you will also have to live there for the house hacking strategy to work for you. Since you are reading this book, you likely work full time and are not looking to move too far away from your job. I will show you how to research the best possible location for your house hack in the next few pages.

Property Types

The first question you need to ask yourself is which house-hacking strategy is best for you to pursue now? Are you looking for the most lucrative (trailer or rent by room), or the least impact to your life (traditional or luxury) house hacking? Once you have chosen your strategy, you can then decide on the property type.

There are many property types that can be used for a house hack. The lender will only require that it is in a livable condition. You will need it to have a structurally sound roof, running water, heat (or air conditioning depending on the location, such as Arizona for example), and all of the exterior walls must be intact. The options for house-hacking properties include single-family residence, duplex, triplex, fourplex, townhome, and condominium.

Single-Family Residence

A single-family residence (SFR) is typically a standalone house. This is the home you envision when you think of the American dream. It has the yard, the driveway, the white picket fence; and no one else is going in or around your property except you, your family, and your friends. Purchasing a single-family residence is what most people are comfortable with when purchasing a home. When doing a house hack, purchasing a single-family home means that you are pursuing either the rent-by-room or luxury house-hack strategy.

If you are seeking a rent-by-room house hack, make sure that you check with your city laws and ordinances. In some cities, there is a limit on how many non-related people can live under the same roof. If you take the rent-by-room route, you do run the risk of breaking the law if you have four or five unrelated people living in the same place.

If you are looking for the luxury house hack, make sure the house has a mother-in-law suite that you can put up for a short-term rental, or that it's zoned for an additional dwelling unit (ADU) so you can build. Luxury house hacking is most popular among families, whereas the rent-by-room is more popular among young professionals.

The rent-by-room strategy in single-family properties tends to be the best for cash flowing. They also tend to benefit from appreciation more than the multifamily properties. The downside is that you are forced to interact with your tenants (or roommates) more than you would with a small multifamily property.

Pros of SFR	Cons of SFR
• Great cash flow • High likelihood of appreciation • People understand and know single-family houses • Maintenance and upkeep is likely cheaper	• You need to live in the same place as your tenants (or roommates) • More difficult to scale with single-family properties • Lots of competition when buying

Small Multifamily Property

Small multifamily properties are duplexes, triplexes, and fourplexes. A property that is larger than four units is considered a "commercial" property and will not qualify for the low percentage down house-hacking loan. The small multifamily properties cater to the traditional house hack where you live in one unit and rent the others. You have the option of living alone this way; and you are neighbors with your tenants instead of roommates.

When you rent a single-family home, your typical tenant is going to be a young professional looking to save money on rent. They do not need a lot of space, and rooms are usually much cheaper than entire units. With multifamily properties, your tenant pool grows. You are now open to families and individuals who are likely earning more money, and want to live on their own.

Small multifamily properties tend to provide great cash flow, but typically do not benefit as much from appreciation. When you sell a multi-family property, you are likely going to be selling to an investor. However, when you sell a single-family property, your potential buyer list will be much larger since families will also want to purchase the property. It is easier for a buyer to develop an emotional attachment to the single-family property, which means they will often pay a premium, versus the average buyer of a multifamily property.

Pros of Small Multifamily	Cons of Small Multifamily
• Tend to have great cash flow • Scalable • Do not have to live in the same unit as tenants	• Still need to be neighbors with your tenants • Harder to sell if you ever want to liquidate • More expensive upkeep • Don't benefit as much from appreciation

Townhome or Condominium

Townhomes and condominiums, or condos, are other great properties that you can buy for a house hack. Before I get into the details, I'll explain what distinguishes a townhome from a condominium.

Townhomes are individual houses placed side-by-side such that they have one or two walls shared between the two homes. A condominium is a single unit, usually within a large building with many similar units. Rather than someone owning the entire building and renting out the units individually, a single party owns each condo.

Condominiums are governed by a governed by an HOA. Everyone who owns a condo in the complex is automatically a member of the HOA, and needs to abide by the rules and regulations it sets forth. A select number of people make up the HOA's Board. The board is typically a group of owners who are interested in having an impact on the building, and its rules. In exchange for a monthly fee, the HOA manages the common areas, maintains the property's exterior, and works to ensure a pleasant living situation for all its residents.

Townhomes, on the other hand, do not typically have HOAs. If they do, the costs are much lower than a condo's HOA fees. There are not any common areas in a townhome, outside of walls with your neighbors. The HOA fee would likely cover the cost of large repairs of the entire building going forward. Owners are responsible for maintaining the property's exterior.

There could be an entire book written on investing in condos and townhomes. However, for now it is important for you to understand that many house hackers choose to begin with a condominium or townhome. They are typically much cheaper than a standard single-family or multi-family residence; and are often in the nicer areas of town, which means they are easier to rent out.

Like any investment property, there are downsides to condos and town-homes as well. The largest being the HOA. You likely will not have much control of what the HOA does within the building, or the monthly fees involved. If the HOA decides to raise its fee by $200 a month, you must pay it, or sell. This is a rare scenario since the HOA typically has the interest of its residents in mind, but anything is possible.

Condominiums and townhomes are also usually smaller than your typical single-family or multifamily residence. For that reason, you can typically charge more in rent per tenant. However, if you are doing a rent-by-room strategy, you will likely only be able to get two to three tenants instead of four to five. In other words, while rent per tenant may be higher, your overall rent may be lower.

Pros of Condos/Townhomes	Cons of Condos/Townhomes
• Condos are cheaper. • Typically in nicer parts of town so can be easier to rent. • Large, exterior expenses (e.g. roof, siding, etc.) are typically paid for by HOA.	• HOA fees are out of your control (unless you get on the board). • Condo and townhome values are volatile. They are typically the first properties to drop in value when the market turns. • HOA may restrict short-term rentals so your house hacking options may be limited.

You will find that many BiggerPockets subscribers are against condominiums for house hacking because of the uncertainty behind the HOA. However, as a house hacker, I highly suggest you investigate this option further. In many cities, a condo or townhome might be all that you can afford in the beginning. Getting into a place where you can eliminate or drastically reduce your living expenses will put you in a much better financial position than waiting until you can afford to purchase a single-family or multifamily property. In fact, I am confident that if you were to purchase a condo to house hack, you would cash flow and have enough income in one year to purchase the single-family or multifamily residence you may have initially wanted.

Pick a Neighborhood

Now that I've discussed the types of properties available for a house hack, the next step is to determine which neighborhood you will choose to begin your investment. As I talked about previously, you are not dealing with the Cheesecake Factory effect of having every possible city in the United States as an option. Your options are limited.

When I first moved to Denver, I knew nothing about the city. I had been there once before (for my interview) and that was it. Yet, in just two months after moving, I was able to choose a cash-flowing property in an up-and-coming neighborhood that was close to work. I could not have asked for a better location. Let me explain how I did this.

The first step was getting to know real estate professionals in the area: lenders, agents, property managers, and fellow investors. I will get into the details of putting together your team in the chapters to follow, but just understand that BiggerPockets is the largest network of real estate investors in your area who you can message for free! That's exactly what I did. Within the first six months of living in Denver, I would meet with five people each week, without fail. I would pick their brains on the Denver market, up-and-coming neighborhoods, tenant screening, property management, the works.

As I met with these people and built my Denver real estate network, I was also a Lyft driver as often as my scheduled allowed. They say that seeing is believing, right? I don't think there is a better way to get to know a city in a short amount of time than driving for a ride share service.

Being a glorified cab driver is not the most glamorous job, and you are still forced to trade time for money. I realize that you're reading this book to get out of that type of work, but put your pride aside for the moment. This is just a stepping stone. When you drive for Uber or Lyft you are meeting hundreds (or even thousands) of people, seeing the most popular areas of the city, and looking at properties as you drive by. You are doing this, and you are making money at the same time.

Each time a passenger gets into your car, tell them who you are, and what you do. Nine times out of ten, they will not be able to help you. However, by talking about yourself repeatedly, you are refining your pitch for when you go to networking events. You never know what might happen. I found my cleaning crew for my Airbnbs by driving for Lyft and asking what my passengers did. They are still my cleaning crew one year later.

After talking with more experienced people than myself while driving for Lyft, I started to get a good idea of my favorite neighborhoods. This allowed me to search for places to house hack while getting paid by Lyft. One last thing that I recommend you do during this research phase is to hop on your bicycle or lace up your running shoes (or walking shoes) and hit the streets of your city. By doing this, you will learn the areas that you like, and even discover new neighborhoods that you never knew existed.

Now that you have narrowed down your desired neighborhoods from an experiential standpoint, let's narrow it down even further by looking at publicly available data about your potential house hack's location.

In the real estate space, you will hear many investors, agents, lenders, and other professionals refer to neighborhoods as Class A, B, C, or D neighborhoods, and if they are in between two classes, you might hear A- or B+. Just like in school, a neighborhood receives a grade, though it is much more subjective than any single exam. An A would imply that it is an overall nice neighborhood and a D neighborhood would be much less desirable. Since there is no governing body that regulates a neighborhood as A, B, C, or D, there tends to be some gray lines between the descriptions. It depends on the person making the description. A class A neighborhood to you could be a class B neighborhood to me, and vice versa.

Here is a quick rundown of the location types:

Class A

A class A location is an area that has the newest buildings, hottest restaurants, best schools, wealthiest people, and highest-cost real estate. This is truly the best location you can find in terms of properties and tenants. In this class, you will find that properties will be very difficult to cash flow because of the higher prices of these properties. You will likely be able to house hack and save on rent, but having the rent cover your mortgage may be difficult. If you are purchasing a property in a class A neighborhood, you are expecting to make most of your money on appreciation over cash flow.

Class B

A class B neighborhood might be slightly older (and I'm not talking charm—I'm talking decrepit) than a class A neighborhood, but perhaps still has decent restaurants, schools, and people. This might be your "middle class" areas, but these will attract more blue-collar workers who live paycheck to paycheck. In my experience, these tend to be the best for house hacks. Prices are reasonable, the crime rates are low, and school districts are good; which all attract good tenants. The only catch for some individuals is that it is farther outside of downtown, so your commute may be longer.

Class C

A class C location is likely a lower-income area with homes that are slightly run down. This area tends to attract people who are either on government subsidies, or they are working low-wage jobs. You'll likely find a lot of check-cashing businesses, pawn shops, and other such businesses in this area.

A class C location can be good for a house hack, but just make sure the property is in one of the safer areas. While prices tend to be lower and you will likely be able to charge rent in excess of your mortgage, you need to be sure to thoroughly screen your tenants.

Class D

A class D location is a usually called a rough neighborhood, where you likely would not feel safe to travel alone. Not every city has a class D area, but you will likely recognize one when you see one. Often, even police officers are nervous about entering these areas, and crime and drug use/sales run rampant. There are probably numerous buildings with boarded-up windows and other indications of being vacant. While properties here will be extremely cheap, do not be tempted, and please do a lot of your own research. Your safety while living in the property is much more important than a couple of bucks.[1]

Location

When choosing a house hack, you will not only find ways to save on housing, but also on your second largest expense, transportation. When

---

[1] https://www.biggerpockets.com/blog/2015/12/09/class-a-b-c-d-real-estate/

I buy my house hacks, the first thing I do is set up a multiple listing service (MLS) search with properties that are five to ten miles from work. I can do this myself because I am an agent. However, if you are not an agent, ask one to do this for you. It's an easy process and only takes a minute or two of their time. The MLS is an amalgamation of all of the properties that are on the market in your neighborhood. You can also purchase properties off market, which means finding someone selling a property that is not listed on the MLS. In most cases, house hackers are content with the options on the MLS when looking to close their first property, and they do not yet have a large enough network to get high-quality off-market properties. For that reason, I'm going to only talk about MLS properties.

My first property was just one and one-half miles from the office, which was a ten-minute bike ride or a thirty-minute walk on those snowy days. Now, I live ten miles away from my office, but intentionally purchased the property close to a bike path. Now, my bike ride is about forty minutes and 85 percent of it is on the bike path. There's little worry of cars, traffic signals, and other road hazards.

Maybe you are not a real estate agent, and do not have access to the MLS. That is okay, there are tens of thousands of agents out there that are more than happy to help you out (more on how to find the best one later). It takes them less than two minutes to set you up with a search. Tell them your criteria and ask them to find a property within a five to ten mile radius from where you work.

Your first option for getting to work should be to either walk or bike. Try to find a property that is close to a bike path. If you can walk or bike to work most days, your life will be much better because you'll be saving on gas, exercising, and saving the planet. Sure, you may have to do maintenance on your bike every now and again, but it will be far less expensive than repairs on a car.

If biking or walking is not an option for you, your second-best bet would be to find a property that is close to a bus or train stop. If you're like me, and you have no idea where the bus stops are located and looking at a map of bus routes is harder than learning a foreign language, Google Maps can save you! Type in your prospective address or drop a pin in a desired location and check out how long it would take to get to work via public transportation. If it is within a reasonable amount of time, public transportation certainly is not free, but it's much cheaper than driving your own car. The best part about public transportation is that you do not need to worry about operating the vehicle. You can read, write, or maybe get a head start on your day at work. Any of these options are better than sitting in traffic and listening to the same twelve songs they play on the radio.

If you are in the third group of people and think there is no way you are giving up your driving commute, that is fine too. I will not be offended if you don't take my advice. But make the most of your commute and turn your car into a "mobile university." What do I mean by that?

There are millions of podcasts, audiobooks, and other forms of audio learning you can listen to while in your car. Why not make the most of your thirty- to sixty-minute commute every day and educate yourself? Learn more about something that is relevant to you. Sorry to break the news to you, listening to music on your way into work doesn't provide much benefit to you. *National Public Radio* or your local news is usually just an endless feed of useless information that you are not interested in doing anything about. Sure, it makes you "feel" like you're in the know. I haven't paid attention to the news in years, and I haven't missed a beat. You gather news from the people around you, by glancing at headlines on your Facebook feed, or as you walk by a newspaper stand. Don't litter your brain with information that is no benefit to you. Learn something relevant. Something you can take action on!

Okay, enough of the commuter talk. You get the idea. Find a property close to your work to save time, money, and your sanity on your commute. And do it all while making the most of that commute by learning something through a podcast or audiobook.

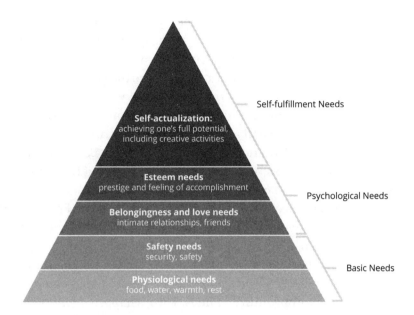

Crime

Abraham Maslow was a psychologist in the early 20th Century who proposed a theory that all humans have basic needs, psychological needs, and self-fulfillment needs.[2] In order for the psychological or self-fulfillment needs to be met, the human must first meet their basic needs. The basic needs are physiological needs (food, water, warmth, rest) and safety needs (security and safety). It was shelter from the cold, rain, and wild beasts during the pre-historic times. It's the same today, except those wild beasts look a little different: They may be job security, health, feeling safe in your neighborhood, and more. For house-hacking purposes, you need to be sure that you are choosing a neighborhood where you can walk down the street without feeling like you are in danger. Not only does it give you peace of mind, but it will also be easier for you to get tenants if they feel safe.

Now that you have narrowed down the location of your house hack, you need to make sure you've researched the neighborhood. In many

---

2 Saul McLeod, "Maslow's Hierarchy of Needs" (Simply Psychology, 2018) www.simplypsychology.org/maslow.html.

cities, neighborhoods can change very quickly. You can find yourself in an unsafe neighborhood by simply walking a block or two off the main street. Fortunately, there are resources that provide the neighborhood's crime rates with details on the streets where the crimes occur.

My favorite place to research crime is www.Trulia.com. Trulia is a real estate listing site just like www.Zillow.com or www.Redfin.com. Trulia has what they call a "crime map" that provides police reports with the details and locations of crimes in the area. Based on the severity and number of crimes, Trulia will shade a portion of the map blue. The darker the shade, the more crime there is in that area.

In my experience, you will always find some sort of crime that has happened in the neighborhood. Don't expect to find a neighborhood with zero crimes. When you are looking for a house hack, the property will likely be in a class B or C neighborhood so there will be some level of crimes in the area. Find out the details about the crimes since it is possible that they were only minor crimes. Things happen. Someone breaking into a car, slashing tires, or vandalizing a nearby building are considered petty crimes. Make sure they are not happening frequently, and you should be okay. If you are not convinced, walk around the neighborhood at multiple times during the day and see if you feel threatened (obviously, use your best judgment). If you are still not convinced, try to find an Airbnb in the neighborhood and see if you can stay for a night. If anything makes you feel uncomfortable, then move on to the next property. If you feel unsafe, chances are that your prospective tenants will too.

School District

I never thought much about school districts when researching properties. I don't have kids and do not plan on having kids for quite some time. Therefore, it makes little sense to worry about the school district where I'm looking for a house—especially if the best houses are in areas where the school district may be average, or even slightly below average.

Talk to a parent about the importance of school districts, and they will likely tell you it is one of the top factors when looking at houses. Even if you have no intention of renting to a family, it is always a better decision to find a property that is in a good school district. At some point, perhaps in as little as one year, you are going to proceed to your next property. You are going to need to rent out the current property. Perhaps your next tenant will be a family. Any family is going to want their kids in the best possible school district, so it will increase the amount you can charge for rent. After your third, fourth, or fifth house hack, you may have few ties to the first property and decide to sell. The same idea applies. The better the school district, the easier it will be to sell, and at a higher price.

Great! You know you need a property in a good school district. How do you figure out whether your property is in a good, average, or poor school district? Fortunately, you can find that out the same way that you learned about the crime rates in that location. You can go to almost any listing site such as Zillow, Trulia, or Redfin, type in the desired property address, and check out what elementary, middle, and high school is in the area. You will find that in most neighborhoods with good schools, the crime is low and vice versa.

To determine the quality of each school, there is a numeric grading system. Each school (elementary, middle, and high school) will have a number next to it that is typically between one and ten. The higher the number, the better the school system.

Path of Progress

Municipalities (cities and towns) are just like businesses. They are constantly finding ways to wisely invest their money to enhance growth and provide a better product to their customers. A municipality's customers are primarily its residents and visitors, while its products are the streets, parks, public school system, law enforcers, and tourist attractions that people use every day. The municipality generates revenue through taxing its residents. It then uses this revenue to maintain (or enhance) the city or town. In many cases, the policymakers who decide on what to do with the tax money focus on improving a single neighborhood, or part of town. You will be in great shape if you can discover this neighborhood and purchase a property before the word gets out. You can benefit from significant appreciation as the neighborhood is further developed.

To do this, look at past development and see which way the city is moving. For example, Denver has been focusing on improving the northern part of the city during these past ten years. They improved lower downtown (LoDo), the Highlands, River North (RiNo), Five Points, and they are continuing to extend north. RiNo, a neighborhood of warehouses, is turning into offices, luxury apartment complexes, shops, and restaurants.

Next, look at the neighborhoods adjacent to the one currently being rebuilt. It is likely that they are still a little rough around the edges. In

Denver, the Cole and Whittier neighborhoods are probably class B- or C+ neighborhoods that are now starting to transform into class A neighborhoods. However, since it is not there yet, home values will likely lag. Purchasing a property in one of these areas will be ideal because there is a high probability that over the next five to ten years, the growth will continue that way.

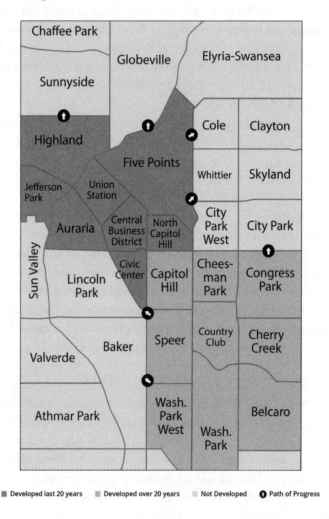

■ Developed last 20 years ■ Developed over 20 years ■ Not Developed ⬤ Path of Progress

If you do this correctly, you will likely be purchasing a property in a class C neighborhood. Friends and colleagues are going to question your decision. Remember what I said about going against societal norms and being uncomfortable? Tell them that you have heard the city or town is really focusing on improving the area and you wanted to purchase a property before values skyrocketed. Warren Buffett is famous for saying, "Be fearful when others are greedy and greedy when others are fearful." In this situation, the average person will be fearful to purchase in that neighborhood, but you have a good reason to believe that it will improve so you have every right to be greedy.

One of the best aspects about real estate investing is that insider trading is perfectly legal. What is insider trading? It is the idea of getting information not known to the general public and making investment decisions based on that information. In the stock market, this is illegal. For example, if an executive or employee of Apple were to purchase a bunch of shares just before they were to release results of their best quarter in history to the public, they would likely be arrested for insider trading (just ask Martha Stewart). In real estate, you can obtain insider information and then make investment decisions based off this information. In fact, I encourage you to do so. Why is this okay in real estate, but not in stocks? It's because anyone can access the information in real estate, but it is not nearly as readily available as it is when researching stocks.

You need to network and get on the good side of the city planners to gain access to this information. In many cities, though not all, there are city planning meetups. Frequently attend these meetings, and become a regular. As you build your network, you will get insights to which parts of the city are going to be developed, therefore, which places are best for your future investments. If your city does not have a meetup, then go to the town hall meetings or other regular meetings that are open to the public and establish relationships with the other attendees. There is a high probability that they will talk about the city's plans, and you will be able to purchase a property before they break ground and the general public learns of the plans.

Making the Decision

Finding the perfect property to house hack is like finding the perfect job. There will be tradeoffs between things you enjoy and things you could live without. As long as the things you enjoy are greater, I would encourage you to submit an offer. Finding a property in a class A neighborhood with a close commute to work and will cash flow you $1,000 per month while appreciating plus-10 percent per year is going to be difficult to find.

It's certainly not impossible, but it is improbable to say the least. Instead, figure out what matters most to you. Separate out your "must haves" from your "nice to haves." Cash flow or appreciation? A crime-ridden area? Or a long commute? How far are you willing to compromise in each category?

For example, I purchased my second house hack in a suburb of Denver. It is ten miles from work along the bike path and in a class B neighborhood, right next to the town's public school district. The property cash flows me about $1,000 per month and I am living for free. Not a bad deal, right?

My must haves were:
1. Rents collectively need to be $1,000 over my estimated mortgage payment (PITI).
2. Near a bike path for my work commute.
3. Not many severe crimes. Some petty crimes are okay. They happen everywhere. I stay away from neighborhoods that have reported homicide and the like.

Nice to haves:
1. Extremely low crime. There is a tiny bit of crime in the neighborhood, but nothing the average person would notice. It is similar to any middle class neighborhood. There are families next door and kids walk by the house to get to school every morning.
2. Appreciation: This property will likely not appreciate as high as a property in downtown Denver. I am okay with that.

As you can see, I was all in on cash flow versus appreciation when buying this property. However, on the tradeoff between price of the property and proximity to work, I was able to compromise a little bit to each. The property was fairly inexpensive for my area (take), but I am ten miles from work/downtown (give).

CASE STUDY
ZACH GWIN

- **House-hacking strategy:** Trailer-hacking
- **Age at first house hack:** 23
- **Location:** Denver, Colorado
- **NWROI:** 1,205%

Meet Zach Gwin. He is doing the strategy that almost everyone is afraid of: the trailer strategy. At 23 years old, Zach knew he had an advantage that most people do not have: time. He wanted to invest in a property, see it appreciate over time, and become much wealthier as a result. Zach did not have a super high paying job so he was limited as to what he could afford.

In August 2017, Zach purchased a newly renovated, one-bedroom, one-bathroom townhome in an up-and-coming neighborhood close to where he worked. He purchased the property for $250,000 with an FHA loan, so he was required to bring a total of $8,500 to the closing. Zach was not interested in paying $8,500 though. He reached out to friends and family who ended up letting him borrow a total of $6,000 so he only needed to bring $2,500 of his own money to the closing table.

After closing, he and his longtime girlfriend moved in and split the $1,650 mortgage payments. Now, rather than paying $950 in rent, he was paying $825 to himself. Things went swimmingly for a few months, but then he and his girlfriend broke up. Zach was now left with a mortgage of $1,650.

After the breakup, well over half of his paycheck every month was going toward the mortgage. This left him in the same trap that many Americans fall into: hardly any savings and extremely limited on the things he could do outside of work. Purchasing a place that is on the upper edge of what you can afford and not being able to save for the future is not a good situation. Zach recognized this immediately, and after his friends started joking about living in a camper, he thought that it actually wouldn't be such a bad idea.

Zach purchased a camper for $1,350 and his goal was to live in the camper while renting out his townhome on a short-term basis though Airbnb, Vrbo, etc. He put the camper in the dedicated parking spot around the back of the townhome and started living there immediately. He lived in the trailer for six to seven months and averaged $2,200 per month in gross short-term rental income.

Rather than paying $1,650 per month, he was making $550 per month. This is a net difference of $2,200 per month or $26,400 per year—not to mention the $5,000 in loan paydown and the $15,000 of appreciation he received after the first year. By putting down just $3,850 of his own money, Zach was able to generate $46,400 of net worth in one year. That's over a 1,205 percent annualized return! To recap:

Rent savings: $1,650 per month

Cash flow: $550 per month

Total additional monthly savings: $2,200

Total additional annual savings: $26,400

Loan paydown after year 1: $5,000

Appreciation: $15,000

Total increase in net worth = $26,400 in savings + $5,000 loan paydown + $15,000 appreciation = $46,400

$46,400 of net worth generated / $3,850 invested = 1,205%+ return

When talking to Zach, I had to address the elephant in the room. How was your lifestyle impacted by living in a trailer? He laughed and said, "not at all." Living in a trailer for a year has taught him how to be more minimalistic, and to appreciate the things in life that matter. Living in a trailer forced him to be more productive. He wasn't going to sit in the trailer and watch Netflix. Instead, he focused more on his 9–5 job, going to the park to relax, and exercising.

After a year, Zach's camper living days were over and he is now renting a studio apartment for $900 a month while continuing to Airbnb the townhome. Since the Airbnb still cash flows him about $400 after setting aside reserves, he is able to offset some of his rent costs with his rental income. That $900 studio apartment becomes $500. The savings continue!

Anyone who is house hacking has a larger purpose. A purpose that is beyond money or growing your net worth. That's Zach's story. An unusual one, but inspiring to say the least!

 "I house hack because I wanted more from life. I've had a tough year. My mom got diagnosed with liver cancer and the doctor only gave her a few months to live. This hit me hard in so many ways. It made me realize the purpose behind the "sacrifices" that I'm making right now. The first being that life is short and it can be even shorter than expected. You need to put yourself in a position where you can live your best life. Secondly, you need to build a financial shield that can cushion these unexpected blows in life. Because I was able to save so much money in just a year, I was able to give my mother a place to live for a few months before she found a more permanent place."

ACTION STEPS

❏ Sign up for Uber or Lyft if you do not know the city where you will be house hacking. Start driving (while getting paid) and get a feel for the different neighborhoods.
❏ Determine the type of property you want to live/invest in.
❏ Determine the location you want to live/invest in, while finding out more about the area (crime rate, school district, etc.).
❏ Find a real estate agent and set up an MLS feed that meets your criteria.
❏ Start researching and analyzing properties.

CHAPTER 4

ASSEMBLING YOUR TEAM

What do you think when you hear the names Michael Jordan, Warren Buffett, Steve Jobs, Serena Williams, and Tom Brady? Regardless of what team you might be a fan of, or which company you admire, there is no denying that these individuals are some of the greatest success stories in their respective fields. How do you think they became the greatest? They certainly did not do so by themselves. They all had teammates and/or a supportive team that they leaned on to make them better and achieve their level of greatness.

Michael Jordan had one of the best coaches of all time in Phil Jackson, and he was surrounded by high quality players such as Scottie Pippen and Horace Grant. Warren Buffett would be worth a fraction of what he is today without his business partner and long-time friend, Charlie Munger. Steve Jobs had Steve Wozniak. Serena Williams had a multitude of personal trainers, nutritionists, and coaches that helped her improve her game. Tom Brady? He was fortunate enough to be paired with one of the best football coaches of all time in Bill Belichick.

The point here is that you are not going to be able to start your house-hacking journey on your own. You are going to need to work with a team. As the old adage goes, "No (wo)man is an island." Along the way, you are going to have good and bad teammates. Be sure that you quickly dispose of the bad, and then do everything you can to retain the good. High quality teammates in real estate are invaluable.

If you listen to the *BiggerPockets Podcast*, peruse the forums, or watch our videos, you will hear almost everyone talk about how important the team is to their success. You must have great bookkeepers, accountants, lawyers, contractors, engineers, lenders, agents, property managers, and many more along the way. That's a lot of people to need, and it can be overwhelming! Do you really need ten people to start investing in real estate? How do you screen all of them? How do you make sure they are good teammates? These are obstacles for many first-time investors and I'm here to make your life easier.

Myth of Team Assembly

The notion that you need a team of ten or more people to start investing in real estate is nonsense. You do not need the majority of the aforementioned people when house hacking. You will have one property so you can do your own books, prepare your own taxes, and manage the property yourself. The only people you absolutely need include your lender, real estate agent, and contractor if you are seeking to make improvements to the property.

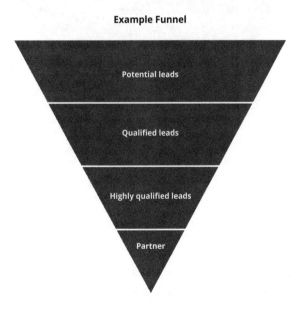

Example Funnel

Potential leads

Qualified leads

Highly qualified leads

Partner

You will find that the process of finding each team member is similar as you assemble your team. At BiggerPockets, we love to think in terms of funnels. Many leads convert to potential partners; and based on a series of criteria, you ultimately decide who you want to work with during this journey. It's much like dating. When you are single and interested in getting into a relationship, you start becoming more flirtatious in your everyday life to add people through the top of your funnel. You make a point to talk to that cute girl (or guy) at the gym, at the grocery store, or at the party. You also might get on the dating apps such as Tinder, Hinge, or Bumble to increase your prospects.

Once a potential girlfriend/boyfriend has been added to your funnel, you start to hang out with that person a bit more. You go on a few dates. If things go well, after a few months, you may end up meeting their parents. If the relationship continues to flourish for a year or more, you might consider moving in together. This is when it gets serious. If you can bear to live with each other, there is a high probability that you may have found "the one." I understand that I am taking all of the emotions out of dating, but that is ultimately what it is—a funnel.

Marriage Funnel

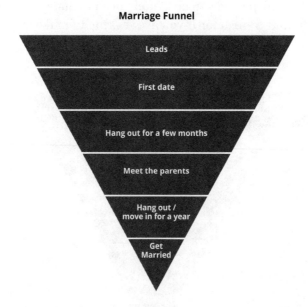

The process of assembling your team will be much quicker, less romantic, and more like the emotionless process described above. You want leads that have a high probability of becoming your team member so recommendations and networking with people you meet through Bigger-Pockets and meetups are likely your best bets. (You can search meetups and events in your area at www.BiggerPockets.com.) If that doesn't work for you, I would resort to more generic platforms such as Google Reviews, HomeAdvisor, Zillow, and others easily accessible. In any case, you will want to increase the leads that go into your funnel.

As you begin to find team members that may be able to help you, bring them to the next stage of the funnel. Schedule a phone call, or meet them for coffee or a drink to begin the conversations. What exactly are you looking for? How do you operate? Are they going to be pleasant to work with? If your prospective team member checks off all of the boxes, you need to make a decision on whether you want to have this person be part of your team. In many cases, you will have multiple people that you like, and you could see yourself working with several of them. Make sure to meet them on multiple occasions to get to know them even better, and don't hesitate to ask for references. Do your due diligence. These individuals can help or hinder your investments.

Hiring Funnel

Leads

First interaction (phone/coffee/drink)

Do you like them?

Can they help?

Additional screening

Teammate

Let's get into more of the specifics. We are going to explain how we go about getting a lender, agent, and contractor on your team in this section, as these are the three team members who you will most likely need for your house hack.

Lender

The first step in purchasing a house hack is finding a lender. With a house hack, you will be taking out a loan that is serviced by Fannie Mae or Freddie Mac. Heard of them? We touched on these earlier, but they are important so here is a brief overview.

Fannie Mae and Freddie Mac are government organizations that provide loans to homebuyers. As of 2019, they offer loan products for one- to four-unit properties. The great thing about these two organizations is that they are by far the cheapest way to finance your house hack. The downside is that they do not budge when it comes to their lending criteria. You need to be a perfectly round peg that fits into a perfectly round hole. This means you need to have a certain credit score, debt-to-income ratio, and down payment; the property needs to appraise at value; and it needs to be livable. If any of these criteria are not met, they can deny you the loan.

Were those last few sentences gibberish to you? I know I didn't know what most of this meant when I first started house hacking. Let's dive in a bit deeper to learn more about the criteria for Fannie Mae and Freddie Mac.

Credit Score

You can think of your credit score as your "debt" grade. Similar to the 90s to 100s you received on your exams in school, the higher your credit score; the less "risky" you are to a lender. The credit score takes into account a variety of different factors, and it combines them into one concise number for you to show your lender. The score is comprised of the following five factors:

1. **Payment History (35%)** —Whether you pay your outstanding loans off in a timely and consistent manner is what most impacts your credit score. In this case, lenders do feel that past performance is indicative of future results. Make sure that you are current on all of your loans. This means your student loans, car loan, credit cards, rent, and revolving lines of credit.

2. **Credit Utilization (30%)**—This is the amount of credit you are using, divided by the amount of credit you have available. For example, if you have a $10,000 limit on your credit card and a balance of $5,000, then your credit utilization will be 50 percent. You want to keep your credit utilization as low as possible. The most obvious way to do this is to make sure you pay off your credit cards in a

timely manner to keep the balances low. Having an outstanding credit card balance can destroy not just your credit score, but your financial position all together. If you use and then pay off a credit card, you will be rewarded with cash back, free travel, gift cards, and many other things that credit card companies offer you to use their card. The trick is, if you don't pay them off in full, you will be paying interest rates of 20 percent or more. This is crippling debt that, over time, will seem impossible to escape.

3. **Length of Credit History (15%)**—This is exactly what it sounds like: It's the average age in years of the loans you have in your name. For example, if you have had student loans for ten years, your credit card for five years, and your car loan for three years, your average length of credit history would be (10 + 5 + 3) / 3 = 6 years. The lower the number, the riskier you are for a lender. This can be frustrating because there is absolutely nothing you can do about it except wait. My recommendation would be to always keep the first credit card, so that it skews the average upward.

4. **New Credit (10%)**—This covers the action of taking out new loans. When you take out new loans, or even apply for them, it signals that you may be in financial trouble and this appears in your credit score. If you are getting ready to be pre-approved, or about to purchase a property soon, I would wait until after you close to obtain the new credit card. When applying for new credit of any type, always ask them if they are going to do a "hard" or "soft" pull. A hard pull will reduce your credit score whereas a soft pull will not. In many cases, such as applying for a mortgage, a hard pull will be inevitable. If you do need to do a hard pull (or multiple hard pulls), try to do them within 30 days of each other. That way, the hard pull only affects your credit score once.

5. **Credit Mix (10%)**—This is often somewhat of a gray area that features the different types of credit in your report. For example, student loans, a mortgage, a revolving line of credit, home equity loans, and credit cards are all different types of loans. Having a good mix of these that you pay on time will indicate that you can handle all kinds of debt, and it will improve your credit score.

After considering all of these factors, the three credit bureaus (Equifax, Experian, and TransUnion) each will provide you with a credit score between 300 and 850. Again, the higher your score, the less risky you are to the lenders, and the more likely it is that you will be able to obtain a loan. Do not be alarmed if the scores are all different; they almost always are different. Your lender will take the middle score and use that when applying for the loan.

You should have an understanding of what makes up your score, but if not, please go back and read the last page again. This is important stuff. Now, how can you tell if your score is good, bad, or somewhere in the middle? You know that the higher the score, the better your position, but you may not know what constitutes the score as good or bad.

300–549 — Horrible. Good luck getting a loan. If you find yourself in this category, you are going to need to take the next twelve to eighteen months to fix your score. I recommend taking action on my advice above, or checking out Dave Ramsey's podcast called *The Dave Ramsey Show* or his best-selling book, *The Total Money Makeover.* He is an expert in correcting people's debt situation.

550–699 — Decent. You will likely be able to get a loan if you find yourself in the upper end of this category, but you will likely not be able to get approved if you are in the lower end. Other factors will come into play here such as down payment and debt-to-income ratio. You are on the fence, and banks are willing to lend to you, but they view you as a higher risk. To compensate them for this risk, you will likely have to pay a higher interest rate.

700–850 — Great. Assuming the other lending criteria have been met, you will have no problem getting a loan from Fannie Mae or Freddie Mac. You will be seen as the least risky borrower. While some people believe there are a tier of "elites" that are 800-plus, the banks look at anything over 700 as top tier.

If you are looking to get a conventional loan from these organizations, you will need to have a credit score of at least 620. If you decide to go the FHA route, you will need at least a 580 credit score. But if your credit score is below 580, you can still apply for an FHA loan. You'll just need to put down a 10 percent down payment. If your credit score is hovering around these amounts, your first step should be to fix your score as much as possible. Otherwise, it will come back to bite you with higher interest rates.

Debt-to-Income Ratio

The next factor that any lender will review is your debt-to-income ratio

(DTI). There are two types of debt-to-income ratios: front-end and back-end. Both of which are shown as percentages, and show the lender how much your monthly debt obligation will be when compared with your gross monthly income. The differentiation is that front-end DTI only takes into account property expenses (mortgage, insurance, taxes, HOA, and PMI) in your debt obligation, whereas back-end DTI takes into account all of your debt obligations (mortgage, student loans, and car loans) and then divides that by your monthly income.

In most cases, the lender will work off of back-end DTI so in the examples below, I will calculate back-end DTI. To get front-end, you would just remove any non-property related expenses such as car loans, student loans, and credit cards. In order to calculate the debt-to-income ratio, you take your monthly debt payments and divide it by your monthly income. Your monthly income is calculated on your base salary. If you work independently, or for commissions, you will need to show at least two years of income in order for it to be considered in the debt-to-income ratio.

For example, let's say you are making $72,000 per year, have $90,000 in student loans, a $20,000 car loan, and you have a credit card that is paid off each month. Your gross income will be $6,000 per month, you will be paying about $750 in student loans, and approximately $350 in a car payment.

Gross monthly income = $6,000

Student loan: $750 per month

Car loan: $350 per month

Total debt: $1,100

Current debt-to-income ratio = $1,100 / $6,000 = 18%

Using this number, the lender is able to tell you how much you can afford. All lenders are different, but most allow for an "after purchase" debt-to-income ratio of 43 percent to 57 percent. For the sake of this example, we will keep it easy and say that the debt-to-income ratio cannot exceed 50 percent.

Now, we need to see what you can afford. A 50 percent debt-to-income ratio would imply that you have $3,000 in debt obligations each month, compared with $6,000 of income. Since your debt obligations right now are $1,100, you are able to afford a mortgage for $1,900. This includes principal, interest, taxes, insurance, and any HOA fees. Now that you know the maximum monthly payment, given your expected interest rate and the term of the loan, the lender will determine the amount of house that you can afford.

As a rough example, a $1,900 a month payment at 2019 interest rates (approximately 5 percent) will allow you to purchase a property priced at approximately $325,000. Remember, these are just for instructional purposes. Each lender has different criteria, so inquire with multiple lenders to determine the best rates for you.

That is what the debt-to-income looks like when purchasing a normal house where you plan to live. However, you're planning to house hack, and by definition, house hacking is living in one part of the house and renting out the remaining rooms. We talked about the different ways to house hack in a previous chapter. Nonetheless, your property is an income generator, and it should be included in the debt-to-income ratio.

If you plan on purchasing a two- to four-unit property, then the lender will take 75 percent of the appraised rents for the unit(s) that you are not occupying and add this amount to the "income" portion of the equation. However, it can get tricky if you are house hacking a single-family residence. If you decide to go the short-term rental route, this will be considered 1099 income and you will need at least two years of short-term rental history to count toward your income.

If you purchase a single-family residence, live in one room while renting out the others, you are collecting what is called "boarder" income. Unfortunately, most lenders will not include boarder income in your debt-to-income ratio unless you are applying for a HomeReady loan offered by Fannie Mae. Again, call around to different lenders to see if they will include boarder income. Even though most loans are sold to Fannie Mae and Freddie Mac, I have noticed that different lenders are often able to offer different loan products.

How does rental income factor into the calculation? For ease of explanation, let's assume that in our example, you plan to house hack a duplex for $325,000. To recap, this is what your debt-to-income ratio looks like now:

Gross monthly income = $6,000

Student loan: $750

Car loan: $350

Total debt: $1,100

Current debt-to-income ratio = $1,100 / $6,000 = 18%

Assuming zero dollars in rental income, you will be able to afford a $325,000 duplex with 5 percent down so your loan balance will be about $310,000. Now your debt-to-income ratio looks like this.

Gross monthly income = $6,000

Student loan: $750

Car loan: $350

Mortgage: $1,900

Total debt: $3,000

Current debt-to-income ratio = $3,000 / $6,000 = 50%

Given that your debt-to-income ratio is exactly where the lender needs it to be, you would be on the cusp of getting accepted for your loan. However, we can add in the 75 percent of rental income. Let's assume that you are able to rent one side of the duplex out for $2,000, and 75 percent of $2,000 is $1,500. So, $1,500 would be added to your income. Now your debt-to-income ratio will look like this:

Wage income: $6,000

Rental income: $1,500

Gross monthly income = $7,500

Student loan: $750

Car loan: $350

Mortgage: $1,900

Total debt: $3,000

Current debt-to-income ratio = $3,000 / $7,500 = 40%

Now, your debt-to-income ratio is well below the lender's minimum standards, which increases your odds of getting accepted for your loan. You may even be able to afford a more expensive place. That is a question that you need to ask your lender when going through the process. As a heads up, they will need to see a lease signed and a deposit into your bank account to confirm that the rental income is in fact truthful.

Down Payment
One way to reduce your debt-to-income ratio would be to increase your down payment on the property. If you increase your down payment, you decrease the loan amount the lender needs to give you and, thereby, decrease your debt-to-income ratio.

Let's go back to the example, but say you increase your down payment to 10 percent or $32,500. (Remember, the home costs $325,000.) Now, you will only need a loan for $292,500 so your monthly payment will be reduced. Unfortunately, the difference between $16,000 over the course of 30 years is not material. It will only decrease your debt obligation by $100 per month. Adding more to the down payment will likely only be feasible if you are just on the cusp.

Livability and Appraised Value
The other factors that a lender will consider when applying for an owner-occupied loan include livability and appraised value. These are all pretty straightforward so I will only touch on them briefly.

In order to qualify for an owner-occupied home, the property needs to be "livable." In other words, you should be able to move in right away with all of your basic needs met. It needs to have a roof that is intact, four exterior walls, and functioning electricity and plumbing.

Typically, lenders will lend on a metric called "loan-to-value" ratio (LTV). LTV is a simple calculation that tells the lender how much buffer they have when giving a loan for a property. You calculate the LTV by taking the loan amount and dividing it by the value of the property. The larger the down payment on the property, the smaller the loan you will need; and the lower the LTV will be. The lower the LTV, the less risky it is for the lender.

For example, let's say you purchase a property for $100,000 and the bank is willing to give you a loan for $90,000 with a $10,000 down payment. The LTV would be $90,000 divided by $100,000 or 90 percent.

When you take out a mortgage, the lender is protected even if you do not pay the mortgage because they will foreclose on you and take your property back. Trust me, they do not like to do this, and will avoid it in almost every situation. In the event that you leave them no choice, they need to protect their investment. They do this with an appraisal.

The appraisal is an assessment of the value of your prospective property done by an unbiased, third party service called an "appraiser" (fancy name, I know). They take into account comparable properties, age/condition of the property, and a multitude of other factors. After they have taken all these factors into account, they establish the true value of your property. The appraiser will use the value of the appraisal in the LTV calculation. For example, if you are purchasing a $300,000 property with 5 percent down you are going to get a loan for about $285,000 ($300,000 × 0.95) and bring $15,000 in cash to the closing table. This means that the LTV is 95 percent. However, if the property appraises at $310,000, you still only need a loan for $285,000, but the value of the property is now $310,000. Now, that LTV decreases from 95 percent to 92 percent ($285,000 / $310,000).

If the appraisal comes back at (or above) the purchase price, you will likely be approved for the loan as the LTV will remain the same, or be less than expected. If not, you will have to reduce the loan amount needed by either negotiating the price down with the seller or bringing a larger down payment to the table.

Now you know what a lender is looking for in these situations, and you have put yourself in a position where you check all of the boxes. To recap, you likely will need the following:

- Credit score of 600+
- Debt-to-income ratio below 50 percent
- Enough savings to make the down payment

Finding the livable property that gets appraised at value will come *after* you choose your lender. It's now time to begin the funneling process of finding your lender.

Finding Your Lender

Let's say that you are taking your first trip to Denver. You know a good friend who used to live there. What are you going to do? Of course, you are going to ask your friend, someone you trust, to give you recommendations on good bars, restaurants, and other things to do while you're in town. The same thing goes for finding a quality lender. Ask for recommendations from people you know and trust who have also purchased real estate. These are the highest quality leads. Secondly, you should be attending networking events with people who are real estate investors. They will likely have plenty of recommendations of excellent lenders. If you still are unable to find a quality lender, I suggest that you go to www.BiggerPockets.com and message local investors to see whom they recommend.

You will notice a pattern when it comes to obtaining team members. You will need to get out and talk to the locals; whether it be grabbing coffee with various real estate investors, going to networking events, or just asking friends and family.

After you find five to seven potential lenders, it is time to really narrow them down. The best way to do this is with a phone call, or perhaps grab coffee with them and ask questions as they pertain to your situation. Essentially, you are interviewing them. Here is the list of questions I usually ask:

1. What kind of property types do you lend on? Do you lend on small multifamily properties (two to four units)?
   - *You will want to find a lender that lends on multifamily property if you are house hacking a two- to four-unit property.*

2. What town or area do you lend in?
   - *Find a lender that lends in your area.*

3. Do you take into consideration the condition of the property? What are the maximum repair costs?
   - *This depends on what you are looking to do. If you have a massive rehab, or the property is borderline livable, you will want to know whether you can purchase it with your lender.*

4. Do you have a maximum or minimum loan amount for a property?
   - *This will help you decide on what you can (or cannot) buy.*

5. What is the maximum/typical debt-to-income ratio you would lend to? Do you focus on front-end or back-end DTI?
   - *If you have student loans, a car loan, or credit card debt, you will be more likely to receive the loan if they focus on front-end DTI because it only spotlights the property. However, I have found that it is most common for lenders to focus on back-end DTI, which takes into account all debt in your name. However, be sure to talk to your lender. Depending on the loan type you receive, some of your projected rent may counter the debt.*

6. What is your loan-to-value (LTV) requirement? What is the maximum/typical LTV you lend on? Is it the same for FHA loans?
   - *The higher LTV that is allowed, the more likely you will be able to qualify for a loan. At this time, most lenders require 75 to 80 percent for conventional investments and 90 to 96.5 percent for owner-occupied.*

7. What credit score do you use for your evaluation, and is it the same for conventional and FHA loans?
   - *You will want to know whether your credit score will satisfy your lender's requirements.*

8. My intentions are to rent part of the property out and pay for the mortgage that way. Do you take that into consideration?
   - *If they count future rents toward your mortgage, this will help you qualify for a larger property. I would go with a lender who includes future rent toward the mortgage.*

9. I'm relatively new to real estate investing. Does lack of experience count against me in any way?
   - *Most conventional lenders do not use lack of experience as a way to penalize you, but always double check.*

10. Do I need any cash reserves to qualify for the mortgage?
    - *You should always have cash reserves because things go wrong,*

and you do not want to lose your shirt. However, you do not need a lender to tell you what they should or should not be.

11. Are there any compensating factors? For example, if I have a great credit score, but my debt to income is slightly above your mark, could we work something out?
    - *If you meet one criterion, but barely meet the other, you are going to want to see if the lender will be flexible.*

12. I want to make the loan approval process as easy as possible for the both of us. What do you need from me so I can get it to you all at once?
    - *The easier you make it for the lender, the more likely it is that they will want to continue working with you, give you the best possible rate, and actually close the deal. Your lender is your friend. Make it easy for them.*

After you have asked the questions that you need to ask, it is time to narrow it down to two or three lenders. You will want to go with someone who you get along with, and someone who meets the majority of your standards. The idea is that you will not need to go through this vigorous process on the second, third, and fourth properties; so be sure to find someone that you know and trust from the beginning.

Once you are down to just a few lenders, start getting pricing and terms from each of them to know how to best move forward. We compare these prices and typically go with the lender who offers us the most competitive (cheapest) monthly payment. Assuming that you are comparing mortgages of the same length, the lender will take into account two differing factors to determine the monthly payment: the interest rate and private mortgage insurance (PMI). PMI is a monthly premium you pay when the loan-to-value is under 80 percent. In other words, when you put less than 20 percent down you are required to pay this premium. The amount of the PMI is typically between 0.5 and 1 percent of the entire loan amount on an annual basis. In our example above, if we had a $285,000 loan amount, our PMI would likely be approximately ($285,000 × .01) $2,850 per year or $237.50 per month. This may sound like a lot, but you just need to be sure to factor it into your numbers when looking for your first house hack.

Once you have decided on a lender, it is time to go through the pre-approval process. This is a preliminary process that will tell you, your agent, and the seller of your prospective property what you can afford. You absolutely MUST get a pre-approval letter from your lender to prove to the seller and agent that you are capable of buying a particular property.

Real Estate Agent

Now that you understand how to find, screen, and decide on a lender, it is time to find yourself a high-quality agent. A real estate agent is an individual who facilitates a real estate transaction. They connect buyers and sellers. On any particular deal, there are typically two agents involved. One represents the buyer (buying agent) and the other represents the seller (listing agent). When a seller wants to sell a property, they hire a listing agent to market the property. The most popular place to market a property is on the Multiple Listing Service (MLS).

After you find a property that you want to make an offer on, you will tell your agent the terms you wish to propose to the seller. Some of these terms include purchase price, date of closing, objections, who pays closing costs, and other details. Once these are all hashed out between you and your agent, your agent will create a "purchase agreement." The purchase agreement is a standardized, fill-in-the-blank form that outlines the price and terms in one document. This will be presented to the seller's agent to then present to the seller who will either accept, reject, or make a counteroffer.

If you are uncomfortable negotiating, it's something you should work on; but for now, your agent will do it for you. Your agent is a fiduciary, which means that they legally must act in your best interest at all times so they'll be on your side. After some back and forth between you and the seller, and an offer is accepted, the agent will then lead you through the process of closing the transaction. They will find the title company, set up the inspections, talk with your lender, and ensure the deal closes smoothly and on time.

The agent typically gets paid 3 percent of the purchase price, and is paid by the seller. As a buyer, you typically do not need to worry about paying the agent.

Okay, so now you should understand the reasoning for a real estate agent when looking to buy a property. If I were to sum it up in one sentence it would be that they hold your hand through the entire purchasing process. Now let's talk about finding a high-quality real estate professional.

Finding an Agent

A great agent is an invaluable resource. They will find you the best deals, negotiate with your best interests in mind, and make sure the deal closes smoothly. Like almost anything, finding a top-notch real estate agent can be looked at through the lens of a funnel:

Real Estate Agent Funnel

At the top of the funnel are all of the real estate agents in your city or town. You can find these people everywhere. Look on Zillow, Bigger-Pockets, friends' recommendations, or just call the number on a bus stop bench. There's a million ways to find an agent, but you can spend years churning through horrible agents. We need to figure out how to find the highest-quality agents that can enter the funnel, especially those who are familiar with house hacking.

What's the best way to source high-quality agent leads? Recommendations are always first. Be sure to attend local meetups and find people that are house hacking or investing in real estate in your area. People are more than happy to share information about their favorite agents. By referring business to an agent, that agent will be more likely to send you the best deals. Like anything else, it is always a game of give and take.

I have found recommendations are the best way to find team members. However, if you are just getting started, or you cannot find anyone who recommends an agent, you have a community of over one million members on BiggerPockets, many of whom are real estate agents. In fact, if you are looking for a house hack, I would recommend only finding agents who have a presence on BiggerPockets. After all, BiggerPockets is the largest network of real estate investors in the United States. Brandon Turner, who is the face of BiggerPockets, invented the term "house hacking." If you are looking for an agent, and you want someone who knows about house hacking, there is a high likelihood that they are using BiggerPockets. If a prospective realtor who you are considering is not on the site, it's likely they do not know much about real estate investing OR just do not care about their agency business.

At this point in your search, you should have five to ten leads in your funnel from personal recommendations and networking on BiggerPockets. The next step would be to meet them in person. I always request to meet at 7:15 a.m. I know what you are thinking. Who in their right mind would meet that early? Listen: Whether you like it or not, you are starting a business. If your agent is not able to wake up for a 7:15 a.m. meeting, that means they won't be there for you when you put an offer in late on a Friday night. And guess what? You need someone who will be there for you, regardless of the time of day.

Setting up a meeting can be a logistical nightmare, since it can be nearly impossible to find a time and place that is convenient for both parties. As far as I'm concerned, no one has meetings at 7:15 a.m., so it works almost every single time. When getting coffee with someone, I always suggest meeting at 7:15 a.m. at the coffee shop closest to work. It has never been a problem!

At the meeting, you want to take the time to get to know the person, as a person. Unless you plan on getting your license yourself, you will likely be working with this person for years to come. You are going to want to make sure that you like them as a person first. I would recommend not treating this meeting like an interview. Instead, have a conversation and casually ask the questions needed. In many cases, the agent will answer these questions themselves without you even needing to ask. That is the best!

Here are some questions I always make sure to get answered:

1. Are you a full- or part-time agent?
   - *You are going to want someone who is a full-time agent. If the person has a W-2 job, that will be their priority for forty hours a week. There are too many full-time agents out there to go with a part-time one.*

2. How long have you been an agent for?
   - *I do not recommend working with anyone who has been licensed for under four or five years. The only exception is if they are on a team with a more experienced agent they can go to for advice.*

3. What percentage of your clients are investors versus homebuyers?
   - *Obviously, the more investors the better, but they do not solely need to be investor agents. However, if they have never done a deal with an investor, then this is a red flag that they will try to sell you on the brand new appliances and granite countertops versus the unfinished basement that can be used to add two bedrooms.*

4. Are you an investor yourself?
   - *It would be great to find an agent who is also an investor. However, this can be a double-edged sword. If your agent is also an investor, they may be competing with you on deals. If they are an investor, be sure that you are looking for different deals.*

5. Have you ever transacted a house hack? Ask them to tell you about it.
   - *An agent who is experienced with house hacking will be able to tell you the type of property, the location, and how they recommended their client to rent out the property. In the 2019 market, deals are hard to find. You need to make deals. A good agent will be able to look at a house and suggest how you can turn it into a money-making machine.*

6. What's your view of the market? What neighborhoods do you like right now?
   - *This is a question I ask because I'm always curious to hear what agents think. They spend a lot more time than I do analyzing my local market, so I expect them to be experts in knowing what places have a high likelihood to appreciate over the next five to ten years. If the agent cannot give you a straight answer, move on to the next one. Every agent should have a pulse on their market.*

Once you have had a few of these meetings, it will be painfully obvious as to who you clicked with the most, and who you feel most comfortable representing you in the next transaction. Move forward with that agent.

Have them set you up with an automatic feed of deals from the MLS.

Okay, so you have decided on who your lender and agent are at this point. These are by far your two most valuable team members when purchasing your first house hack, and the two you need to find first. If you are planning to buy a property with some forced appreciation, you are likely going to need to find contractors to help you.

Contractors

Finding a good contractor is like finding a gold mine. They are very rare, but when you do find them, you will want to hold on to them as long as possible. For this reason, quality contractors can be hard to find. Most active investors may not want to share their contractor's information with you because they're doing work for them. And, of course, they don't want to lose their contractor to someone else. Your best bet when finding a contractor is to find a part-time investor who has done a few projects with the same contractor, and has seen good results.

If you are buying a house hack, the property will need to be livable so we will assume that you will not be in need of a general contractor. In a house hack, the projects you will likely be doing are adding a bathroom, a bedroom, or doing minor repairs around the house.

Just like finding an agent or a lender, the highest quality leads will come through your network. It is crucial to attend these networking events and meet local investors in your area. It may be slightly more difficult to get recommendations from the big-time investors, but the local investors you will meet through BiggerPockets and at the BiggerPockets meetups will likely be part-time investors with full-time jobs. These are the resources who will be happy to recommend more business to their contractor as it does not interfere with their primary source of income.

In many cases, it may be difficult to find someone in your network who has done a similar project that you are looking to do. Luckily, you are not the first person to have this problem, and there are billion-dollar companies looking to solve this problem for you. The largest one, and one that BiggerPockets highly recommends, is HomeAdvisor. If you go to www.BiggerPockets.com/Contractors, you will be led to a page that is powered by HomeAdvisor and will allow you to describe the project you are working on through a series of questions. The tool will then send you a list of contractors that have been reviewed by others. Call the highest reviewed contact and have them give you a quote. Be sure to get quotes from a few different contractors. You will be surprised as to how different each quote may be. When you get them on the phone, here are questions that I typically ask:

1. How long have you been in the business?
   - *The more experience the contractor has, the better. Every house is different. The more problems they have experienced, the higher the probability that they will know how to deal with these situations as they occur.*

2. Do you have a contractor's license?
   - *Many states require contractors to have proper licensing. Make sure he/she has a license that corresponds with their area of expertise.*

3. Can I see your certificate of insurance?
   - *Contractors should have both workers' compensation and liability insurance in case something happens on the job. If they do not have this insurance and they get hurt on the job, you as the owner might be liable for any injuries that occur to them while they are working on your property.*

4. Will you obtain permits and set up inspections required for the job?
   - *If you are looking to add a bedroom, bathroom, or touch the plumbing or electrical, you will likely need to pull permits. If so, you need to be sure that the contractors will indeed pull the permits to remain in compliance with the city or town.*

5. How long do you expect it to take to complete this project?
   - *You want to have an expected timeline. We highly recommend incentivizing the contractors to finish early or on time. We do this by giving them a $100 premium for every day they are early and charging a $100 fee for every day they are late.*

6. What is the payment schedule?
   - *Make sure you understand the payment schedule. You will not want to pay in full up front. You will never see those contractors again. The more money you can pay at the end, the better. However, the*

most common payment schedule is typically 50 percent up front, 25 percent halfway through, and 25 percent upon completion.

7. What is the best way to be in touch?
   - *You will want to be in contact with these contractors throughout the process. You will want to be sure what method of communication they prefer so they can get back to you quickly.*

8. Do you clean up after your project?
   - *Find a contractor who cleans up after they are done. Nothing is worse than coming home to a bunch of dust from a drywall project.*

9. How do you deal with unforeseen expenses?
   - *As you start to invest in more and more properties, and complete more and more rehabs, you will deal with unforeseen expenses. Ask the contractor how they deal with these. You will want someone who is very open, communicative, and does not hide anything from you.*

10. Is there a warranty for your services?
    - *You will want the contractor to provide at least a one-year warranty for their services. That way, if they are the cause of any problems, then they are required to come back and fix it with no additional costs to you.*

11. Can you please provide a list of references that I can contact?
    - *Be sure to contact the list of references they give you to make sure that their prior customers are happy with the outcome of their work. If not, this is a huge red flag, and you know to keep searching.*

When it comes to contractors, going with the cheapest one is not always the best option. I highly recommend that you ask for a list of two to three references when you call to get the quote. In other words, talk to customers who they have done similar work with in the past. By taking the time to do this, you can confirm that the contractors are capable of doing high-quality work.

There you have it: your three essential team members when it comes to purchasing a house hack. You should now know who they are, and how to find them. As you continue to add more people to your team such as accountants, lawyers, and property managers, you will go through this same exact funneling process. Generate potential leads, screen, and then decide.

CASE STUDY
LAURA HINES

- **House-hacking strategy:** Traditional
- **Age at first house hack:** 24
- **Location:** Lawrence, Kansas
- **NWROI:** 85%

Meet Laura Hines. Laura was just any ordinary 23-year-old American a year ago. She had finished her undergraduate degree in environmental science at the University of Kansas and did not know what she wanted to do next. Laura was a recent graduate (and newlywed) who was scared to take on the real world. She was comfortable going to school, so she strongly considered going back for a nursing degree. That career would allow her to make more money when she is older and put off any real-life decisions for a few more years while she continued to live a similar life to what she had been living for a number of years.

It is funny how you can stumble onto something at the perfect time. Shortly after she found herself in this position, Laura found BiggerPockets. She discovered the strategy of house hacking. Her mind was blown. She thought that house hacking seemed like a great way to build a strong financial position so that she could enjoy life with her husband and future kids. She was sold.

Laura used her undergraduate degree in environmental science to obtain a W-2 job with the state of Kansas. Because of the steady income and flexibility of this job, she was able to qualify for a loan and start submitting offers on properties. She asked a friend to be her realtor, and they submitted an offer on a duplex in the college town of Lawrence, Kansas. Unfortunately, her friend/realtor did not understand what the seller wanted, and they ended up losing out on the deal by $5,000.

There are not a lot of multifamily properties in Lawrence so they had to wait four months before making another offer. Finally, a property came on the market that would be perfect for her first house hack. It was a side-by-side duplex with each unit separated by their own garage for $163,000. There was no way they were missing out on this one. They put in the offer for $5,000 above asking at $168,000 and wrote a letter detailing how she was a newlywed purchasing her first home with friends in the neighborhood. The sellers had over five offers on the table, but went with Laura because they felt that she would take the best care of the place.

They went under contract and since she was relatively new to the idea of house hacking and real estate investing, she decided to play it safe by putting down 20 percent on a conventional owner-occupied mortgage, making their monthly payment $965 per month. There was a slight problem in this case. They were closing on the property in February, but both sides of the duplex were rented until July. Unless she and her husband could convince one set of tenants to move out in the next sixty days, there could be no deal.

After some convincing, one set of tenants decided to end their lease early and move out at the end of February instead of waiting until July. Bullet dodged. These tenants occupied the less desirable unit, which would be where Laura and her husband would live. After a $6,000 cosmetic rehab of redoing the floors, replacing the kitchen cabinets and countertops, and making updates to the bathroom, the new value of the property was about $200,000.

The tenants in the next unit were paying $675 in rent, significantly below market value. Once the tenants moved out in July, she and her husband put in another $5,000 in cosmetic upgrades and were able to rent the unit out for $850 to $900.

Once the rehab was completed, she and her husband paid the mortgage of $975 per month while collecting $900. They paid $75 per month (before reserves) to live in a two-bedroom apartment by themselves. Before stumbling upon the idea of house hacking, they were renting a much smaller apartment for $615 per month. A total savings of over $500 per month! After you add in $30,000 of added value through the renovations, and about $5,000 of loan paydown throughout the year, this is what her NWROI looks like:

$5,000 of annual savings + $30,000 of appreciation + $5,000 of loan paydown = $40,000 of net worth increase

She put down $36,000 to purchase the property and $11,000 to rehab, which brings us to:

$40,000 / $47,000 = 85% return

Laura and her husband received an 85 percent return on investment, and they did not even leverage as much as they could have. If they had put 3 percent down on the deal instead of 20 percent, they would be looking at a return closer to 400 to 500 percent.

With all of the savings from their first house hack, Laura and her husband plan to purchase another property in the next year or two. This time, they are going to look for a slightly larger property, likely a triplex or fourplex. Now that they have seen the strategy work, they may even use a little more leverage by putting 3 to 10 percent down instead of the full 20 percent.

WHY

"I'm house hacking because, while kids are not in our near future, we will likely be parents in the next seven to ten years. By that time, I'm going to want to have mine and my husband's time be completely freed so that we can spend unlimited time with our child. We want to attend every baseball game, every dance recital, and be home as the child matures. This is invaluable to us, and it is what drives us to tackle all of the obstacles, something that just money cannot accomplish."

ACTION STEPS

- ❏ Reach out to ten local investors on BiggerPockets and ask them to grab coffee. Ask them who they have used for a lender and an agent.
- ❏ Sign up and attend a real estate meetup in the next month.
- ❏ Generate a list of three to five potential lenders. Screen them.
- ❏ Get pre-approved for your first loan.
- ❏ Generate a list of three to five potential agents. Screen them.
- ❏ Sign up for the MLS feed.

CHAPTER 5

FINANCING

If you have ever watched Brandon Turner's webinars on BiggerPockets.com, he talks about having tools in your toolbox. In a literal sense, it certainly does not hurt, especially if you are doing a large rehab project. However, he uses this as an analogy when talking about how to finance deals. The more ways you know how to finance a deal (tools), the more likely that you can complete a deal.

Imagine building a house, and the only tool you had was a hammer. The house would probably be in poor shape: wood cut unevenly, messed up electrical, useless plumbing, and circular paint globs from your hammer. However, if you start adding tools such as a circular saw, reciprocating saw, wrenches, drills, and paint brushes, your house will start to come together nicely.

The same thing happens when we talk about financing. If the only way you know how to finance a deal is through a 20 percent down conventional loan, it is going to be much more difficult for you to find a deal. However, if you understand all of the methods that I describe in this chapter and more, you will get the deal done. For those times that you cannot "find" a deal, so you need to "make" a deal. Making a deal all begins with the financing.

Since this is a book about house hacking, you will most likely be occupying the property that you buy. With that being said, this opens up a lot of options for "owner-occupied" loans as the government (Fannie

Mae and Freddie Mac) advocate for home ownership. It is part of the American dream, right?

As I mentioned in chapter 4, loans that are purchased by Fannie Mae and Freddie Mac are typically the least expensive route, which is why I believe this should be the chosen route for any house hacker. However, it may involve cleaning up your credit score, paying down some of your other debts, and purchasing a house with an affordable down payment.

Don't worry though, as there are methods that people with little money (and bad credit) can use when house hacking—they just involve a bit more work. First, let's talk about all of the owner-occupied loans, which require the buyer to live on the property for at least one year.

Conventional Loan

The conventional loan is the most common. When the non-real estate investor purchases a house, they believe that the only way to do it is to put down 20 percent. This, of course, is the most obvious way to purchase a property, and I would be doing you little good if only telling you what everyone already knows. What many people do not know about conventional loans is that they can go down to as little as 5 percent on a single-family property. Why doesn't everyone do this? There is this thing called private mortgage insurance (PMI). PMI is required at any point you put less than 20 percent down, and this is why many people do not think to put less than 20 percent down. They do not want to pay the PMI. My answer to this: Factor it into your numbers. If you can still cash flow with PMI, then it is worth it to still do the deal.

Unfortunately, the 5 percent down option only works if you wanted to house hack a single-family residence. If you want a two- to four-unit property, then you will need to either put a minimum of 20 percent down, or pick another loan option.

FHA Loan

The Federal Housing Administration, commonly referred to as the FHA, insures a type of loan that they creatively named the FHA Loan. The FHA program was created in response to the seemingly insurmountable amount of foreclosures and defaults that happened during the Great Depression. To help provide lenders with more comfort, and to stimulate the housing market, the FHA made it possible by insuring loans with lower interest payments that require the borrower to bring less cash and have a lower credit score to purchase a property.

Although you do not need to be a first-time homebuyer, the FHA Loan is popular with first-time homebuyers and house hackers because of the 3.5 percent down payment, and the lower credit score requirements. However, as a result of lending to riskier borrowers, FHA Loans come with PMI, a monthly premium that is added to your principal, interest, taxes, and insurance (PITI).

To qualify for an FHA Loan, the borrower needs to have a credit score of 580. However, the credit score can range from 500 to 579 if the borrower decides to put down 10 percent as opposed to the 3.5 percent. The broader list of requirements are as follows[3]:

- Steady employment history or worked for same employer for two or more years
- Must be a U.S. citizen
- At least a 3.5 percent down payment
- FHA Loans are only available for a primary residence
- Borrower must obtain an appraisal from an FHA-approved appraiser
- Front-end DTI (debt to income) needs to be less than 31 percent
- Back-end DTI needs to be less than 43 percent
- Minimum credit score of 580 if you wish to put 3.5 percent down
- Minimum credit score of 500 to 579 if you wish to put 10 percent down
- Property must be livable

If you check all the boxes on these requirements, then there is a high probability that you will qualify for an FHA Loan.

The biggest downside of an FHA Loan is that darned PMI. How much is that insurance exactly? That depends on the amount of the loan and the loan-to-value ratio. Here is a chart of what you can expect on a 30-year term.

---

3   https://prosperopedia.com/finances/mortgages/2018-fha-loan-requirements/

Loan Amount	Down Payment	PMI
Less than $625,000	5% or more	0.80%
Less than $625,000	5% or less	0.85%
Over $625,000	5% or more	1.00%
Over $625,000	5% or less	1.05%

For example, if you purchased a $300,000 house hack and put 3.5 percent down, you would be paying 0.85 percent in PMI or $300,000 × 0.85% = $2,550 annually or $212.50 monthly.

Unfortunately, the PMI remains with the loan even as you pay off and gain more than 20 percent equity. The only way to get out of private mortgage insurance on an FHA Loan is to replace your existing FHA mortgage with a conventional mortgage. This process is known as refinancing. The process of refinancing a property is identical to the process you go through when obtaining your first mortgage.

Another downside to FHA Loans is that there is a limit as to how much they are willing to lend. The specific amount differs between the city and state you are purchasing in, but this typically is not a problem for house hackers since we are always looking for a place that is reasonably priced.

The FHA Loan is used by house hackers across the country who are looking to purchase a small multifamily property (two to four units) and house hack the traditional way: live in one unit and rent out the others. The reason we do not suggest the FHA Loan for a single-family residence is because there are conventional loan products that offer similar benefits to the FHA Loan. In other words, you can get the same benefits of an FHA Loan without actually having to use it. Now, when you move on to your second project, which may be a small multifamily property, you will have access to an FHA Loan without having to refinance.

203k Loan

If you are looking for a property that can realize some forced appreciation, the 203k Loan is one that you should consider. It is a type of FHA

Loan that allows you to lump any rehab costs into the same loan that is used to purchase the property. All of the requirements previously mentioned for the FHA Loan are also required for the 203k Loan. However, with the added element of rehab costs, there is more work involved.

Your contractors will need to do a lot more paperwork, and you will need to estimate rehab costs before you close on the deal so that the lender can give you the proper loan amount. There is an area on www.HUD.gov that assists you in doing this, but understand that there is more work involved.

When the rehab begins, you will have the lender release the funds for the project into an escrow account. The funds will be released according to the timeline agreed upon by you and the contractor. There is not much of a restriction on the type of repairs that need to be done. Anything from a major rehab and/or structural repairs to new additions or the elimination of safety hazards are all fair game for the 203k Loan. However, you are on a tight timeline and need to make sure the project is finished within six months.

When choosing 203k Loans, you need to know that there are two types: the standard and streamline loans. The standard 203k Loan is a bit more involved, but there is no limit set for the amount of repair funds you are able to receive. You just need to abide by the standard FHA requirements.

The streamline 203k Loan involves less paperwork than the standard 203k Loan. The only difference is that you will get a list of recommended repairs along with bids from a contractor with $35,000 being the maximum amount you can spend on repairs.

The FHA and 203k Loans are best for those looking to house hack a small multifamily property. This is not to say that you cannot do an FHA or 203k Loan on a single-family property, but there are much better programs out there for single-family residences, which I'll dive into next.

United States Department of Agriculture (USDA) Loan

A USDA Loan is a mortgage option that requires a zero down payment, and is available to owner-occupants who wish to purchase in a qualified rural or suburban area. The USDA defines "rural" as any area with a population under 35,000, which has very few low to moderate income earners purchasing houses. The USDA Loan's base annual income limit is $82,700 for a one- to four-member household or $109,150 for a five- to eight-member household. To find out if you are in a rural area you can google "USDA loan map" and determine whether or not your area is eligible for a USDA Loan.

USDA Loans are issued by private lenders, and are guaranteed by the USDA (yes, the same people who grade your meat). The purpose of the USDA Loan is to allow low to moderate income earners in rural areas to get a taste of that "American Dream" of homeownership.

Have you heard of the Pareto principle, aka the 80/20 rule? Vilfredo Pareto was an Italian economist who discovered that 80 percent of Italy's wealth was owned by 20 percent of the people. This principle, or a variation thereof, applies to almost every scenario. It is no different for USDA loans and where people are located in the United States.

Despite there being approximately 325 million people in the United States, 225 million of them live in just 3 percent of the United States' land mass. The last 100 million? They live in the 97 percent of the United States that is considered "rural" or "suburban" and will qualify for the USDA loans. Please visit www.USDALoans.com/Program to see a map of the United States that shows you where USDA loans are eligible and ineligible.

Because of the USDA Loan guarantee, lenders are willing to take more of a risk and offer certain homebuyers more competitive rates and terms than a conventional mortgage. The main benefits include:
- No down payment
- Lower interest rates
- Lower PMI
- Flexible credit requirements

In order to keep balance in this world, every yin has its yang, and the USDA Loan is no different. Not everyone can just walk into a bank and obtain a USDA Loan. The minimum requirements include:
- U.S. citizenship
- Dependable income, meaning salaried income or at least two years of self-employment income
- Acceptable DTI ratio, which can vary by lender so it's difficult to put a number on it
- Annual income that does not exceed 115 percent of the area's average income
- Property must be located in a rural/suburban area
- Minimum credit score of 640, but typically can be negotiated

Of course, the USDA is part of the government, and nothing is smooth sailing with the government. They do not just take your family's income and compare that with the county's requirements. There are also a series of adjustments that take acceptable deductions into account, such as childcare and medical expenses.

Unfortunately, the USDA Loan only works for single-family residences so the only house-hacking strategies would be the rent-by-room, the short-term rental, or the trailer strategy. The traditional method of house hacking will not work with a USDA Loan.

Veterans Affairs (VA) Loan

In the World War II era, the United States had a huge problem. Veterans who had risked their lives to preserve the values of their country were thrown to the curb when they returned home. In order to combat this problem and incentivize U.S. citizens to join the war, the United States government created the VA Loan, allowing returning service members to purchase a one- to four-unit property without a down payment or good credit.

If you are a veteran of the U.S. military, or active member, I would like to first thank you for your services and highly suggest you continue reading to learn more about the benefits of the VA Loan. Unless you are a veteran, active-duty servicemember, or the spouse of a veteran, this loan will not apply to you. Feel free to skip to the next section.

The backend process works similarly to the FHA Loan. The government does not lend directly to homebuyers. Instead, they go through typical lenders. The Department of Veterans Affairs only offers a guaranty, which allows lenders to offer loans with better terms. The terms that you will typically see on a VA Loan include:

- Zero percent down payment
- No PMI
- Competitive interest rates
- Relaxed qualification standards

Besides not being available to everyone, the two largest downsides are that the VA Loans have a loan limit and corresponding funding fees. The most expensive home a veteran can buy is $484,350. If you live in an area with generally high average home prices, you could be eligible to borrow up to $726,525.

The fee due at closing goes directly to the VA to ensure the program can continue running for future generations of military homebuyers. The fee varies depending on each homebuyer, but usually ranges from zero percent to 3.3 percent of the purchase price.

Hold on a second! I just told you that you do not need to put anything down, but this is essentially the same as a 3 percent down payment. The good news about this fee is that borrowers can roll the funding fee into their loan OR you can have the seller pay the fee. In most cases, the buyer can purchase the home with absolutely nothing down.

The VA Loan is one of the best options for veterans who are looking to build wealth through real estate. It can be used for any property up to four units, as long as the purchase price is below the established threshold.

HomeReady

HomeReady is a program offered by Fannie Mae that helps low to moderate income owners purchase a property. The HomeReady Program reduces the down payment and mortgage insurance requirements. What really separates HomeReady from the rest of the options is that it is more flexible about allowing contributions from other lenders. For example, in many cases, lenders will not allow you to take gifts from family members, friends, or other down payment assistance resources. With the HomeReady Program, you can truly purchase a home with zero down.

Believe it or not, you do not have to be a first-time homebuyer to use the HomeReady Program. The requirements to qualify for HomeReady include:

- You must earn income less than, or equal to, the average income in your area. If you are unsure of where your income lies, you can find the average income in your area on www.FannieMae.com.
- You must have a minimum credit score of 620.
- You must take a home ownership class.

If you qualify for the HomeReady Program, there are numerous benefits, including:

- Down payment and credit score requirements are lower.
- You may accept gifts as part of down payment and closing.
- Mortgage insurance is reduced. Once you have paid down the loan

to have 20 percent equity (or 80 percent LTV), the mortgage insurance disappears.
- Family or friends can co-sign your home loan.
- Income from others in your house can help you get approved.

The HomeReady option works best for those looking to house hack a single-family home. If you wish to purchase a two- to four-unit property, the lending requirements change slightly. If you purchase a two-unit property, you will have to bring a 15 percent down payment to the table, and you will need a 25 percent down payment for three to four units. However, these amounts can still be funded from a family member, friend, or assistance program. But it will certainly be more difficult to obtain more money.

HomeReady is Fannie Mae's option. I don't want Freddie Mac to get mad so let's talk about his option next.

Home Possible

Home Possible is Freddie Mac's version of HomeReady. Home Possible allows those with low to moderate income to purchase property with a low down (or no down) payment. The main distinction between Home Possible and HomeReady is that the borrower with Home Possible needs to be a first-time homebuyer. If you have already purchased a property in the past, this section will have little use to you. Feel free to skip ahead.

The down payment with Home Possible will be 1–5 percent depending on your income, the type of property, and location. As it is with almost any type of financing, when your equity stake is less than 20 percent, you are required to pay PMI. However, the good news is that unlike FHA Loans, once you reach a 22 percent equity stake (78 percent LTV), the PMI automatically burns off. You can increase your equity stake by either paying down principal or obtaining an appraisal by a bank-approved appraiser that proves your property has appreciated since a prior appraisal.

Just like the rest of the "specialty" loans, Home Possible has limitations as well. In order to qualify for the Home Possible Program, you need to:
- Be at or below your area's average income
- Have a 1–5 percent down payment, which may be money that's been gifted

- Live in the home you are purchasing as your primary residence
- Have a credit score of 620 or more
- Have a maximum debt-to-income ratio of 45

You can use the Home Possible Program to obtain any property that is up to four units. This program will work for any first-time house hacker, and it's a program I strongly recommend.

As you can see, there are a plethora of owner-occupant financing options for house hackers that your one lender can provide. Make sure you ask him/her about these programs, and get their opinion on which of these options they feel would be best for you. I know that was a fire-hose amount of information spit out at you and I'm sure reading about loan terms was not all that entertaining. Here is a table that summarizes the seven loan types described above.

	Conventional	FHA	203k*	USDA	VA	Home-Ready	Home Possible
Down Payment	5% to 20%	3.5%	3.5%	0%	0%	3% to 5%	3% to 5%
Minimum Credit Score	~620	580	580	640	620	620	620
Maximum DTI	43% to 50%	43%	43%	Varies	41%	45%	45%
PMI	If under 20% down	Yes	Yes	Lower	No	Yes	Yes
Property Type	Single family	1–4 unit	Yes	Lower	No	Single family**	Single family***
Annual Income Restriction?	No	No	No	No	No	Yes	Yes

*Main difference from FHA is that rehab costs are included
** Can purchase up to 4 units with 15% to 20% down
*** Must be your first home

You should now have a good idea as to what loan might work best for you based on your situation. If you have a poor credit score or have too much debt, your first order of business will be fixing these things. There can be another full book on how to fix your credit score, but as a start, go back and read chapter 4 to remind yourself how to determine your credit score. If you have too much debt, there are really only two ways to combat this issue. Make more income, or pay down your debts.

What if you are unable to qualify for any of the aforementioned mortgage types? As the great Bob Marley once said, "Don't worry about a thing. 'Cause every little thing gonna be alright." There is this thing called private financing. Private financing is a completely different beast. If you would like to learn more about it, BiggerPockets's own Matt Faircloth wrote an entire book on it, *Raising Private Capital*, which can be purchased at www. BiggerPockets.com/Store. Here is a quick overview of private capital.

Home Equity Line of Credit (HELOC)

Have you already purchased a property before your desire to purchase financial independence? If so, and you have some equity in the property through appreciation or loan paydown, then you can go to a bank and get a loan that is secured by the equity in your house. For example, let's say you purchased a house for $187,500 three years ago with a $150,000 loan. The house is now worth $200,000 and the loan has been paid down to $125,000.

This means that you have $200,000 - $125,000 = $75,000 of equity in your house.

Banks will give you a loan for 80 percent of the equity you have in the house.

In this example, it would be $75,000 × 80% = $60,000.

Depending on your area, this might be enough money to purchase a smaller house hack outright. However, in most areas, it will be hard to find a property for $60,000. What you can do, though, is combine loan types.

You can take the HELOC from your current residence and apply it toward the down payment on your next house hack. Let's say you pulled $60,000 out of your current residence and wanted to put the entire $60,000 down as a down payment on a 5 percent conventional loan.

Ignoring all other factors (credit score, DTI, etc.), you would have the purchasing power for a $60,000 / 5% = $1.2 million property.

Think you could buy a house hack with that amount being available to you? Absolutely! Be careful though, properties that are more than $400,000 will be difficult to house hack in many markets. So, just because you *can* qualify for a $1.2 million property does not mean that you should take that leap. You will need to make sure the rents that you can garner will provide you with the necessary cash flow.

HELOCs are only useful for those who already own a property with a significant amount of equity. If this is not you, it is something that you can consider in the future. If you are able to obtain the HELOC, and purchase a property with only the HELOC, then there are few requirements as to what you do with the money. If you are using the HELOC as a down payment on a larger property, you will then need to adhere to the bank's criteria in order to get the conventional loan approved.

Private Capital

All of the mortgage types described above need to be approved by a higher power. That higher power is comprised of the two government programs we have discussed, Fannie Mae and Freddie Mac. Private capital can come in many forms (e.g., hard money, portfolio, or seller financing), but the underlying commonality is that they are kept on the lender's books. Since the lender holds onto the loan and does not sell them to Fannie Mae or Freddie Mac, they can be much more flexible with their lending requirements.

Let's dive into the three main types of lending: hard money loans, portfolio lending, and seller financing.

Hard Money Loans

We are not going to spend too much time on hard money loans because they are outrageously expensive, and typically not feasible for house hackers.

Hard money loans are called "hard money" because they are based on the hard asset and nothing more. The lender is not concerned about your income, credit score, or any of your personal finances. They only care that you are purchasing property that has a high likelihood of appreciating in value, usually through forced appreciation (e.g., rehab, raising the rent, or decreasing expenses).

Hard money loans are easy to obtain, but they are compensated for the risk. These are best suited for flippers who can use the money to purchase a property quickly, do the rehab, and quickly refinance out to a cheaper mortgage. Most hard money loans have a term of three to twelve months. If you are trying to house hack, I would suggest leaving hard money loans alone.

Portfolio Lending

A portfolio loan is the closest thing to a conventional loan. The only difference is that it is not sold to Fannie Mae or Freddie Mac. The loan is kept on the bank's books so it is the bank who makes the ultimate decision as to whether or not they will provide you with a loan. Unfortunately, I cannot give you a list of criteria you must meet in order to qualify for a portfolio loan, but I can say that they do look at the same factors as a conventional loan. How much weight they put on each piece of criteria will differ from bank to bank. Your best bet is to increase your debt-to-income ratio, down payment, and credit score to help your odds of getting approved for the loan.

How you go about getting a portfolio loan is like most things in life: not as easy as it sounds. You can't just walk into a bank and ask if they do "portfolio" loans. The bankers will stare at you like a three-headed dog guarding the Sorcerer's Stone (I'll call you Fluffy). You need to go into a bank—local banks and credit unions work best—and ask them if they sell their loans to Fannie Mae or Freddie Mac, or do they keep the loans on their own books. If they keep them on their own books, they are portfolio lenders and they may consider lending to you.

Not every bank will do this, so it is truly a numbers game. Remember the funnels? Same thing applies here. The more banks you ask, the more likely it is that you will find one that offers portfolio loans. I know of a guy who was looking to obtain a private loan and he wanted to look the part so he dressed up in a suit and tie, walked to the bank, and really sold himself on being a quality borrower. Do you know which bank it was that he entered? It was one of those local banks inside Walmart. You really can obtain them anywhere—it's just a matter of searching.

When you do find a lender that keeps their loans on their own books, make sure you are prepared with the following information:
- Credit score
- Monthly debt payments
- Monthly income (W-2) or last two years of self-employed income
- Cash reserves (including retirement)

If you know all of this information, the banker should be able to tell you whether or not you will be able to qualify for one of their loans. If you decide to go with this particular private lender, that is when they will be sure to verify all of the information you provided.

Portfolio lending is much more flexible than any of the loans that the government backs. For this reason, they can be used for any type of property. Be careful though, because with great power, comes great responsibility. The more flexible the terms, the easier it is to close on a deal that will not work for you. Always, always, *always* run the numbers! We will talk about analysis in chapter 7.

Seller Financing

When Brandon Turner was 24 years old, he bought a twenty-one-unit apartment complex with no money down. He was not making very much money at the time, and there was no way a lender would approve him for a loan. Knowing this, he asked himself: "How do I buy an apartment complex if no one is willing to lend to me?"

Turns out, there was one lender that would: an older couple at his church. He went around telling everyone that he wanted to purchase a medium-sized apartment building and, lo and behold, he stumbled upon a couple looking to sell their building. The couple did not need the lump sum of cash, but instead preferred to have monthly installments paid to them, along with an interest rate. After a couple of years, he paid them off, and went with a cheaper loan option.

That's the idea of seller financing though. Honestly, I did not get too creative with the name, but sometimes simple is better. Seller financing is when the seller turns around and becomes the bank. These standards are even looser than the portfolio lending because it will likely just be an average Joe selling you the property. A good seller financer will be sure to check your credit score, income, and the same things that a typical bank would evaluate. It is certainly not required though.

If you are looking for a low down payment, have a bad credit score, or low income, and the seller simply trusts that you will pay, that is good enough. Nothing else required!

This is a great way to purchase your house hack with zero to little down. It works for any type of property, and it can be extremely powerful. Again, just be careful. The seller does not care that you cash flow each month; that is something you need to analyze and check for yourself.

Partnering

The CEO of BiggerPockets, Scott Trench, began his journey by partnering with one of his best friends, Walker. These two joined forces and bought their first house hack in 2014 when the term was relatively new, and there were not nearly as many success stories. So, by nature, Scott was nervous. This was the largest investment of his life. He was 24 years old. It was scary. To settle the butterflies, he asked his best friend if he wanted to go in on the deal. He said, "yes."

Scott and Walker found a side-by-side duplex for $240,000 where each side had two bedrooms and two bathrooms. They both brought half of the 3.5 percent FHA down payment to the table and were all in together. Their mortgage payment, which included principal, interest, taxes, insurance, and PMI was about $1,600 per month. They rented the other side out entirely for $1,200 and were each paying $200 to $400 a month for rent. Not a bad situation.

Arguably, the best part of this partnership is that although they purchased the house together, Scott was the only one with the loan under his name. If you remember, you can only have one FHA loan out at a time. That means that they could purchase another house hack together in one year with an FHA loan where Walker signed off on it. This is exactly what they did. A little over one year later, they purchased a duplex on the other side of Denver. This one is an up-down duplex where they both lived in the bottom unit while renting out the top unit.

If you are nervous about getting started, partnering up with a friend is a great way to calm the nerves. You put less down, get to live with a buddy, and you can effectively have two FHA loans out at once.

The flipside (or downside) to this method is that you have a partner in the deal. Sure, you get to split the expenses down the middle, but that also means you split the cash flow and equity down the middle as well. For example, if Scott was able to purchase this property by himself, he could rent out the room that Walker occupied for about $800 per month. With that, he would have had rental income of $2,000 per month on a $1,600 mortgage. He would have been living for free and would have had $400 of cash flow. Some of which, I know he would put aside for reserves.

Financing is usually the largest obstacle when it comes to getting a deal done, which is why I just made you drink from the fire hose as you read this chapter. The idea is that I wanted to give you a whole set of tools that would allow you to finance a deal regardless of your financial situation. Whether that be because you are just getting your financial house in order, or because you just can't afford a down payment or have bad credit, you will be able to find financing.

In today's seller's market where housing prices are at all-time highs, it is hard to find deals, so you need to *make* deals. That is where these financing options come into play. Using one or a combination of these ideas will give you the option to make a deal that you may not have found because it wasn't conventional.

I have taken you through why you should house hack, researching the area, building your team, and figuring out what type of loan will work best for you.

CASE STUDY
JOE SADUSKY

- **House-hacking strategy:** BRRRR/rent by room
- **Age at first house hack:** 23
- **Location:** Edgewater Park, North Carolina
- **NWROI:** Infinite

Meet Joe Sadusky. He went to Pennsylvania State. No, there is no "n" in his last name. Therefore, there is no relation to "Sandusky." If you don't know what I'm talking about, look it up. If you do know: There is no relation. Now that we got that out of the way, let's get into his house-hacking story.

Joe graduated from Pennsylvania State at 22 years old with over $110,000 of student loan debt. He was a civil engineer by day, and unknowingly a contractor and house hacker by night. Joe's first house hack was unintentional. He closed on his first property just after he graduated at age 23, which was originally meant to be a wholesale purchase. Because Joe had so much student loan debt and not an incredibly high paying job, there was almost no way that he would be able to obtain a loan. So, what did he do? He started to ask around. Eventually he found a private lender: his grandma. His grandma was able to lend him $30,000 at a favorable rate for the five-bedroom, two-bathroom townhome built in 1875 that he purchased outright.

Can you believe Joe purchased a $30,000 property? I couldn't at first, but then he went on to explain his thought process. It needed a lot of work. Part of the roof was missing, there was mold damage, cracked floorboards, holes in almost all of the walls, copper was taken from the electrical, water in the basement, and there were structural problems with the basement floor joists. It was time to get to work. His father owned a construction business, so Joe was always handy and is never intimidated by large projects. Since he was doing most of the work himself, he estimated that he would only need about $20,000 for the entire rehab. He got a personal loan through Citizens Bank. In total, Joe purchased and rehabbed the property for $50,000 using none of his own money.

When the rehab was complete, he refinanced the property for $115,000. He paid off his debts to grandma, the bank, and was still left with over $65,000 in his bank account. The monthly mortgage payment on the refinance was $1,200. He was perfectly content with paying $1,200 for him and his girlfriend to live in a newly renovated, five-bedroom townhome. However, he was not satisfied with this for very long. In the back of the townhome, there was a separate staircase that led to an additional bathroom and bedroom that were not being used. He knew this could be rented out, so that's exactly what he did. He rented it out to his girlfriend's cousin for $450 per month. A screaming deal for her cousin, but that's what you get when you choose to live with friends or family. Joe and his girlfriend split the rest of the costs so now instead of paying $1,695 to rent a nice two-bedroom apartment, they were paying $750 per month while building equity in the property through both appreciation and loan paydown.

While Joe was fixing up his first property, the owner of the townhome that was attached to his property stopped making payments and abandoned the townhome. It then went into foreclosure. Joe saw that it was on www.Auction.com and used the $65,000 in his bank account to purchase the attached townhome and repeated the process. He obtained another personal loan for $20,000 to fix it up and refinance. Since the second property was almost identical to his first, they both appraised for $115,000.

After rehabbing the second property, Joe moved out of both properties, and is renting them out full time. He now gets $1,775 in rent for each property with a monthly mortgage payment of $1,200. While almost everything in the property is newly updated, he still sets aside $200 each month for reserves and maintenance. His net profit on each rental is $375 per month. This all started with him putting zero dollars of his own money into the deal.

Now, Joe lives with his girlfriend in a larger townhome just a few towns over in Mount Holly, New Jersey. He has no plans to halt his real estate investing anytime soon. Next up, they are going to go after multi-family properties with the hopes of retiring by the time they are 35 years old, using real estate investing as his main vehicle.

WHY

"I house hack to do more than just increase the amount of money I have in my bank account. What is the point of that? It goes much deeper. I just had my first child in April of 2019. (Congratulations, Joe!) Having this child has already changed my ambitious outlook on life. Now, rather than hustle, I want to be able to have the freedom and flexibility to put my family before all else. I've grown up seeing good friends and family members bound to their jobs where they have no control of their future. And the most important things in their lives pass by before they know it. I'm not going to fall into the same trap, and I'm using house hacking as a way out."

ACTION STEPS

- ❏ Figure out your credit score, debt-to-income ratio, and your assets.
- ❏ Understand what financing strategy you want to use for your next house hack.
- ❏ Contact your lender to make sure this is a feasible financing strategy for you. If you are not using a lender, start networking with people that you can seller finance or partner up with on projects.

CHAPTER 6

HOW TO FIND DEALS

There is a story of a man who was struggling to attain some level of wealth. He had been poor his entire life (obviously, he did not house hack). Burned out from working for thirty years with nothing to show for it, he did what many of us would do. He started to pray. Every night, he would kneel down by his bedside, cross his hands, and pray to God that he would win the lottery. One, two, three nights passed and no luck. Years passed and God still had not answered his prayers. Frustrated one night, he screamed, "Are you even real?! Years have passed and every night I have prayed that I would win the lottery, but I have never received a dime!"

Finally, God responded, "Kind sir, I have heard your prayers. In order for me to help you, you need to first purchase a lottery ticket."

For all of his days he was praying that he would win the lottery, he never even purchased a ticket. This could be you when it comes to your real estate deals. You can pray and pray for the best real estate deal, but if you do not go after deals, you will never get one.

I will talk about many of the different strategies you can use to find a deal in this chapter, and whether or not they are feasible for house hacking. If you remember from chapter 5, most people who house hack do so with an owner-occupied loan. This means that the house must be livable, so getting a dilapidated property will do you no good if you want to go with the cheapest and most common financing route. Where do you find these deals? That's where we will go next.

The Multiple Listing Service (MLS)

The multiple listing service (MLS) is a collection of all homes listed for sale by real estate agents in your area. Historically, a seller's agent would send their physical lists to a buyer's agent around the area so that they know what is for sale. The internet has simplified this immensely. Now, all of these lists from the different seller agents have been combined into one list that can be accessed online and is referred to as the MLS. Before you run to your computer to try to figure out this list, understand that you will not be able to—unless you are an agent yourself. The MLS is a tool owned by licensed real estate agents, so unless you or your spouse have your license, you will have to do this search elsewhere.

There are several websites that upload properties from the MLS to their marketplaces that are accessible to anyone. A few of the most popular include www.Zillow.com, www.Trulia.com, www.Redfin.com, and www.Realtor.com. However, none of these will give you the complete picture like the MLS provides. This is the primary reason why investors get their license. However, if you do not plan to get your license, you will need to find a good agent that can set you up with the automatic notifications.

Once you get your agent to set up notifications that are sent directly to your inbox, it is then up to you to look over each one. There are going to be tons that will not work for you. When you do find a deal that checks off most (or all of) your boxes, it is time to set up a showing with the agent. I will probably review fifty deals that come through my inbox before setting up a showing. There are lots of bad deals on the MLS, mainly because people are putting the highest possible price rather than trying to move the properties. It does not take that much effort to list your property on the MLS while trying to get top dollar for your property, especially if you are not in a rush to sell. Don't let this discourage you because I have found almost all of my deals on the MLS. Many successful investors find the majority of their deals through the MLS. You just need to be smart with how you find and offer on MLS properties.

Here are some tips on how to make the most of your MLS searches.

1. *Make Sure the Search is Set Up Correctly*

   When setting up the search with your agent, make sure that the criteria you set are specific and narrowed down. Otherwise, you are going to get properties that are outside of your price range, or just simply not what you are looking for in your search. For example, if you are looking to house hack a single-family home by renting out the rooms, you might ask your agent the following:

I am looking for a single-family residence that is under $350,000. I am looking for something with three-plus bedrooms and two-plus bathrooms that is over 2,000 square feet. I want the property to be within five miles from my office.

With this description, you will be getting properties sent to your inbox that are specific to exactly what you want, and almost every one that comes your way will be a possibility.

2. ***Act Quickly***

One of the downsides of the MLS is that there are a lot of eyes on the properties you want to consider when they are listed. That means there is going to be a lot of competition, and you are going to want to act quickly.

Having specific criteria will help you act quickly. This way you know that only the deals that have the highest probability of winning your interest will come through to your inbox. However, there will still be some bad deals that slip through the cracks. Screen these out immediately and take a closer look at the ones you do like. Once you see one that has potential, immediately contact your agent and have them set up a showing for as soon as humanly possible.

3. ***Look for Hidden Value***

What is the best way to make money in life? You need to add value. The best properties you can find are those that you are able to add value to. Remember, though, the property still needs to be livable. My favorite strategy is to look for a three-bedroom, two-bathroom house with an unfinished basement that is over 2,000 square feet. With that much space, there is a high probability that you can add an additional one or two bedrooms and a bathroom. Not only does the value of the house increase when you do this, but you will also be able to garner 40 to 50 percent more in rent by adding and renting the extra two bedrooms.

Other value add opportunities could be adding square footage, a garage, or an accessory dwelling unit. You could do a cosmetic rehab where you redo the flooring, cabinets, countertops, and light fixtures. Find something that you can add value to, and your wallet will thank you later.

4. ***Make Offers When No One Is Working***

When you find the property you love, it is time to make an offer. You always want to make an offer as soon as possible. Don't be afraid of denial. Don't be afraid to fail. If you are going to fail, fail hard, and move on to the next one.

One of the best times to submit offers is when no one else is working. My favorite time is on a Friday or Saturday night, or even over a holiday. It is unlikely that there will be any other offers coming in during those times. And if the seller sees it at the right time and your offer seems "good enough," then they might just want to move on with the process and accept your offer.

This happened to me when purchasing a single-family residence. I saw a property that I really liked on a Friday afternoon. I scheduled a showing for that evening. On the listing, I noticed that there was supposed to be an open house just a few days later. After looking at the property on that Friday afternoon, I went home and made an offer that same evening. I set the expiration date to just before the open house. The seller did not want to have the open house, so this was perfect. They accepted my offer and canceled the open house.

5. ***Increase Earnest Money***
Buying a house is a scary investment for most people. Sellers understand this simple fact, and as a result, there are a lot of people who explore the idea of buying a house, make an offer, but then get scared and back-out last minute. If you are 100 percent sure you want to purchase this property, increase the amount of earnest money you put down. This lets the seller know that you are serious about purchasing the property, and the only way you will back out is if your contingencies (likely financing and inspection) do not play out.

The MLS is my favorite method of finding deals as a house hacker. The reason? You are looking for just one deal. You cannot do multiple house hacks in a year without breaking the law. For this reason, it is not extremely difficult to find a deal that works well enough for you to live cheaply or for free on the MLS. However, there are additional strategies if you have been on the MLS for months, or even years, and still unable to find anything worthwhile.

Driving for Dollars
Have you ever driven past a house and thought, "Man, that is a nice

property." If you have, then that is essentially all driving for dollars is. It is driving up and down the streets in the neighborhoods you like and scoping out houses that have potential. Instead of admiring the house and moving on with your day; you now write down the address, go to the county website to determine who owns the home, and you ask them if they are willing to sell.

When looking for a house hack by driving the streets, it is important to remember that you will need to live in this house for at least one year. If you are in a neighborhood that you do not want to live in, then go find another neighborhood. If the house is in a state of disrepair, the bank will not approve the loan, so move on to the next one.

With driving for dollars, you will likely have a lower success rate than you will have on the MLS. When a property is on the MLS, you do not need to convince the seller to sell. They are already doing so. If you are driving for dollars and the property is not already on the MLS, there is likely a reason. If the owner wanted to sell and wanted the highest probability of a sale, they would want the most people to see it, which would involve listing it on the MLS. For that reason, you are likely going to have to convince them to sell, and then offer them a price to make it worth their while.

Don't get me wrong! Some people just have not found the time to inquire with an agent about listing the property. If that's the case, you put yourself in a great position because you eliminate a large step for the seller, and you can purchase the property before thousands of other people even know that it's on the market.

Although driving for dollars has a lower success rate, it is a great method to scoop up deals before they hit the market. Not only that, but it costs you nothing more than your time and a couple of tanks of gas. Better yet, ride your bicycle around these areas. You'll save money, get exercise, and can stop at any time to write down addresses without stopping traffic.

Direct Mail Marketing

Direct mail marketing is one of the most common methods for house flippers, wholesalers, and real estate investors who are looking to do lots of deals. The idea behind direct mail marketing is to obtain a list of property owners who have a high likelihood of selling and send them a postcard letting them know that you are interested in purchasing their property. Owners who have a high likelihood of selling are those who have owned the property for 30+ years, absentee owners, or landlords going through an eviction.

I know that direct mail seems to be something from the previous century, but it still works, and it works very effectively. Similarly to everything else, direct mail marketing is a funnel that is driven by the conversion percentages. If you send out 1,000 postcards and 5 percent of the people respond, you will get fifty phone calls. Out of these fifty phone calls, maybe 10 percent of those deals are about a property that you would sincerely want to purchase. Out of the five deals that are of interest to you, there are three you want to make an offer on now. Out of the three you make an offer on, one gets accepted. The funnel looks like this:

Direct Mail Funnel

Postcards

Calls

Interested properties

Offers made

Offers accepted

Direct mail marketing is not popular amongst house hackers for a few reasons. You typically make your money back right away when flipping or wholesaling; however, you make your money back over an extended period of time when house hacking. You are only looking for one deal when house hacking so putting in all of the extra time and money to obtain the list, create the postcards, and then mail the postcards is a bit of overkill. It's also very rare to see your first mailing work in your favor since success comes to those who are persistent in sending these postcards out to their database. You may not receive any calls until your second, third, or fourth round of mailing the postcards. Lastly, you are likely not seeing the property that you are inquiring about when doing direct mail marketing, so you are not sure if you even have the ability to purchase the property. If it is not in livable condition, you will not be able to use an owner-occupied loan.

In most cases, direct mail marketing does not make a whole lot of sense for house hackers. However, if you are having trouble finding deals in your market, you might want to start a direct mail marketing campaign to find deals that other investors and potential house hackers are not seeing. It is a great way to increase the funnel of potential deals. If you do find a great deal through a direct mail marketing campaign that you cannot purchase with an owner-occupied loan, then you can always wholesale the property. If it truly is a deal, someone else will be willing to purchase it from you at a slight premium.

BiggerPockets Marketplace

BiggerPockets has completely revolutionized the marketplace. Rather than just being a series of forums, it looks a lot more like www.Zillow.com. You can filter houses based on location, price, cap rate, and many other real estate metrics. We even estimate the rents you will receive and give you an estimated cash-on-cash return. Note, that many of the rental estimates are as if you were going to be renting the house out as a true investment, not as a house hack. You will need to make some adjustments, but the cash-on-cash return provides a good metric that you can compare across properties on the BiggerPockets marketplace to determine what the best deal might be for you.

Craigslist

Back in the dinosaur era (okay, maybe not that long ago), people would put listings in the classifieds section of the newspaper. The internet-version of the classifieds is www.Craigslist.org. If you are not yet aware, Craigslist is an online classified section where it is free to post and browse, so it is a great resource for finding and selling things, including real estate deals.

There are three main strategies that have proven to be effective when using Craigslist:

1. **Search for sellers:** The most obvious way to use Craigslist is to look at the list of classifieds and see if there is anything for sale that you might like. You can do this very easily. The only problem is that there are a lot of other people looking on Craigslist as well.

2. **Post an ad:** Rather than trying to find a deal, make the deal find you. Create an advertisement that tells all of the sellers you are looking to purchase a property. This might bring a motivated seller to you since they are actively looking for someone to purchase their property. If you do get someone from this method, I would recommend figuring out their motivation and using that in your negotiations.

3. **Search for rentals:** Another strategy that has proven to work is to contact landlords who have listings to rent their property. Many people stumble into being a landlord. It could be that they could not sell their previous property, they inherited it, or various other reasons. These people do not want to be landlords, and they are often not good at being landlords. To find these people, you search for the Craigslist rental listings that have been placed by "mom and pop" landlords. You can usually determine the "mom and pop" operations when they have photography that is not professional, lack details in their description or if they have a phone number listed in the ad. If there is a phone number, call them and tell them exactly what you are trying to do. You will likely get denied, but it only takes one "yes" to get you that deal.

Craigslist is a great way to find house-hacking deals. You can see pictures, the location, and the price (except when you use strategy three). The best part? It's all free, and it takes very little time. Take five to ten minutes and peruse the Craigslist advertisements to see if there is a property perfect for you.

Wholesalers

Finding a good wholesaler is like finding an honest used car salesman. They are out there, but are few and far between. A wholesaler is someone who finds the deal for you. Their entire business involves finding great, usually off-market deals, and then selling (or assigning) them to an investor for a percentage of the sale.

For example, if I were to find a property that was exactly what you wanted at a price of $125,000, I would put it under contract and immediately sell it to you for $135,000. You get exactly what you were looking for and I get $10,000.

The problem with wholesalers is that there are no barriers to entry. You do not need a certification or schooling. All you need to do is start opening up your deal funnel likely through one of the methods we described above. For that reason, there are lots of wholesalers out there who are newbies just trying to make an extra buck, but do not actually know what they are doing. To be a good wholesaler you need to be incredible at every point of the real estate transaction: from marketing and analyzing, to selling and negotiating. Tread carefully when working with wholesalers and make sure to do your due diligence to find a successful deal!

The largest problem with house hacking is that investors usually need to purchase wholesale deals with cash. Wholesalers do not want to wait around for a month while Fannie Mae and Freddie Mac assess your risk with an FHA Loan. They typically only accept cash or hard money. Since house hacking typically involves getting a low percentage down loan, it is unlikely that a wholesaler will want a house hacker as a customer.

If you do find an amazing deal through a wholesaler that only allows cash or hard money, I would recommend taking out a hard money loan and then immediately refinancing with the low-down owner-occupied loan. You will lose $2,000 to $5,000 doing this, but that may be well worth the costs to secure a great deal. When doing this, make sure that all of your bases are covered:

1. Rents and property value are where you expect.
2. The property is in livable condition so you can obtain the proper bank loan.
3. You have enough reserves to cover hard money holding costs in case the bank does not accept the deal.

Friends and Family

The final way to get a great real estate deal is by the tried and true method of word of mouth. Most people feel good when they are helping others. It's in our nature to want to be helpful and to want to provide value in other people's lives. For that reason, you should tell everyone you know what you are looking for in a property. Tell friends, family, even that random person you meet at the bar. Notice that I say, "tell" people. Do not "ask" them. You will get some weird looks, but keep putting it out there and if someone can help, they will. You never know who knows someone who might be selling a property that is perfect for you!

CASE STUDY
TRAVIS WYLIE

- **House-hacking strategy:** Traditional
- **Age at first house hack:** 29
- **Location:** Harrisburg, Pennsylvania
- **NWROI:** 102%

I would like you to meet Travis in Harrisburg, Pennsylvania. Travis has been a resident of Harrisburg for much of his life. During the day, Travis works a typical W-2 job as a financial systems analyst. Believe it or not, Travis's primary passion is not being a financial systems analyst.

When Travis first began house hacking, he knew absolutely nothing about real estate. He did remember that he used to rent a property from one of his friends who owned the place back in college. He knew that he was covering the mortgage, but he thought nothing of it at that time. Fast-forward almost a decade later, and he is realizing just how smart his friend was back in the day.

Travis was looking for his first property in midtown Harrisburg in September 2015. For those unfamiliar with central Pennsylvania, midtown Harrisburg was a gentrifying area at the time. Restaurants and breweries were starting to pop up, but there were still some houses that were relatively inexpensive. Initially, he was looking to find a single-family home for a maximum price of $150,000. In his search, he found a newly renovated fourplex for just $275,000. There was just one problem. He did not have any liquid cash for the down payment. This brings us back to the "I can't" versus "How can I?" mentality. If Travis were to have just given up right then and there, then he would never have invested in real estate. Instead, he did some research.

Travis discovered that he could take a personal loan for up to 50 percent or $100,000 (whichever is less) against his 401k. At the time, Travis had $80,000 in his 401k so he had $40,000 available. This was more than enough to put down 3.5 percent (about $10,000) for an FHA loan on a $275,000 property. He closed on the property with $10,000 and no further problems.

When he first moved in, only two of the four units were rented. One was rented for $1,100 and the other for $850, so the total rental income was $1,950 and his mortgage payment was just $1,880. From day one he was covering his mortgage. Travis was able to fill the third (and final unit available) quickly as a friend was looking to move. He charged his friend $750 so he was making $2,700 on a $1,880 mortgage. After setting aside $300 in reserves, he was making $520 per month and living for free. Before purchasing the house hack, he was paying rent of $400. Now, rather than paying $400 to live, he was making $520—a difference of $920 per month! That's crazy savings. In case I lost you, here is a recap:

Total initial rental income: $1,950

Monthly payment: $1,880

Total rental income after filling vacancy: $2,700

Total income over mortgage: $2,700 - $1,880 = $820

Reserves: $300

Cash flow in pocket: $820 - $300 = $520

Rent before house hacking = $400

Total savings = $520 + $400 = $920

It was not all rainbows and unicorns though. The rehab on this property turned into a major project. In the first year, he ended up having to redo some concrete work, repave the sidewalk, waterproof the basement, and replace all of the appliances for a total of $25,000. In hindsight, he wished that he asked for a one-year warranty on the house, which would have made the seller financially responsible when major home system components broke down in that first year. A lesson that you, as the reader, can take away from this story. Always try to get a warranty anytime it's possible.

Since the rehab was more to maintain the property versus improve it, the rehab did not add much value to the property. After one year, it appraised at $295,000 or $20,000 more than when he purchased it. All in all, Travis had experienced $11,040 in rent savings/cash flow plus $20,000 in appreciation, and $5,000 in loan paydown for a total of payback of $36,040 in the first year. With the $10,000 down and the $20,000 rehab, he was all in for $30,000 that he had borrowed as a loan against his 401k. His NWROI on the deal was $36,040 divided by $30,000 or 120 percent.

Purchase price: $275,000

Value after year 1: $295,000

Year 1 appreciation: $295,000 - $275,000 = $20,000

Year 1 cash flow: $11,040

Loan paydown: $5,000

Total payback: $20,000 + $11,040 + $5,000 = $36,040

Initial investment: $30,000

NWROI = $36,040 / $30,000 = 120%

After this first year, Travis experienced the power of real estate and house hacking in particular. He has gone on to purchase seven more properties for a total of fifteen units, and is growing fast. He now lives in a large single-family house with his fiancé. The house has an accessory dwelling unit that he rents out so he has moved toward the less aggressive end of the house-hacking spectrum to luxurious house hacking. Travis's ultimate goal is to reach fifty units.

WHY

"I house hack so that I can quit my job and focus on boxing fulltime. I have been a boxer for nearly my entire life and now am a volunteer coach for a college in Harrisburg. Knowing that I wanted to dedicate the majority of my life to boxing, I realized that there was no way I could continue working my W-2 and box at the same time. That's why I turned to real estate investing."

ACTION STEPS

❏ Contact an agent and get automatic notifications sent to you from the MLS.

❏ Drive, walk, or bike around the neighborhoods where you are interested in buying. Write down the addresses and call three owners to see if they would be willing to sell. Get ready to hear a rude, "NO!"

❏ Write a post on social media that tells the world exactly what you are looking for.

❏ Next time you meet someone new, let them know you are wanting to invest in real estate and the type of property you're looking for. If they know of something, they will help for sure.

CHAPTER 7
ANALYZING DEALS

Investing in real estate, and investing in general, is all about the numbers. Do not make the excuse that you are not a numbers person. Do you think some people came out of the womb with a calculator practicing long division? Of course not! Anyone who is a numbers person had to work to become a numbers person. If you are planning on investing in real estate, then you are going to need to become comfortable with numbers.

Luckily, you do not need to be the next Fibonacci. Real estate investing is basic math. Rarely are you doing anything at a higher level than percentages or division. There are no trigonometry, calculus, or quadratic equations needed here. It is math that a fifth grader can do.

I hope that most of your stress surrounding numbers has been alleviated, but that is only the start of the stress. Analyzing deals and submitting offers are typically the scariest part of real estate investing and understandably so. It is likely the largest investment you will make to date. Not to mention all of the unknowns. How will you know if a property will rent? What if the market tanks? What if the roof falls apart? What if the foundation is off? What if the tenants stop paying rent?

So many "what if" scenarios run through your head and it can be scary. All of these variables are potential problems, and there is some probability that they will happen. That is why you analyze deals and, lucky for you, that is what this book is all about. I'm pouring everything I know about house hacking into this book so that you can lower the probability that any of these disasters happen. Keep reading, and I hope that your nerves will be settled.

Deal Metrics

If you have listened to the *BiggerPockets Podcast*, read the blogs, or perused the forums, you have likely heard what seems to be thousands of different metrics. You have PITI, ROI, ROE, cap rate, PMI, vacancy rate, capital expenditures, and the list goes on and on. If you can wrap your head around all of these, great! I believe though that one of the biggest reasons people do not take action is that they get overwhelmed with all of the terminology.

All of these metrics are important for tracking when you become a seasoned real estate investor and start bringing on partners who give you money. If you are just starting out and doing a house hack, do not be overwhelmed by these terms. There are just four things you need to know to analyze a deal:

1. Monthly payment
2. Monthly rent
3. Reserves
4. Net worth return on investment

Monthly Payment

The beauty of house hacking is that you are able to purchase a property with such a low down payment. As a result of that lower down payment, the loan you will need to purchase the property will be higher and, therefore, your monthly obligation to the bank will also be higher. The monthly payment will be comprised of the following:

- **Principal**: Paying down the money that you borrowed from the lender.
- **Interest**: Paying the lender a premium for letting you borrow the money.
- **Taxes**: Almost every county will require you to pay an annual property tax. That will be included in your mortgage, and deducted monthly.
- **Insurance**: Almost all lenders will require you to carry insurance on your home, in the event of an accident.
- **Private mortgage insurance**: I already talked about this, but as a reminder, it is the premium you pay when you put less than 20 percent down on a property.

Now that you know what makes up the monthly payment, how the heck do you figure out what it is? The answer is quite simple. Ask your lender. By this point, you will have already been pre-approved for a property up to a certain amount. Your lender should be able to give you an estimate within a couple hundred dollars of what your monthly payment will be at your pre-approved purchase price. As you are looking for properties, you will then be able to adjust that monthly payment slightly based on the price of the property to see that it works for you.

For example, let's say that you were pre-approved for a $350,000 house. With 2019 interest rates, your monthly payment will be about $2,000. You know that is your base. Now, you just make any needed adjustment. If the property is below $350,000, you know your monthly payment will be slightly less and you will have more room to cash flow.

Reserves

While the monthly payment is easier to estimate, you must pay it on time or you will get yourself into a lot of trouble. Reserves are quite the opposite. Reserves are money that you set aside for all unexpected expenses such as vacancy, maintenance, repairs, and capital expenditures. How much you put aside is completely up to you, and your risk tolerance. However, no matter who you are, there are factors to consider when deciding how much money to put aside. These include:

- **Location**: If you are in a less than desirable location, vacancy will be higher, and so can your monthly reserve.
- **Age of the property**: The older the property, the more you should put aside.
- **The size of the property**: The larger the property, the more you should put aside.
- **Known upcoming expenses**: Do you know you are going to need a new roof in a couple of years? Start saving for it now!

Let's take the two house hacks that I have for example. My first one is a duplex that was completely remodeled in 2017 and only has 1,250 square feet. I put $250 in my reserve account each month. My second house hack, however, is a 2,400-square-foot single-family home that was built in 1973. It's almost twice the size and quite a bit older than the duplex. I set $400 a month aside for this property.

There is one huge fault in this methodology though. What if a large expense occurs in the first couple of years after purchasing the property and you have yet to build up a significant reserve account? There are two ways that I have found to solve this problem. The less risky way to is to make sure that your reserve account always has at least $10,000 in it. In other words, you will need to have $10,000 of cash beyond the down payment that you can use towards any repairs needed for the property within those first few years.

If you don't have an extra $10,000, or do not want to wait to save an additional $10,000, you can check out the available credit card options. Be sure to find one that has zero percent interest for the first twelve to eighteen months. That way, if something goes wrong, you can charge the expense on the credit card and you will have enough time to pay it off. Personally, I do not advocate this method for obvious reasons. If something does happen and you are unable to pay off the credit card, you may be stuck with debt that has an exorbitant interest rate attached to it.

I hope that I simplified the thoughts behind the amount you will have to put aside each month when it comes to the reserves. Again, the amount will range depending on the aforementioned factors. However, I typically see people setting aside between $250 and $600 a month for reserves. Next, let's talk about how to estimate the amount of money you will bring in.

Monthly Rent

The monthly rent is the sum of all of the monthly payments your tenants will pay to occupy your property. If you are doing the rent-by-room strategy, add together the monthly payments per room. If you are doing a traditional house hack, add together the rent from the other units and do not forget to include rent from your roommate (if you are going to have one). For a short-term rental, estimate your daily rate, and then multiply that by the number of days you believe you can have it occupied.

This can be a bit tricky as well. How are you supposed to know the appropriate price to charge for rent? The best way to do this is to look at other properties that are similar to your units or rooms that are within a couple of miles of your property. These are called comparables, or "comps" for short. Look to see what they are charging for rent. If you know someone who is also renting in that area, ask them how much they charge.

In most cases, you probably will not know someone who has a similar property within one to two miles of you. In these instances, use your resources. There are plenty of them. My top three are listing sites (Zillow, Trulia, and HotPads), Facebook Marketplace, and Craigslist.

There are a lot of listing sites out there. The most popular and the sites that I've had the most success with include Zillow, Trulia, and HotPads. These will only work for the traditional house hack though, since they only do full units, not rent-by-room rentals.

Facebook Marketplace

In the last few years, Facebook has been working to replace Craigslist with its Facebook Marketplace. Given that the Craigslist website still looks like it is from 1995, it has done so with relative ease. On the Facebook Marketplace, you can look at properties for rent in all shapes and sizes. Rent by the room or full unit options are available. Just set the radius to within three to five miles of your desired location, and you will have an estimate as to what you can charge for rent.

Craigslist

While it seems that less and less people are using Craigslist, they do still have a unique feature when it comes to estimating rental income. They have a "map" feature. You can go to this feature, filter your search to match the property you will have for rent, and see what others are charging in your entire city or county. You can then narrow in to see what rate places are going for that are closest to you.

Alright, so now you know where to look to get a good idea as to how much you can charge for rent. You can make further adjustments if your property is slightly different. For example, if there is a garage parking or a private entrance, you may be able to charge a little bit more. If the room is smaller and does not have a large closet, you may have to charge a bit less. Use the comps as a base, and make small adjustments as they relate to your property.

After doing the above, you should have a good idea as to how much you will be able to collect in monthly income. Those are really the three metrics you will need to decide on whether a deal will work, or it will not work in your favor. However, it's not always so black and white. The next metric I'll discuss is called the net worth return on investment, and it determines just how good a deal will be.

Net Worth Return on Investment (NWROI)

Your net worth return on investment (NWROI), similar to a cash-on-cash return, summarizes exactly how good an investment will be (or has been) through a percentage. The higher the percentage, the better the deal. Unlike cash-on-cash return, NWROI takes into account all wealth generators of real estate: cash flow, appreciation, and loan paydown; and it shows the overall impact it has on your net worth. We are going to ignore tax advantages because it is different for everyone but keep it in the back of your mind that every NWROI mentioned throughout this book will be slightly understated for this reason.

The NWROI can be forward-looking when analyzing and predicting how good a deal will be for you. It can also be backward-looking when determining how good the deal actually was for you. Either way, to calculate the NWROI, you are going to add together your increased net worth through: cash flow/rent savings, loan paydown, and appreciation. When you get that sum, you will divide it by your total initial investment to determine your net worth return on investment. The initial investment is any cash coming out of your pocket to initially secure the deal. Examples may be the down payment, closing costs, and rehab costs. In a formula it looks like this:

$NWROI = (cash\ flow\ and\ rent\ savings + loan\ paydown + appreciation) / initial\ investment$

Let's use my first property as an example of how to calculate the NWROI. I purchased my first house hack for $385,000. It was a newly renovated, up/down duplex with each unit having one bedroom and one bathroom. I did a 3.5 percent down FHA loan. After the down payment and closing costs, I was all in for $17,000.

$Cash\ flow/rent\ savings = x$

$Loan\ paydown = x$

$Appreciation = x$

$Initial\ investment = \$17,000$

There are many ways to generate wealth, but the first is cash flow. My strategy with the duplex was to rent out the top unit full time and Airbnb my bedroom while I slept in the living room. The top unit made me $1,750 per month and the bedroom generated about $1,100 per month on Airbnb. My total rental income was $2,850 while my entire mortgage payment (PITI and PMI) was $2,000. Because it was a new build and in a great location, I set aside $250 for reserves each month.

My cash monthly cash flow: $2,850 - $2,000 - $250 = $600 per month

It does not stop there though. I was also paying nothing to live there. My rental expense was zero dollars and I was making $600 per month. Understand though that I was sleeping on a futon behind a curtain in the living room so it would not be a long-term situation. However, if I had not house hacked, but had the same living situation, I estimate that I would have paid approximately $400 in rent. My cash flow and rent savings was $600 plus $400, or $1,000 per month. Because we are looking at net worth return on investment after the first year, we will multiply this $1,000 by twelve to make it an annual number.

Monthly cash flow and rent savings = $600 cash flow + $400 rent savings = $1,000

Annualized cash flow/rent savings = $12,000

Loan paydown = x

Appreciation = x

Initial investment = $17,000

Next, let's talk about the loan paydown as it relates to the NWROI.

A portion of your monthly payment is principal. That is the "P" in PITI. Principal is the balance you owe the bank. As you pay a portion of the balance each month, the principal reduces, which lowers your loan amount and thereby increases your net worth. I started off with a $378,000 loan and at the end of one year had paid it down to about $370,000. In other words, after one year the loan paydown increased my net worth by $8,000.

Monthly cash flow and rent savings = $600 cash flow +

$400 rent savings = $1,000

Annualized cash flow/rent savings = $12,000

Loan paydown = $8,000

Appreciation = x

Initial investment = $17,000

Last but not least is appreciation. Appreciation is where you take the most risk, but you also get the most reward. There are two types of appreciation. There is natural appreciation, which is the steady 6 percent you expect real estate to increase year after year from doing nothing. But you never bank solely on natural appreciation. Instead, find a nice cash-flowing property in an area that has a high likelihood of appreciating, or a property where you can force the appreciation.

Forced appreciation is when you increase the value of the property by improving it yourself. This can be by adding bedrooms or bathrooms, square footage to the house, an ADU, or just cosmetic enhancements such as new cabinets or floors.

The duplex I purchased was fully remodeled so there was no forced appreciation to be realized, only natural appreciation. Luckily, the Denver market did improve from 2017 to 2018, and it was worth approximately $435,000 one year after I purchased the property. (Remember, I bought the property for $385,000.)

The impact on my net worth from appreciation was $50,000.

Monthly cash flow and rent savings = $600 cash flow + $400 rent savings = $1,000

Annualized cash flow/rent savings = $12,000

Loan paydown = $8,000

Appreciation = $50,000

Initial investment = $17,000

Now that we have all of the pieces to the equation, we can enter them in and calculate my net worth return on investment. If we add up all of the ways I generated wealth in my first year, we would get $70,000. Divide that by $17,000 and you get a return of 412 percent.

$$NWROI = (\$12,000 + \$8,000 + \$50,000) / \$17,000 = 412\%$$

A 412 percent return sounds crazy right? It's not! You've already seen from the case studies how house hacking can build your wealth. The main reason why you can achieve these high returns can be attributed to the fact that initial investment is incredibly low relative to what you can make on the returns.

The example I gave was a backwards-looking example, and it illustrates just how good my deal was after the first year. As I'm sure you noticed, the factor that propelled my return was appreciation. This will likely be the case for you too. However, appreciation is speculative, especially natural appreciation. When using the NWROI to analyze and predict the outcome of a deal, I would highly suggest being conservative and use zero percent as your appreciation assumption.

Let's return to the example of my duplex. This time let's calculate the NWROI as if I was still analyzing the deal. Since I do not know what the market is going to do over the next year, and I was not planning on making any renovations, I am going to assume that appreciation is zero percent. Let's run the numbers back through the equation:

$$NWROI = (\$12,000\ cash\ flow + \$8,000\ loan\ paydown + \$0\ appreciation) / \$17,000\ initial\ investment = 118\%$$

Before knowing what the market will do over the next year and without taking into account any tax advantages, I knew that I would see a return of 118 percent. This is still a better return than almost any other investment option.

To summarize, your net worth return on investment is an important metric that can be used to evaluate the health of your deal as it relates to your personal wealth. It is a rather simple calculation, which is why I like it. You sum up all of the wealth generators of real estate and then divide it by your initial investment. Here is the formula one more time:

$NWROI = (cash\ flow\ and\ rent\ savings + loan\ paydown + appreciation) / initial\ investment$

I hope that was not too confusing for you. Even if you are not a numbers person, math in real estate is not that difficult. It is just adding, subtracting, multiplying, and dividing. Now that you know how to figure out each metric, let's get into the application.

Applying the Metrics

Just by learning the first three metrics, you will be able to safely analyze a deal and confidently be able to move forward with a high probability of success.

You have all the tools you need to start analyzing deals. A box of tools that you can't use is the same thing as a box full of paperweights. You need to be taught how to properly apply these tools. Thankfully, it is ridiculously easy. When analyzing a house hack, you should completely disregard any form of appreciation. The only thing to analyze is the cash flow, which also encompasses the loan paydown. The equation you will want to satisfy is the following:

$Monthly\ rent - monthly\ debt - reserves = expected\ profit$

The monthly rent is how much you believe you will be able to charge for rent. As described in the previous pages, this involves a bit more research, but you should be able to get a good estimate—and one that will not change drastically assuming that you are looking at similar properties.

The monthly debt payment is given to you directly by your lender. If you have already decided on an area and a property type, it is likely that the property values you are searching for will be similar in price so the loan amount will not drastically change.

Figuring out the right number to set aside for reserves is akin to Goldilocks picking the perfect bed to sleep in. There is really no right or wrong answer, just reasonable and unreasonable. Setting aside too little is unreasonable and you will end up losing your shirt. Setting aside too much is unreasonable and you will never find a deal that works for you because all of your cash flow will be going to reserves. You need to find a sweet spot that allows you to set money aside while still increasing your financial position.

The reserve number is the highest variable in the equation so that is the one you will be toggling to satisfy "expected profit." As shown in the equation above, expected profit is taking your monthly rental income and subtracting out your monthly debt obligation and reserves. Your expected profit should be above the profitability bar that you have set for yourself.

What should that bar be? Unfortunately, I cannot choose it for you. In many cases it will change based on your market and investing strategy. If you are in a market that has a high likelihood of appreciating, it is expected that the prices are already high, which means lower cash flow. If this is the case, then your profitability bar will be lower because you are betting that the property will appreciate, and appreciation is not accounted for in the formula above.

I know what you are thinking . . . "I thought we weren't supposed to bet on appreciation." This is true. However, betting on appreciation is like speeding on the highway. We are not supposed to do it, but we do anyway—within reason. When you speed on the highway, it is likely you are going five to ten miles per hour over the limit. In other words, you will get to your destination a little bit faster, but the odds of you having a car accident are not that much higher. It's a risk that most people are willing to take. Real estate investors treat appreciation the same way. We will invest in a market that has a high likelihood of appreciation; even if we do so while sacrificing cash flow.

In this scenario when you are taking a lower cash flow for higher odds of appreciation, your profitability bar will be lower. Depending on your market and your strategy, it is up to you.

In Denver, the properties I have purchased to date are in the $300,000 to $400,000 range. In order for me to do these deals, my profitability bar was set at $750 per month above the mortgage. This allowed me to set aside $250 to $400 in reserves each month while still cash flowing $250 to $500 per month.

However, in Jacksonville, Florida I am doing a few rehab projects that I will rent out upon completion. This is called BRRRR (buy, rehab, rent, refinance, repeat), a strategy that involves buying a run-down property, fixing it up, renting it out, refinancing, and pulling all of your money out so you can do it again. There is an entirely different book written on this strategy so I will not dive in too deeply here. The properties that I have purchased and am rehabbing there are valued at closer to $150,000. For that reason, my profitability bar is slightly lower. In Jacksonville, I hope to get $500 above the monthly mortgage in rent.

Once you start analyzing deals in the market where you are invested, you will find that determining your profitability bar will be easy. But finding a deal that meets your criteria will be difficult. With that being said, everyone has different profitability bars and each deal will have a different expected profit. House hacking will almost always be beneficial to your financial position. The question usually is just how much of an impact will it have? That is why I tiered them based on the expected profit below.

Tiers of House Hacking

There are three different tiers of house hacking when it comes down to it, all of which are beneficial to your financial position at varying levels of severity.

The first tier, and most beneficial, is the positive cash flow house hack. In this scenario, you are living in part of your property and renting out the remaining parts. The rent from your units is 100 percent covering your mortgage, reserves, and you still have some left over. In this scenario, you are living for free and making additional cash flow.

The second tier would be a break-even house hack. In this scenario, the rent from your tenants/roommates will cover your mortgage payment completely, but you will still need to dole out maybe $100 to $300 per month for utilities and reserves. Because you are still living for free and completely eliminating what likely was your largest expense, it will still be beneficial to your financial position.

The third tier (the least lucrative), though still helpful, is what I call the false-positive house hack. In this situation, the rent you receive will not cover the full mortgage but is helpful, and it will cover the mortgage when you move out. For example, let's say you purchased a two-bedroom, one-bathroom townhome. The mortgage is $1,500 per month, but you are only charging $900 for the extra room. You are still responsible for paying $600 to cover the rest of the mortgage plus another $200 to $300 for reserves.

At first, this may not look like a deal (hence the false-positive name). However, it will still be helpful to your overall financial position. Although you are spending the same amount in paying off part of your mortgage (plus reserves) as you would be in rent, you are still paying off equity in your property and when you move out, you will likely be making $200 to $300 over the mortgage. In other words, you'll have a property that is paying for itself. Over time, you will be able to increase rents and the equity in your property will increase, but the mortgage payment will remain the same.

To quickly understand what type of deal your house hack falls into, you can make the quick calculation in your head:

Expected monthly rent – monthly mortgage payment

Here is a simple breakdown of where each tier will fall. The higher the tier, the higher the probability that this deal will enhance your position.

Tier	Rent Minus Mortgage*
1: Positive	$500 or more
2: Break even	$0 to $499
3: False positive	Less than $0

*Does not include reserves. Remember to add a few hundred dollars for reserves.

There was a lot of information thrown at you in the past couple of pages, so here is a brief recap of the metrics:

- **Monthly payment (PITI):** The estimated amount you will need to pay (including PMI) the lender each month given a property in a certain price range. This is the start of your analysis.
- **Monthly rent:** The estimated rent you will be charging to your tenants/roommates. The rent minus your monthly payment will help you determine the tier of your house hack.
- **Reserves:** This is the total amount that you will set aside each month for vacancy, capital expenditures, and repairs. It will differ based on a number of factors (property age, size, and location). However, it is crucial that you are setting money aside each month for when things go wrong.

These three variables are really all you need to analyze a deal, and determine what tier of house hack you are doing. If you wanted to take it a step further, we could calculate the net worth return on investment.

- **Net worth return on investment:** This takes into account appreciation and loan paydown as well as cash flow from the property. It takes all wealth generated from the property and divides it by the amount invested to get a return on investment.

While this is a great, all-encompassing metric, we look at NWROI as a backwards-facing metric. It allows you to see just how good a deal was looking back on it, but it is extremely difficult to get this correct through prediction. The main reason for this is that the majority of your wealth will likely come from appreciation of the property. However, it is impossible to predict the future, or accurately predict the market. For these reasons, this metric is great when illustrating the power of house hacking, but may be tough to get right when analyzing a deal.

Analysis for When You Move Out

Before we get into actually making the offer, we need to talk about one more thing. The whole idea behind this house-hacking strategy is that you will get into your first deal in year one, save enough to move out, and get into your second deal in year two, third in year three, and so on. You do this until you either have enough properties with enough passive cash flow that exceeds your expenses, or you can accumulate enough cash for a down payment on a non-owner-occupied loan.

With that being said, when you run your numbers, you are going to want to see what it looks like when you move out as well. For example, if you are doing a traditional house hack or renting by the room, you will have additional rent coming in when you move out and someone fills your space. The only additional expense associated with this would be property management; whether it be you hiring a professional property manager, discounting the rent of one of your tenants for them to manage, or paying yourself. You will want to include this as an added expense going forward.

You will want to ask yourself the question: *Does your strategy work if you move out?* In many locations—Denver to name one—there are laws that require all short-term rentals to be a primary residence. Once you move out, the short-term rental strategy will not be a sustainable strategy for you. If you are pursuing this strategy, you will want to make sure that the property works as a full-time rental as well as a short-term rental.

I was pursuing the short-term rental strategy (less than 30 days) with my duplex in Denver while I was living there. Then I moved out and continued doing the short-term rental strategy. My profits were through the roof. After about a year though, the big bad city of Denver gave me a call and asked me to shut it down. Fortunately, I ran the numbers and made sure that the property still worked as a full-time rental before purchasing it so I wouldn't be forced to sell, had the short-term strategy not worked out. Now, I am converting it to a medium-term rental where it gets rented for more than 30 days, but less than a full year. My cash flow will be slightly less, but so will my work, and I will still be cash flowing.

With all of that being said, I hope that you now feel more comfortable analyzing deals. Now it is time to start making offers.

CASE STUDY
ZAC BURK

- **House-hacking strategy:** Traditional
- **Age at first house hack:** 25
- **Location:** Lincoln Park, Michigan
- **NWROI:** 44%

Zac Burk is a man of action. He is great at looking up to his elders, observing what they are doing, and then implementing it into his own life. It all started when he was 21 years old. He and his family were part of the same church for fifteen years, and Zac had always looked up to his pastor. The pastor was not only a man of the church, but a great businessman as well. The first house Zac ever rented was from his pastor. But Zac quickly realized that he was paying the pastor's entire mortgage for him. Zac did not get mad, but he was envious. He decided to figure out how to go down the same path. The first thing he needed to do was build up for that down payment.

How did he do it? Straight hustle. Zac moved in with his parents for six months to save on rent while he worked three jobs. Two jobs were just to bring in a paycheck at an animal shelter and a warehouse while the other was setting himself up for a career: an internship at an architectural firm. After six months of living with his parents, they kicked him out and he found a place to rent in Lincoln Park, Michigan. Lincoln Park is about a mile away from the Detroit border. He was paying $550 per month for a 550-square-foot one-bedroom single-family house. Over the course of the next year, he continued to work and save until he had $25,000 saved up after the 18 months of living with his parents and renting the place in Lincoln Park. It was time to start looking for properties to house hack.

Duplexes were sparse in Lincoln Park. After a few months of looking, he found one three blocks away from where he was currently renting. It was an up/down duplex for $74,900. With 25 percent down and closing costs, his total initial investment was $18,750 and the monthly payment was $545. The downstairs unit was move-in ready, so he did just that immediately. The upstairs unit, however, needed a little bit of work. All of the floors needed to be redone thanks to an ancient shag carpet that was covered in cat urine. Zac ripped up all of the carpet and redid the floors with a friend. It took him about a week and cost him $400 to do this entire rehab.

Once the top floor was finished, one of his friends had nowhere to live and was slightly desperate so she moved into the upstairs unit for $525 per month. After paying for his share of utilities and setting aside $100 to $200 for reserves, Zac was living in this duplex for just $300 per month. This is $250 less than his smaller, one-bedroom place just three blocks away, and a great example of a successful, third-tier house hack where the rent partially covers the mortgage. Because he continued to work his three jobs, he was able to save up another $12,000 after ten months so he was ready to house hack again. Note that he put 20 percent down on this property so there was no obligation to live there for a year.

Once he and his friend moved out of the townhome, Zac redid the upstairs. He put in a new toilet pump, replaced the PVC under the sink, sanded all the trim and stairs, painted the entire place, and sanded the floors. He worked about 100 hours himself, along with some help from friends and family; but he only spent $525 on the upstairs rehab. He now rents the top unit out for $625 and the bottom for $750 (including pet fees). His total income on the duplex is $1,375 on a mortgage of $550. After putting aside money for reserves, Zac is cash flowing $500 to $600 a month on this property.

The second property he found was a two-bedroom single-family house in a great neighborhood. However, the house itself was in a state of disrepair. The gutters were busted, the basement flooded, etc. Before

Zac purchased this property, a contactor purchased it for $74,000, and in just three weeks redid the plumbing, water-proofed the basement, put in a new HVAC system, a new furnace, and new water tank.

After the rehab, the property was sold to Zac for $105,000. He put down 3 percent or $3,000 with the seller paying all closing costs. This is his current house hack and he is paying a monthly mortgage of $1,150 thanks to the high taxes paid in that part of town. When looking at the property, admittedly, Zac did not do the due diligence he should have done. After a few weeks of moving in, he noticed a large vertical crack in the foundation behind one of the doors and the plumbing to the downstairs bathroom was not hooked up. He felt he did not do a good job at looking for these issues when he first visited the property, and he did not get a full inspection. He had a contractor that he knew give him the thumbs up.

Zac's plan with this property is to spend about $50,000 in rehab to make the repairs and enhancements. He is going to fix the foundation, replace the roof, hook up the plumbing downstairs, and do some cosmetic work to modernize the place. He expects that he will be able to sell the property for a net gain of $50,000.

 WHY *"I house hack so that I can have the freedom to take some time off. Once this project is complete, I plan to purchase a skoolie, a school bus that has been converted and refurbished into a home on wheels. I plan to take six months to a year off and travel throughout the United States. From there, I will come back to work and continue building my real estate portfolio."*

ACTION STEPS

❏ Go on Craigslist, Zillow, Facebook Marketplace, and other rental sites to compare local rents.
❏ Figure out your estimated monthly payment from your lender.
❏ Even if you do not have the means to buy a deal yet, start running through that simple formula to see if it is a deal you would want to buy.

CHAPTER 8

MAKING THE OFFER AND GOING UNDER CONTRACT

Crafting an offer is more than a large math problem. It is a large math problem nestled into a fine painting that must attract the seller. It needs to both work for you and look pretty enough to make the seller accept the offer.

Before making an offer, you need to make sure the numbers work. The number that has the most impact on the deal is by far the purchase price. Without a purchase price in your range, your deal will fall apart worse than an oil-based painting on a Florida summer day.

The purchase price has the largest impact on your monthly payment, which affects all of the real estate wealth generators: cash flow, appreciation, loan paydown, and tax advantages. When you get pre-approved from the bank, the lender is going to tell you a maximum purchase price that you can afford. The way they do this is by estimating an interest rate, and then estimating what your monthly principal and interest payment would be on the deal. They then tack on the taxes and insurance premium to arrive at your estimated payment. As long as that monthly debt payment does not put you over the debt-to-income threshold, you will be approved for the loan.

Just because you are approved for a loan does not mean that the deal will work in your favor. Remember what I just talked about? You need to make sure that the rental income you garner will exceed your monthly payment by your profitability bar. Once you know what your maximum purchase price is for a particular property, it is time to craft the offer.

Don't worry, unless you are your own agent, you will not actually have to fill out the paperwork. You just tell your agent the price and terms of the deal. A good agent will gather information from the seller to understand their motivation for selling. With this information, they will craft an offer that will meet your numbers, while still looking attractive to the seller.

For you, the future house hacker, the glue that holds together your offer is going to be the purchase price. For the seller, the purchase price will be important, but it may not be the most important factor. If the sellers are an older couple who have lived in the property for thirty or more years while raising a family, they will be more emotionally invested than someone who just owns it as a rental who may want to sell it fast. You will want to cater to these needs as you are crafting your offer.

Before we get too far into the emotional side of crafting a deal, let's do an overview of the primary items in an offer that you will be able to change. Note that when crafting an offer, anything goes. You can be as creative as you want. You can make up your own terms and clauses. Just be careful not to confuse the seller, the seller's agent, and maybe even yourself. My advice would be to keep your offers as simple as possible by just toggling the following terms:

Purchase Price

The price of the property. This is going to have the largest impact on you so be sure that you know what your monthly payment will be given a certain purchase price. This will also have a large impact on the seller. Like Goldilocks figuring out which bed she likes, there is a spectrum of offer prices. At some point they become unreasonably high and pass your maximum purchase price. They can become unreasonably low and go below the seller's minimum sale price. The goal is to find that sweet spot that is as close as possible to the seller's minimum sale price, while still accepting the offer. Because the purchase price will likely be what you care for the most, you will likely need to cede on other terms.

| Minimum Sales Price (Your Offer) | **Sweet Spot** | Maximum Sales Price |

Closing Date

The closing date is the date chosen for the closing on the property. The seller will want this to be as fast as possible. The lender is typically the reason that a deal takes so long from the buyer's side. The underwriting process will take an estimated three to four weeks. Once you are approved for the loan, the deal can close. For that reason, it is pretty standard for the closing date to be almost exactly one month after the offer letter is submitted.

Earnest Money

Earnest money is the amount of money you put into a third-party account called escrow. The amount can be anything you deem it to be. It can be $1 or it can be the entire down payment. The higher the earnest money, the more serious you look to the seller, and the more likely the seller will accept your offer. This money will do one of two things. It will either be refunded to you in the event that one of your contingencies are not met (explained next) or it will be deducted from the cash you owe at closing.

For example, let's say you are purchasing a $200,000 property with 5 percent down. You will need to bring $10,000 cash as the down payment. However, the earnest money will be deducted from that total amount so you will only need to bring $5,000 (plus any extra fees) to closing since you already paid that earnest money. On the other hand, if the deal does not get to closing due to one of your contingencies, then you will be refunded your money back in full. The only way you lose the earnest money is if you decide to back out on a deal for any reason not originally specified.

Earnest money is my favorite variable to play with during the deal. I always err on the side of giving more earnest money. I am always confident that if I am making an offer on a property, I will be happy if the offer gets accepted and I want the deal to happen. The properties that I offer on typically require $15,000 to $20,000 down so my earnest money is almost always $10,000 or higher. This proves to the seller that I am serious about buying the property, and as long as there are no surprises, I will be purchasing it.

Contingency

A contingency is clause in the contract that covers you in the event of any surprises. You determine what your contingencies are when crafting the initial offer. If during your due diligence period, something catches you by surprise and falls into one of your contingency buckets, you will be able to back out of the deal and get your earnest money back in full.

You can have a contingency on anything. When I say anything, I mean anything. The deal can be contingent on the seller wearing a pink tutu each time you meet, calling you by "master [enter first name here]", or by taking the little man off his glass each time he has a sip of his drink. Rather than combining your offer with a college drinking game, it's better to have the contingencies be few, and serious.

I always make sure to include the financing and inspection contingencies in my contract. The financing contingency says that in the event a lender denies you a loan for the property at hand, you will not be obligated to purchase the property. The lender can back out if the appraisal does not come in at or above the purchase price or if they find something in their underwriting process that disqualifies them from lending to you.

The inspection contingency allows you to hire a licensed inspector to give you a full inspection of the property. If the inspector finds something that you did not like such as the foundation is not stable, the roof is going to need to be replaced soon, or there are remnants of a meth lab in the cellar. You have the ability to back out and recover your earnest money. The three examples I said are extreme (one more so than the others), but at this point, you can truthfully back out for almost anything.

Another contingency that used to be popular (but is becoming less so) is the home sale contingency. If you already own a home, you might be looking to sell that one in order to get into your house hack. You may need to use the proceeds you retain from selling that property to purchase the house hack. For that reason, you will want to include a home sale contingency. This says that in the event you do not sell your current home within a specified amount of time, your earnest money will still be refunded to you.

When it comes to contingencies, the fewer the better. Then the seller doesn't need to be surprised and if they have nothing to hide about their property, they should not be wary of accepting an offer with these contingencies.

Closing Costs

In a real estate transaction, there are many parties involved in the deal. There is the lender, title company, the agent, the inspector, the appraiser, the lawyer, the accountant, the surveyor, and many more. Unfortunately, these folks do not work for free. Fortunately, I have no intention of diving into the purpose of each closing cost and turning this book into a bedtime story. If this is of interest to you, I am going to give you the advice my grandfather gave me. "Look it up, kid."

In total, closing costs will typically be 2 to 5 percent of the purchase price of the property. It sounds crazy that you need to essentially put an extra 2 to 5 percent down on a property you are already putting 5 percent down on. The good thing is that you may not have to pay these closing costs. This is the negotiation piece of the offer. In your offer, you can suggest that the seller pays all of the closing costs, or that it be split evenly.

If you really want the deal, paying for the closing costs is something that is not incredibly expensive relative to the overall purchase price. Offering to pay for the closing costs goes further than the few thousand dollars it costs, and it is sometimes the difference between a seller choosing to accept your offer, and not another offer on the table.

The good thing about closing costs is that in many cases, the lender will add most of the costs into the loan so there is nothing you owe the bank at closing. It will mean that there is a slightly higher monthly payment, but not enough to make or break a deal.

Offering to pay closing costs ultimately comes down to how badly you want the deal. Gauge interest by asking the listing agent how many offers are on the table. If there are a lot of them, it makes sense to offer to pay the closing costs. If there are not a lot of offers and the seller almost seems desperate, let them pay these costs.

Fixtures/Appliances

When you purchase a property, it is assumed that anything physically attached to the property comes with it. This includes all lighting fixtures, appliances, and cabinets. Some examples include a fence around the property, the refrigerator, the nice chandelier above the kitchen table, and even doorknobs. It's anything that is tied to the property.

As part of your offer, you are allowed to include (or exclude) any of these fixtures. If you really dislike the chandelier and want it removed, you can have a clause that says the seller will remove the chandelier. Same thing works the other way around. If you really want the hot tub in the back, you can say that the owner must leave the hot tub as part of the offer.

Typically, you will have your agent talk to the seller to see what they want to take with them when they go. This is usually a very easy conversation and they leave everything you would expect. If there is a disagreement, you need to decide how badly you want the deal to succeed. Typically, these items will cost $2,000 or less to replace, so whether you get a fixture should not be a deal breaker.

By now, you should know how to simply analyze a deal and how to make an offer. If making an offer seems intimidating, don't worry. Your agent will be there to help you. They have closed hundreds of deals (you confirmed, right?) so this process is second nature to them.

Other Items

Like I said previously, you can include anything when crafting an offer. One clause that I like to include is that the seller should not be responsible for any items less than $1,000. This is actually a huge selling point. In many cases, during the inspection, buyers will try to nickel and dime the seller to fix the place up perfectly, which is just not going to happen. This way, you are protecting yourself by ensuring that you will not be responsible for any large expenses (plumbing, electrical, structural, etc.), but lets the seller know that you are not concerned about minor issues. And you are not going to be a nuisance to the seller, which they will appreciate. Put yourself in the seller's shoes and imagine the buyer asking you to fix all of these petty items such as changing a lightbulb or patching a piece of drywall.

Ding. You hear your phone go off alerting you of a new email. You open it and there it is. The buy-sell agreement that has been filled out by both parties. Congratulations! You are under contract! You will probably be going through a roller coaster of emotions. Happy, nervous, excited, confused, lost, sick, you name it. Don't worry, this is totally normal. However, if you are reading this book, the only feelings you should be having are excited and confident.

First Actions

In the next few pages, I'm going to tell you exactly what to do, as the buyer, after your house hack goes under contract. This is called the due diligence period.

Tell Lender

The first step is going to be to call your lender. They will likely have already written a pre-approval letter for you so they will know the property. Just call them and tell them that you are under contract. That way they can begin with their underwriting process. They have a lot of work they need to do to ensure you get accepted for the loan. By getting them everything they need quickly, you'll make their life easier, and the higher the probability will be they will accept you for the loan and that you will close on time.

Set Up Inspection

After you call the lender it is time to get the inspection set up. If you have friends that are investors or have recently purchased a property, ask them for recommendations. If there are not any good recommendations, ask your agent. They likely close on multiple properties a month and need to have a team of inspectors to meet their client's needs. Ask them. They are usually pretty good.

After you have found your inspector, take a look at the buy-sell agreement and note the inspection deadline. You are going to want to make sure your inspection takes place at least three to five days before this deadline. Give the inspector enough time to do this inspection and get the report back to you. In my experience, an inspection will be completed in one to two days, but things happen. The earlier you can get the inspection done, the more time you have to assess the results and decide whether you want to act on the "inspection contingency" or not.

Due Diligence

That takes much of the administrative stuff out of the way, and now it is time to get down and dirty with the due diligence. This is the most important part of doing a deal and luckily you will have a lot of help from the title company, your real estate agent (if they are good), and your lender.

The single most important thing that the title company will do is a title review. In performing this review, the title company will surface any hidden liens or encumbrances on the property that may cause problems later. If there is a lien on the property that means that the prior owner is indebted to a third party who has the right to take possession of that property should it not be paid. The most common liens are tax liens (owner did not pay taxes), mechanic's lien (owner did not pay contractor for agreed work), and mortgage lien (the owner did not repay the lender).

If the title review is performed and there is a lien on the property, you and your agent will need to renegotiate with the seller. Either you or the seller will need to pay the creditor in order to remove the lien. If it is you, then you need to make sure that the purchase price is reduced.

Luckily, you do not need to do much work as it relates to the title review. Let's get into the diligence you actually need to be present for: the inspection.

Inspection

Remember the second person you called after you went under contract? The inspector. The inspector is like a middle school bully who can point out anything and everything you are self-conscious about. The inspector is going to come to your property, dissect it, and tell you everything that is wrong with it. We highly suggest that you attend the inspection as well. Be sure to ask the inspector if they are okay with you shadowing them and asking questions. Most of the time, they will say yes. Believe it or not, they love inspecting properties and love talking about it. In most cases, they do their inspection alone so most do not mind the occasional companion. By shadowing the inspector and asking questions, you become more knowledgeable in what to look for when you view future properties. It's a very valuable skill to learn when determining whether or not you want to purchase a property.

As you are going through the property with the inspector, I recommend that you take notes of the things you are going to want to fix, and the things that you are going to want the seller to fix. For anything that's less than $1,000, put it on your list and for anything over, put it on the seller's list to fix.

When the inspection is complete, the inspector will go back to his office and craft a report with pictures and captions. Be sure to carefully look through this report, but hopefully nothing will come as a surprise. If you do have any questions, do not hesitate to call the inspector. Their job is to make sure that you are getting the property that you pay for.

Once the inspection is complete, you and your agent need to craft up the inspection objection. This is fancy for saying you need to tell the seller what they need to fix if they want the deal to close. Remember, nothing on this list should cost under $1,000 to fix. There very well might be nothing on this list. If you decided to do away with my $1,000 recommendation, or you decide to lower the threshold, then you might have quite a few things on the list.

Once the inspection objection gets sent to the seller, they will either agree or disagree to fix what you suggested. If they agree, there is no problem. If they disagree, then you will likely have to renegotiate the purchase price or make other arrangements.

Appraisal

Once the inspection and inspection objection are complete, you have done almost all that you can do in terms of your due diligence when purchasing a house hack. The only other thing that could influence your decision to buy is the appraisal. I talked about appraisals in chapter 4, but as a refresher, this is when a bank hires a third-party appraiser who comes and takes a look at the property. The property is compared with comparable properties (comps) in the same neighborhood that have similar features to the home being appraised.

For example, if you are purchasing a duplex where each side has two bedrooms and one bathroom, the appraiser will look for similar properties that have sold in your area. If they find a handful of duplexes similar to your prospective property that have sold from $350,000 to $400,000, you can bet that the property you are looking to buy will appraise for somewhere in that range. The appraiser will make adjustments for certain things such as a garage; more/less square footage; and the size of the lot. The comps are a great way to establish a base.

If the appraisal comes back at (or above) the purchase price, everything is hunky-dory, and there are very little ordinary occurrences that will prevent the deal from closing. Anything can happen, especially in real estate, so I choose to never say never. If the appraisal comes in lower than the purchase price, there will be a problem.

In this scenario, the bank will likely not be willing to supply you the loan because they underwrote the deal as if it was valued at the purchase price. When the appraiser comes in and tells them that it is lower than expected, the lender is at a higher risk. There are two easy ways to solve this problem. The first, and most advantageous for you, the buyer, is to ask the seller to come down to the appraised value. They likely will be willing to do this if it is the difference between closing and not closing a deal. In the event that they are not willing to come down to the appraised value, you can pay the difference by increasing your down payment. Any reasonable lender will accept either method so long as their risk profile has not changed.

Once the appraisal is completed and all objections are resolved, there is not much else you can do to get the deal done besides count down the days. However, finding and closing on the property is only half the work. In the next chapter, I need to teach you how to advertise your property and screen your tenants.

CASE STUDY
TYLER BLACKWELL

- **House-hacking strategy:** Traditional, Airbnb, and more
- **Age at first house hack:** 29
- **Location:** Olympia, Washington
- **NWROI:** 259%

Let's take a look at Tyler Blackwell, a house hacker from Olympia, Washington who is house hacking in a creative, yet unique way that has not been mentioned in this book. First, let's talk a little bit about Tyler's life. Tyler is a medical physicist by trade and works particularly in the radiation oncology department about forty-five hours per week. He is 34 years old and happily married to Hallie Blackwell with two young kids; one is 18 months old and the other is 3 years old.

In 2013, Tyler and Hallie were living the typical American dream, owning a three-bedroom, two-bathroom property. They knew they were planning to have two kids so they had room to expand. Although they did own some investment real estate, they were certainly not house hacking. That was until one day Hallie was looking on Redfin and asked if Tyler wanted to go check out a property she thought was interesting. Tyler had no intention of purchasing this property. He went to appease Hallie, but was ready to say that they were not going to put an offer on anything.

When arriving at the property, he saw a large, rundown house with a basement apartment, a small cottage in the back, and a horse arena on 4 acres of property. By that description, you might think that it was somewhere in the Podunk. Nope. This property was actually in Olympia, Washington, the capital of Washington and very close to the downtown area of the city. Tyler and Hallie not only saw a lot of income potential from this property, but also that there was lots of room for forced appreciation.

With a 5 percent down conventional mortgage, they purchased the property for $290,000. The property came with one inherited tenant, a family that lived in the main house and a marriage counselor who used the back cottage as an office. He was very nice, always paid rent on time, and certainly not a problem. For that reason, Tyler decided to continue leasing the space to the counselor at a discount of $300 per month. If the counselor were to ever leave, he could always put that back cottage on Airbnb, but they would need to do major renovations. His plan is to keep renting to the counselor for as long as he can.

There were no initial renovations done to the cottage, but let's move on to the actual house. The first order of business was to get the basement ready for rent. There was already a separate entrance and a carport for the tenant, but Tyler and Hallie contributed an additional $25,000 to put in a new roof, soundproof the basement, redo the floors, paint, and complete other cosmetic finishes. After doing these renovations, the house then appraised for $400,000! In case you missed it, just after $25,000 of renovations, the house appreciated by $110,000.

Initially, they rented the basement out on a full-time basis to a woman who was recommended by a friend. Foolishly, they did not screen her. It was a recommendation from someone they trusted so why would they need to tenant screen? This woman was a nightmare tenant. She always paid rent late and her dog peed all over the carpets. At the end, Tyler ended up collecting all of the rent from the tenant (including late fees) and kept her entire security deposit because he had to rip out the dog pee stained carpets. They have since converted the basement to an Airbnb and get on average $1,200 per month from that.

Remember the four acres and horse arena in the backyard? Believe it or not, Tyler and Hallie are not horse people, but saw the income potential. Rather than rent out each stall to individual horse owners, they rent out the five stalls to a woman for $850 per month who has several horses. This makes management much easier for them, and they do not need to provide any additional services.

To recap, Tyler and Hallie purchased this property for $290,000 with a total PITI of $2,500. The monthly rent from the counselor, Airbnb, and horses are $300, $1,200, and $850, respectively. The total rent collected each month is approximately $2,350. After utilities and reserves, Tyler and Hallie are paying about $300 a month to live in this property. To rent a comparable place in the area, Tyler would pay about $2,000 per month. This is a total of $1,700 in savings per month. That's just from the cash flow. At the end of his first year, he had about $5,000 of his mortgage paid off as well. Before I run the net worth return on investment calculation, let's check out what they did to force appreciation in the property.

Up to this point, they have already invested $25,000 and increased the value of their home by $110,000 to $400,000. They did not stop there. Knowing that they were going to live there for a while, they pulled out $90,000 of equity they generated to rehab the upstairs unit. They put in an updated heating system, took down some walls to open the kitchen and dining room area, added an island, upgraded the bathrooms, redid the roof, and painted the interior and exterior of the house. When all of the rehab was done, they got the property appraised for $600,000. That's $310,000 of value for $115,000 of total rehab costs.

With $1,700 per month added to their net worth in cash flow and rent savings, $5,000 of loan paydown, $310,000 of year one appreciation, and $129,500 of initial investment. Their net worth return on investment from house hacking their forever home in the first year is 259 percent. Again, not a bad deal!

 WHY *"I house hack to gain more freedom with my money. I plan to stay in this place for a while and grow our investment portfolio (currently at 26 units) to eventually replace my income. Sure, I love my job but I don't want to be bound to it. I have a wife and two kids and don't want to miss out on those precious moments: first steps, first homerun, first dance recital. My ultimate goal is to free up my time so I can create memories with my family."*

ACTION STEPS

❏ Write down the deadlines outlined in the contract in your calendar.
❏ Get in contact with a few inspectors.
❏ Compose your list of rehab items that you will complete and what the seller will need to complete.
❏ Start thinking about advertising your listing.

CHAPTER 9

MARKETING THE PROPERTY

Let's pretend you are writing a book. You have crafted the best written book of all time. Shakespeare, Hemingway, and Dickens have come back from the dead just to congratulate you on such a wonderful masterpiece. There is only one problem—you can't sell it. You've always been a masterful writer, but a horrible salesman. What good is a book that you can't sell? Unfortunately, the best written books do not always get praise; it's the best-selling books that do. For that reason, if you want your book to be a success, you will have to learn how to sell the book.

This idea can also relate to purchasing real estate. You can purchase the most beautiful property in the world that any tenant would give their right arm to live in. If you can't market it, how is anyone supposed to know about it? How are you supposed to garner the rents that you were expecting in your analysis? That's what this chapter is about: teaching you how to market and sell your property to prospective tenants.

Fair Housing Laws

Before I delve deep into how to list and market your property, let's talk about fair housing laws. In December 2018, a New York landlord was fined $15,000 because they refused to allow a woman with mental disabilities to keep an emotional support animal. If a landlord does not want a pet on their property, why should they have to let one in? In most cases where the pet is not an emotional support animal, the landlord has every right to deny the tenant. However, people with mental disabilities are a protected class so the landlord cannot deny a person with a mental disability tenancy because of their emotional support animal. Before you market your property, you need to understand the local, state, and federal fair housing laws.

What Is Fair Housing?

The Fair Housing Act was created in 1968 and amended in 1988 to protect tenants against illegal discrimination from landlords.[4] The classes that are protected include[5]:

- Race
- Sex
- Color
- Religion
- National origin
- Familial status (pregnant women, and parents with children)
- Disability

The U.S. Department of Housing and Urban Development (HUD) is the primary enforcer of the Fair Housing Act. According to HUD, no person may do any of the following because a potential tenant is in one of the protected classes:

- Refuse to rent or sell housing
- Refuse to negotiate for housing
- Deny a dwelling
- Set different terms, conditions, or privileges for sale or rental of a dwelling
- Provide different housing services or facilities
- Falsely deny that housing is available for inspection, sale, or rental
- For profit, persuade owners to sell or rent
- Deny anyone access to a membership in a facility or a service related to the sale or rental of housing

---

4   The Editors of Encyclopedia Britannica, www.Britannica.com/Topic/Fair-Housing-Act.

5   https://www.hud.gov/program_offices/fair_housing_equal_opp/fair_housing_act_overview#_The_ Fair_Housing

- Threaten, coerce, intimidate, or interfere with anyone exercising a fair housing right or assisting others who exercise that right
- Advertise or make any statement that indicated a limitation or preference based on race, color, national origin, religion, sex, familial status, or handicap. The prohibition against discriminatory advertising applies to single-family and owner-occupied housing that is otherwise exempt from the Fair Housing Act. [6]

Apart from the above being protected, your local city and state may have additional protected classes. If you are not sure what these are, do a Google search for "fair housing laws" in your state and you will get a bunch of information. For example, if I search "Fair housing laws Colorado," I get the following protected classes in addition to the ones above:

- Religion or creed
- Sexual orientation
- Marital status
- Ancestry

Please be sure to do your research on fair housing laws in your area. Investing in real estate gives you the opportunity to grow your wealth substantially. Make sure you are doing that in a lawful way and following the guidelines in the Fair Housing Act.

There are, in fact, many rules you have to follow when it comes to fair housing laws. There is more leeway if you decide to go a less traditional house-hacking route. If you are doing a short-term rental (via Airbnb, Vrbo, or HomeAway), you can decline people for a variety of reasons. One reason can be simply because you want to use your place for the desired time.

In the case when you are seeking longer-term tenants, you will not have to worry too much about fair housing laws if you are occupying the same dwelling as the prospective tenant. For example, if you are doing the rent-by-room strategy where you will double as roommates with your tenants, then discrimination laws are much more relaxed. However, if you are pursuing the more traditional house-hacking strategy by purchasing a two- to four-unit property and renting out the other units, you will be subject to penalty if you violate the fair housing laws.

The fair housing laws are much less strict when you house hack than

---

6 https://www.chfainfo.com/Pages/nondiscrimination.aspx

when you have a traditional rental. However, it is still best to abide by fair housing laws. One, it saves you from a lot of potential lawsuits. Whether you win or lose, they are still a pain. Secondly, it builds good habits. When you move out of your first house hack and start renting that fully, you will now be required to follow the fair housing laws. Why not just do so initially so you have the systems and methodologies in place to screen tenants legally?

Loopholes of Fair Housing

I already described one of the loopholes of fair housing. That is house hacking! However, there are a few others. The fair housing laws say that you are unable to deny protected classes tenancy because of their protected class. You need to treat them equally as any other tenants or prospective tenants. Because you need to treat them *equally*, you can still deny them tenancy based on a number of factors such as: credit score, background history, or insufficient income.

For example, I had an applicant who had an emotional support dog look at one of my properties. I do love dogs, but given the fact that many people are allergic and I did not want the added mess in my house, I really did not want to accept this tenant. Luckily, I require a background and credit check for every person who wants to live in the property. This gentleman's credit score came back below 500, which if you remember from chapter 4, is horrible. For that reason, it is clear that I denied him based on his credit score and not the fact that he had an emotional support animal.

If you aren't so lucky with the credit score or background check, another option would be to undersell the property. As you are walking through the property with your prospective tenant, you can mention all of the good things you would to a tenant that you do want. However, you can also mention the bad things just like Spongebob Squarepants so eloquently does, "The floor creeks, the roof leaks, there is a terrible draft. The winters are harsh, the summers are brutal! There's a man-eating clam in the backyard!" Okay, maybe you don't go that far, but just be honest. Are the walls thin? Have you been having problems with the plumbing? Is the house not well insulated? Do the roommates not get along? Let these unwanted prospective tenants know *everything*. That way, you are being a 100 percent honest landlord while also giving them a reason to not want to live in your place.

You now should have a good idea about the fair housing laws, and how to abide by them. The place where landlords and property managers are most vulnerable to these fair housing laws are in their listing advertisements. Let me explain how you should go about marketing your property.

Advertising the Property

The strategy for marketing your property will change based on the type of house hacking you plan to do. I talked about the different ways to house hack a while ago. In case you forgot, here is a reminder:

1. **Traditional:** Purchase a two- to four-unit property. Live in one unit, rent the rest.
2. **Rent by room:** Purchase a large single-family, live in one room, rent the others.
3. **Airbnb:** Purchase a property with an accessory dwelling unit or mother in-law suite. Rent the extra space while you live in your house.
4. **Trailer:** Buy a trailer, park it in your driveway or backyard. Rent the house and live in the trailer. You could also live in the house and rent the trailer, but you'll likely get less income this way.
5. **Living room:** Make a sleeping quarters out of the living room and rent out your bedroom.

If you are planning to pursue the traditional or rent-by-room methods, you will be seeking a long-term tenant with a lease. If you are pursuing either the ADU, trailer, or living room strategy, then you will likely be doing the short-term rental route, which calls for a different marketing strategy. Let's dig into each.

Marketing Long-Term Rentals

Your Ideal Tenant

The first step in marketing your property is to determine who would be your ideal tenant. Are you planning on renting to a family? A young professional? Someone in the military? The choices are endless, but you need to decide so that you can cater your ad appropriately. If you are going the traditional route and offering an entire unit, your options are much greater. Families and young professionals who make more money are more likely to rent out a unit rather than just a bedroom. That does not mean the rent-by-room strategy does not work though. It is just that your ideal tenant will come from a smaller pool: a single young professional with no pets.

Please do not forget what we just talked about in the fair housing laws section! Just because you have an ideal tenant in your mind, you should not describe them exactly in your listing. Be very careful with your wording. To avoid running into a fair housing lawsuit, it is best to describe the property or community that attracts the type of person you want, rather than directly describing the type of tenant you want.

For example, if you are renting the other side of a duplex that is a one-bedroom apartment, you will most likely want a young professional or a young couple as tenants. Do not mention "young couple" in the advertisement, just advertise the place as a one-bedroom that is close to bars, restaurants, breweries, etc. This will attract the young couple without saying "young couple." Do not mention anything about the school district or things that may attract families.

Creating the Advertisement

When creating the advertisement, you want your prospective tenant to know as much as possible about the property. If you are renting by the room, you will also want to sell them on the roommates. Because the rent-by-room strategy encompasses both selling the place and the roommates, that is the example I'm going to use in this book. If you are doing the traditional route, you can obviously ignore the selling the roommates section.

Advertising the Property

What makes your property stand out from the others? You want to make the features and benefits incredibly clear to any viewer of your advertisement. Is it large? Do you have a big yard? Is the kitchen beautifully done? Are you close to restaurants, bars, coffee shops, public transportation? Or is it a quiet neighborhood, down a country road, or at the end of a cul-de-sac? Whatever it is, make sure that you craft your advertisement so that it is one of your first items, and is emphasized in your pictures.

After you are done "selling" the property, you will want to tell them what they need to move in. What is the rent and security deposit? Do they need to do a background and credit check (yes!)? Are the tenants responsible for utilities? If so, how much do they run each month? Today, people hate calling to ask questions. I know I do! Try to answer as many of the obvious questions as possible in your ad description so the phone call can be about getting a feel for your future tenant and talking next steps.

Advertising the Roommates

Would you rather live in a nice house with horrible roommates or a horrible house with nice roommates? Believe it or not, most people would choose a dilapidated house if their roommates were okay. Luckily, you do not have to make this choice. The question was just to show you how important it is to live with people that you like.

If you are house hacking while living in the same unit as your tenants, you should think of it as building a small community, or family. You will want to attract people who are like you. The way to attract people that you like is to advertise in your listing what everyone in the house is like, including yourself. What do you do for work? What do you do for fun? Are you a stay in and play board games type? Or do you prefer to go to bars and clubs? Are you outdoorsy? Do you like sports? Are you into video games, anime, and comic books? Describe your day-to-day life in your advertisement, and you will attract people who are similar to you.

EXAMPLE ADVERTISEMENT

Are you a little nervous about posting the advertisement? Don't know where to start? Don't worry, I was too. To give you a boost, here is a sample advertisement for one of my bedrooms.

One room available!
Move in as soon as you can.
- *120-square-foot room on the top floor*

The Area:
- *Very nice, quiet neighborhood in Thornton (easy parking!)*
- *5-minute walk to bus that takes you into downtown Denver*
- *1-minute drive into downtown Denver*
- *Less than a mile away from a grocery store*
- *2 minutes from grocery store, $1 tacos, and many other places to eat/shop*
- *Close to bike/running paths*

Who We Are:
- *One financial analyst (male), two government workers (male), and one graphic designer (female). We all get along great!*
- *Everyone is typically out of the house most of the time between careers and weekend activities.*
- *We are all between the ages of 25 to 30.*
- *Everyone in the house likes spending time outdoors—some of our hobbies include hiking, snowboarding/skiing, golf, basketball, sports, live music, and camping.*

The Space:
- *5-bedroom / 2-bathroom single-family house*
- *2,400 square feet*
- *Fully remodeled and nicely updated over the past 12 months*
- *Large open floor plan for kitchen/living room*
- *Completely furnished with two living spaces (upstairs and downstairs)*
- *A nice backyard with a table, couch, and fire pit to hang out around*
- *Laundry located in basement*
- *Carport, space in driveway & street for parking*
- *All utilities are split five ways (gas, water/sewer, Comcast internet, and garbage), which average out to approximately $50/month per person.*
- *Security deposit of one month's rent due to secure spot. First month's rent due on move-in.*
- *One-person occupancy*
- *Applicant must be non-smoker (cigarette)*
- *No pets*

Must be clean and tidy

If interested, please reach out with name, a social media link (Facebook, Instagram, or LinkedIn preferred), age, hobbies, occupation, etc.

The Photos

You know how the old saying goes, "A picture is worth a thousand words." If that rings true, the above description only has 271 words so it is less than a third of one picture's worth. The photos of your space will be the most important thing in your advertisement. Make sure that they are high quality. I am sure you were a renter once (or maybe still are). What do you do when you see an advertisement with poorly lit pictures taken from a cellphone camera? I'd bet you move to the next advertisement. How about when you see an advertisement with beautiful, well-lit pictures of a clean house? Your interest is piqued, and you move to the next picture. Here are some photo tips for your listing.

Lighting

A few years ago, my girlfriend at the time and I were camping in the Grand Canyon with some friends. There were four people in a two-person tent. Needless to say, we did not get much sleep that night. Rather than lie there and stare at the ceiling of the tent for the next six hours, my girlfriend and I decided to go out to a lookout spot where we could catch the sunrise. We slept for a couple of hours on an embankment and when the sun was about to rise, we noticed hundreds of professional photographers taking pictures. Not of the sunrise, though. They were taking pictures of the iconic Grand Canyon landscape with the bright sun behind them. Why did they wake up so early to snap a picture of a landscape that would be illuminated for most of the day? In the morning, the sun would be at the perfect spot to capture the photo.

The sun plays the same role when it comes to taking pictures of your property. You want your pictures to make the space look open, warm, and inviting. You want your future tenants/roommates to envision themselves enjoying a cup of coffee in the backyard, watching their favorite sports team on the big screen TV, or going on a short walk to enjoy the nearest public attraction. It is going to be hard to envision themselves doing any of this with poorly lit pictures taken at night or in the middle of a rainstorm. Be sure to take your pictures on a bright, sunny day. To add even more lighting be sure that all of your curtains are open and all interior lights are turned on. This will make the place as warm and inviting as possible.

The best time to take the pictures is going to be when your house is exposed to the most natural sunlight. If there is a large bay window on the east side of your house, the sun will be shining through that window in the early to late morning (just a reminder: the sun rises from the east). However, if that window is on the west side of your house, you'll want to take it in the early afternoon.

Staging

Before taking the pictures, you are going to want to make sure the inside of your property is clean, orderly, and rent-ready. Do not take photos that are mid-rehab or before the unit is ready to show. Look to make sure there is nothing weird in the photos, such as open cabinets, random things on the counter, unmade beds or open toilet seats. If you want to put in the extra effort, I would suggest staging the interior with a few items. Maybe put a fruit bowl on the counter, nice curtains in the windows, or a vase of flowers on the dinner table. These little things go a long way when it comes to making the place look and feel like "home."

The exterior is often the first picture that people see. You are going to want to make sure that the property is free and clear of any items that don't belong. Your car should not be in the photo. The trash barrels should be hidden. If you have a flower bed or plants, make sure there are no weeds growing. The grass should be freshly cut. If there is a mulch bed, a fresh layer will not hurt. The goal here is to make the property look as attractive as possible.

Equipment Needed

The property is all dolled up and the photos are ready to be taken. A crappy camera can ruin all the work you just went through to make the property look nice. It's time to donate that Etch A Sketch and 2004 Motorola Razr to a museum.

You do not need to go crazy here. A regular point and shoot camera or the one you have on your smartphone should do the trick. However, if you plan on owning more than one rental property, consider investing in a DSLR camera for a more professional look. A DSLR camera is going to give you a higher quality photo with crisper images, wider angles, and allow you to focus in on the objects you want to emphasize in your photos.

If you are charging $1,000 for rent, and you can get a renter two weeks earlier, the camera has already paid for itself. Plus, you get the bonus of having a nice camera when you go on vacation. Maybe you can join the fleet of photographers at the Grand Canyon now that you know the best time to go.

Taking the Photos

Be sure to take a lot of photos! Again, the pictures are the most important part of the advertisement. Making sure that your description accurately describes the pictures and has all of the information a tenant would need is crucial in making sure your property is the one that prospective tenants must have today.

When placing your pictures with the advertisement, you will want to give the feeling that the prospective renter is on a virtual tour of the property. The first picture should be the exterior of the property. That is followed by what you see when you enter the unit. Then you take pictures of the main rooms such as the kitchen, living room, dining rooms, recreational rooms, bathrooms, and bedrooms, as well as the backyard, garage, and any landscaping that you worked hard on to showcase.

Most listing sites will have a limit as to how many pictures you can include in a listing. Be sure to take lots of photos so that you can display your best options on the advertisement.

Where to Advertise Long-Term Rentals

You wrote the description, you took your photos, and now it is time to get your property rented-out. Remember the funnels we talked about when finding lenders, agents, and contractors? The funnel is coming back to haunt us again. When you are searching for tenants, you will want to get the most exposure as possible. The more exposure you get, the more people will apply to be your tenant, and the higher probability that you will get your ideal tenant. For that reason, we market the property in a variety of different ways that we will cover now. Regardless of where your advertisement is showcased, be sure that all the pertinent information (rent, security deposit, utilities, lease term, and any other details) is clearly featured.

Word of Mouth

How many people have you met in your life? Hundreds? Thousands? Hundreds of thousands? How many people do you think those people have met? There are likely hundreds of thousands, if not millions of people that are within two degrees of separation from you. They all need a place to call home. These usually make the best tenants because if you know them or someone in your network knows them, there is a high probability that you will have similar interests. It's always best to get along with your tenants/roommates than to fight.

Craigslist.org

Craigslist is one of the largest classified websites, and it is still an effective way to obtain tenants. The best part about it? Surprisingly, it's not the name. It's the fact that it is free in ninety-nine percent of the United States. Sorry for all of you in New York City. On Craigslist, tenants are able to search for available listings in their desired locations that meet their criteria. For example, if a prospective tenant is looking for a two-bedroom, one-bathroom place within two miles of downtown, they can easily find this on Craigslist. Unlike many listing sites, Craigslist also allows you to post individual rooms (as opposed to entire units) on their site.

You can list the exact address on Craigslist, but for safety purposes I prefer to just list the cross streets. By doing this, people get a good idea of the location, but will not come knocking on the door. To upload an advertisement on Craigslist just go to www.Craigslist.org and start crafting.

Facebook Marketplace

While Craigslist is still one of the most popular ways to find an apartment, Facebook Marketplace is starting to slowly take over. Each year, I notice that the amount of quality leads I get is shifting from Craigslist to Facebook. There is something about Facebook that is less sketchy. Perhaps it is the fact that you can easily research the person directly on Facebook, and see their recent pictures, posts, and interests? Anyway, if you do not have a Facebook account or are one of those "cool kids" who ditched Facebook for Instagram, it is time to swallow your pride and get back on there. Facebook Marketplace is now one of the best places to advertise.

You can copy and paste your description word for word from your Craigslist advertisement when uploading to the marketplace. One downside to Facebook is that they only allow ten pictures so make sure to choose the best to showcase the beauty of the property.

Once you have uploaded your listing to Facebook Marketplace, you will want to find the Facebook groups where people are looking for places to live. There is at least one group in almost every city. If you are renting by the room, this will be your gold mine. Post the Facebook Marketplace advertisement with the appropriate Facebook groups, and then wait for people to reply. If you want to take the extra step in finding potential tenants, you can proactively look at the group and see if anyone has posted a status mentioning "place wanted." Reach out to these people directly and point them in the direction of your advertisement. They might be interested.

Zillow

Zillow is the crème de la crème of real estate marketplaces, and is probably your best bet when it comes to finding tenants for a traditional house hack. That's right. Zillow does not allow postings for individual rooms, only entire units. However, it is the go-to resource for those looking for a place to rent. Like Craigslist, Zillow is free for landlords to advertise, and it enables users to search for certain criteria such as location, size, type, and price. You can post a Zillow advertisement directly on their site, or you can use the Zillow-owned tool called Zillow Rental Manager.

Zillow Rental Manager is a great way for landlords to advertise their listings. Not only does it allow you to create a listing, but it also distributes it to the most popular rental sites, including Zillow, Trulia, HotPads, and many more. Zillow Rental Manager is free and easy to use, but only works if you are renting out an entire unit. It is not helpful if you are pursuing the rent-by-room or short-term rental strategy.

Yard Signs

Let's take it back to some of the old school methods for advertising your property. Yard signs. Get your property rented by putting a "for lease" sign in the front yard. Please make sure it is actually a sign. A ripped-out piece of notebook paper taped to a stick in the ground is not going to do the trick here. Please go ahead and purchase a "for lease" sign and write your phone number in the space provided. If there is room, I would suggest putting the amount of bedrooms and bathrooms as well as the rent price on the sign so only people with serious inquiries will call you. It's old school, but it works. Yard signs are an extremely effective strategy if your place has a lot of people passing by via cars on the street and/or foot traffic.

These are all the strategies that I have successfully used over the years. If you are still having trouble finding quality tenants, you can increase the top of the funnel by also posting an advertisement in the newspaper, or print flyers to distribute.

Newspaper

I know. It's hard to believe that newspapers still exist. It's even more difficult to believe that there are people who still look in the newspaper for open listings, but they are out there. While newspaper advertising may not work in every market, it can still be effective—especially if house hacking in a small town. Make sure to include all of the most important information such as general location, bedrooms, bathrooms, and price. Whatever you do, do not put the exact address of your home. Put the cross streets. There are a lot of criminals out there, and if they have your address then your property can easily become a target. Also, it forces people to call you so you can have a one-on-one conversation.

Here is an example:

Newly remodeled, 1-bedroom, top-unit apartment available in a well-maintained triplex in the RiNo neighborhood. In-unit laundry. Walking distance to bars and restaurants. All utilities are included. Pet and smoke free. Rent $1,300/ month + deposit. Call us ASAP! 555-555-5555.

Flyers

Flyers are a fast, easy, and cheap way to get your listing advertised to a wide audience. Think back to your target market. Post your flyer in a place where your ideal tenant frequents. Looking for young professional? Perhaps put the advertisement on a bulletin board at a coffee shop. Want a family? Try putting it in a grocery store. You get the picture. Just like with the newspaper advertisement, please be sure to not solicit the exact address. Include all of the pertinent information that will enable them to disqualify your property as an option should it not meet their criteria. No one has time for unnecessary phone calls.

You are not going to be watching these flyers. It is entirely possible that someone takes *all* of them if they really want the property. Unfortunately, this is not something that you can prevent. Just make sure your listing is available through other means so you are not limited to just one potential tenant.

Putting up flyers helps people remember your place. When you start to show it, everyone should get a flyer. In many cases, people are going to be looking at five to ten places. It's hard to keep them all straight. Help them remember your rental by giving them a flyer.

Where to Advertise Short-Term Rentals

As I've mentioned, advertising a short-term rental is quite different from advertising a long-term one. Let's dive in a little deeper. Short-term rentals have two flavors. The first is the one you are probably envisioning. These are vacations, business trips, and short one- to five-day stays. The second flavor is what I like to call medium-term rentals. These are for those who travel for work. Examples may include traveling nurses, contractors, corporate renters, and interns who just need a place to stay for thirty to ninety days. Either way, the advertisement for a short-term rental will be much different than one for a long-term rental. The biggest difference? People expect any short- or medium-term rental to be fully furnished.

Similar to all of these dating apps that have popped up over the years, there are tons of marketplaces for short-term rentals. Since short-term rentals are only a subset of this book, I'm only going to touch on the behemoths of the industry: Airbnb, Vrbo, HomeAway, and Furnished Finder.

Airbnb

Airbnb is by far the most recognized name in the short-term rental space. When you go look something up online, what do you do? You "Google" it. When you are going on a vacation and opting for a non-hotel experience, what do you do? You "Airbnb" it. With over 150 million users and six million property listings in 191 countries (of 195 countries) around the world, Airbnb is the standard in the industry, and it knows it[7]. It gets the most traffic, and many people (especially millennials) are going to look here before they look anywhere else. As a result, it does charge some of the highest fees to list your property on their site. Though, it puts most of the fee on the guests, as opposed to the host.

While Airbnb can be used for both short (less than thirty days) and medium-term stays (thirty-plus days), it is most commonly used for the short-term stays. If your plan is to solely do short-term stays, you will want to have your listing on Airbnb. If not, you will still want your listing on Airbnb for the in-between periods of longer-term stays.

For example, you have a guest who will be in town for two months and their stay ends May 15. But your next guest isn't booked until June 4, so you'll have a couple of weeks of vacancy between guests. For these in-between periods, you will want to put the property on Airbnb to limit your vacancy time.

---

7   Craig Smith, 105 Airbnb Statistics and Facts (2019)| By the Numbers, (2019) https://expandedramblings.com/index.php/airbnb-statistics/.

Vrbo/HomeAway

Vrbo, also known as "Vacation Rental by Owner," and HomeAway were among the original vacation rental sites. Now owned by Expedia, these sites get a lot of traffic from people searching for flights or booking their own vacations.

Since these sites are a little bit older, you will notice that the demographic of the guests is older as well. It may not be your grandma and grandpa looking for a place to stay, but you will definitely get more middle-aged to retirement-aged folks.

Vrbo and HomeAway are almost solely for vacations. If you are looking for a medium-term rental, this should not be your primary place to advertise. Though, like Airbnb, it is great for those times when you are between guests.

The price point for Vrbo and HomeAway is slightly higher than that of Airbnb. Hosts will pay about eight to ten percent of the booking price (or an annual fee), whereas the guests pay less. The great thing about Airbnb and Vrbo is that you can sync the calendars together to prevent getting double booked. If you get a booking on Airbnb, it will block the date(s) so no one can book on Vrbo and vice versa.

Furnished Finder

Apart from all of the places you can list a long-term rental, Furnished Finder seems to be the largest that focuses in medium-term rentals. If you are looking for a corporate rental, or an intern to occupy your space for just a few months, Furnished Finder is the place to go. For $100 per year, the site will allow you to advertise your listing with no other fees included.

Furnished Finder allows for both incoming and outgoing inquiries. If someone stumbles upon your place, they can reach out to you. On the other hand, if someone knows they are moving to your area, Furnished Finder will alert you that there might be someone interested in your place. It is then up to you to reach out to them to see if they are interested.

Admittedly, the site seems to be in its infancy with poor design and longer load times. However, it is effective and I know a lot of people who use Furnished Finder to find their thirty- to ninety-day guests. With as much success as they have had, I am sure that Furnished Finder will work their kinks out.

Advertising your property accurately is incredibly important. You want to make sure that you are getting your advertisement seen by the correct demographic, as well as creating the advertisement to grab their attention. For example, if your place is going to cater to young couples, it's silly to put an advertisement in the newspaper.

Tracking Your Results

Even though you are house hacking, you need to treat your real estate endeavors like a business, not a hobby. It is helpful to understand what strategy works best. That way, you can double down on the most effective strategy and do away with the ones that do not work. I suggest tracking the number of inquiries you receive via email, phone call, and other sources in a simple spreadsheet. Be sure to update this list and see what strategies have been the most effective for you. This will help your real estate business run much more efficiently.

Short-Term Rentals: What to Advertise

The above strategies all work if you are house hacking for a traditional, long-term rental. If you are planning to pursue the strategy where you Airbnb a room in the house, this is an entirely different approach.

There will not be much difference in creating the advertisement. You'll still need to take high-quality photos and write clear descriptions. You will need to state that your place is sold as a temporary stay rather than a long-term stay. What is the difference? When people do a short-term stay, they care less about the details, and more about overall comfortability of the home. You can describe the spacious kitchen with a six-burner stove, but I would highly recommend emphasizing the location and amenities of the property. When describing your short-term rental, be sure to tell your potential guests a bit about you as well. In almost any house-hacking situation, you are going to want to attract guests or tenants that are like you. The reason is that the more you get along, then the happier you will be, the happier the guests will be, and the happier your reviews will be in the end.

Creating the Short-Term Rental Listing

The quality of your listing is always important. With short-term rentals, they are even more so. When creating your advertisement for a short-term listing, this is the only thing your potential guests are seeing. In many cases, they have never even been to your city. They are not going to come look at the place before they book a stay. You need to make sure that what they see is what they get. If you lie, take false pictures, or give a false representation of the place, this will be reflected in your reviews and it will impact your future bookings.

Remember the funnel? The more eyes you get on your listing, the more likely that it is that your place will be booked at the highest possible rate. If you haven't already, you are going to want to create an account on Airbnb, HomeAway, and Vrbo. There are tons more out there, but these are the main sites that capture the majority of the market.

Profile Photo

The first thing you do when creating your account is upload a profile photo. Make sure you have a high-quality headshot of yourself. You may even consider getting one done professionally. As the host, you are going to want to look fun, nice, and welcoming. Your profile picture is a guest's first impression of you. You are going to want to make it a good one.

Description of Yourself

The description is putting words to your picture. It is what makes someone want to stay with *you* and not the identical property down the street. This is super easy to do. Just describe yourself in three to five sentences. What do you do for work? Where are you originally from? What do you do for fun? Why do you like to host? If you are planning to interact with the guest, this is extremely important as you are going to want them to feel comfortable sleeping in your home.

Here is an example of my profile description:

Hey there!

My name is Craig Curelop. I am originally from Boston, but moved to Denver from San Francisco in April 2017 to work my dream job as the finance guy at BiggerPockets, an online community for real estate investors. If you are into real estate or personal finance and want to chat while you're here, I always love chatting about this stuff!

When I'm not working, you will find me taking advantage

of all of the things Colorado has to offer. I enjoy biking around Denver, hiking, hanging out with friends, snow-boarding (still a work in progress), and traveling. I've been an Airbnb host since June 2017 and really enjoying it! I love talking to and meeting new people as well as making sure your impression of Denver is as great as can be!

Get Verified

At this point, these sites are trusted between both the hosts and guests. Although, it makes you look a lot more legitimate if you get verified. Be sure to verify in as many ways as possible: email, phone number, social media, and more. This gives your guests the peace of mind that you are who you say you are.

Creating the Property Listing

The last section was all about you. It's not about you anymore. Now, it's all about the property. Let's switch gears for a second. Pretend you are scrolling through your Facebook feed and you stumble upon an article that seems interesting. What do you do? You click it. What got you to click on that article? It probably was not the author's name, the website it came from, or even what the article had to say. What got you to click was the title and perhaps the cover art associated with the article. The same thing goes for your short-term rental listing. The title and your first picture are crucial in getting people to click on your listing and book the place. Use your title and the first image to make your property stand out from the rest. From there, your stellar pictures and descriptions will close the sale.

Creating your listing title for a short-term rental is much different than what it would be for a long-term rental. This is because they are looking for different things. A place to stay for a few nights is much different than a place to live. When crafting your title, it would be silly to say, "two-bedroom, two-bathroom apartment with utilities included." They can filter for the two-bedroom, two-bathroom units on the site and utilities are obviously included! Instead, you are going to want to use descriptive words that really sell the place.

Here are some examples of high-quality titles:

"Newly Renovated Basement Unit Apartment Steps from Downtown"

"Modernized, One Bedroom next to Central Park"

"Relaxing Bungalow Right on the Beach"

"Spacious Condo in the Heart of Downtown Denver"

The Listing Description

At this point, you have crafted your personal description, the photos, and the title. Now it's time to set up the description of your property. Craft your description in such a way that allows the readers to imagine what their stay is going to look and feel like. Describe the experience they will have while staying in your home rather than just outlining what is obviously depicted from the pictures.

People are not on these short-term rental sites looking for something to read. They are looking for a place to stay. Please do not write a novel in your descriptions. Keep them short and sweet. Use bullet points because this allows the reader to easily skim the description and glean the information they need when deciding which property they want to reserve. If you make this information hard to find, I can almost guarantee that they will end up booking elsewhere.

What is it that makes your place stand out? This should be the first line in your description. Is it near a park? Are you right downtown? Is there a beautiful view from the top floor? Whatever it is, do your best to convince your guests that staying at your place will be a one-of-a-kind experience that they cannot get anywhere else.

Take your guests room by room in the property to make them feel like they have already been there.

Picture Description

Have you ever walked into a property that looked nothing like the pictures? I know I have. Nothing is more frustrating than getting less than you expect. Make sure that your photo descriptions are accurate and if there is anything that may negatively impact someone's stay, let them know. Otherwise, it will show up in your reviews and will negatively affect the amount you can charge. For example, one of my short-term rentals is an up/down duplex. The floor/ceiling between the two units are paper thin. Therefore, I say it front and center that the guests may hear noise between the units. If they expect the problem, there is a lower probability that they will complain.

House Rules

In your short-term rental listing, you are going to need to create house rules. Everyone has different expectations and yours need to be clearly stated if you expect the guests to follow them. All of the sites have a space where you can outline your house rules. Some of the most common rules address issues like:

- Whether or not they can throw parties
- Whether or not they can smoke
- Whether or not they can bring pets
- Off-limits areas
- Temperature settings for the thermostat
- Cleaning procedures
- Quiet hours

This list is not fully comprehensive. If you have additional rules, then by all means, include them in your house rulebook.

Pricing

Unlike a long-term rental when a lease is signed and the monthly payment remains the same, short-term rental rates are volatile. They are subject to supply and demand, which is impacted by seasonality, nearby events, and the quality of your place. For my first few months, I was looking in the area to see what other people were charging and I would charge the same or slightly lower. Doing market research and adjusting prices can end up being a full-time job. That's not the goal. This should be passive. In Michael Gerber's *The E-Myth* he writes, "Work ON your business, not IN your business." His point is that if you get caught up in the minutiae of your business, you will have trouble scaling.

Let's relate this back to price setting. You could set your prices to be the same rate each night, but you would most definitely be losing out on money given the seasonality of short-term rentals. On the other side of the spectrum, you could test the supply and demand of short-term rentals in your area while adjusting for seasonality, events, and amenities that you provide. If you do this, that will take up a lot of your time and you will likely not be perfect at determining the pricing structure. Instead, why not pay $20 per month to have a service that does this for you? You now get your life back and can scale your business.

Rather than setting your own prices, there are a variety of tools out there that can set the listing price for your short-term rental. They do this by looking at similar properties in the area, testing the supply and the demand, and charging the highest possible price while still ensuring your place is booked 90 percent of the time. On every booking, I check to see the price that was paid, and in many cases the price is much higher than I would have ever set. These price setting tools pay for themselves not only in time and hassle, but in money made from bookings.

Airbnb has their own Smart Pricing tool as well. However, I highly recommend you do not use it. Airbnb only makes money if someone books a stay. For that reason, they always set the prices extremely low to ensure a booking while you are leaving money on the table. The pricing tool that I use is called PriceLabs, but there are others including Beyond Pricing and Wheelhouse, to name a few.

Outside of the base nightly stay rate, there are additional fees you can charge. These include a cleaning fee and an extra guest fee. If you are cleaning the place yourself or hiring someone to do so, no one should be cleaning for free. That's why you charge the cleaning fee. There is no set formula on what you should charge, but typically the larger the place, the higher the cleaning fee. Similar to how you should not be tinkering with the pricing, you should not be the one cleaning your property. Why? Well, you are going to get real sick of cleaning. Also, I highly doubt that you can clean better than a hired professional. Getting reviews that complain about your place being dirty can really set you back. Cleaning yourself is not a scalable model because as you start to acquire two, three or four properties in the next few years, you will not be able to clean them all. Another thing to consider is what happens when you go away? Lastly and most importantly, you can make a profit on just the cleaning fee. For example, my cleaning crew charges me $35 per clean. I charge the guests $55 so I profit $20 just from the cleaning fee. I need to be paid for all of the toiletries, goodies that I provide, and for my constant interaction with the cleaning crew. That's where the $20 per stay comes in. Remember that this is a business. If you are renting a short-term rental, you are in the short-term rental business, not the cleaning business.

Another additional fee is the extra guest fee. For example, if you have a one-bedroom apartment that sleeps four people (two in the bed and two on the sofa), you might want to charge a flat fee per person over one or two people. The reason for this is that the more people you have in your unit, the riskier it is. With more people, it is more likely things are going to break; and they are going to use more water and make more noise. If you can make an extra $10 or $20 per person, why wouldn't you?

Boom! Just like that you have your listing. Whether it is short term or long term, you should now have a good idea on how to get people interested in staying with you in your house hack. Just remember when marketing your property, be sure to identify your ideal tenant, take quality pictures, write accurate descriptions, and get the listing out to as many places as possible to garner the best odds of having the place rented-out.

Now that you have people knocking on your door to rent your place, let's get into screening them. But first, check out some action steps and a case study of a fellow house hacker.

CASE STUDY
RICK ALBERT

- **House-hacking strategy:** Rent by room
- **Age at first house hack:** 27
- **Location:** Los Angeles, California
- **NWROI:** 110%

Let's meet Rick Albert. Rick is a top performing real estate agent and investor out of Los Angeles, California. That's right! One of the most expensive destinations in the United States, and he is still making it work. Let's see how he does it!

In 2015, Rick was on the hunt for his first house hack. His ideal property was a cheap two-bedroom, two-bathroom condominium in a class B neighborhood. He wanted to be close to work and within a mile of bars and restaurants. He was looking in a neighborhood called Tarzana where he found exactly what he was looking for: a two-bedroom, two-bathroom condo for just $225,000. As you would expect, anything offered at a price this low in Los Angeles is going to be a major fixer upper. The previous owner had lived there for thirty years, and she had done nothing to the property with the exception of updating the furnace. To top it all off, she was a heavy smoker.

Like any smart investor, Rick walked in there, saw the state the property was in and thought he could definitely fix the place, and make it worth much more, and then rent it out. That's exactly what he did. He put an offer down for $225,000 and financed it using a 10 percent down owner-occupied loan. He replaced the entire kitchen, scraped the ceiling, added ceiling fans, and got rid of the smoke smell by deep cleaning what could be salvaged and replacing what could not be. Rick paid a total of $18,000 for his rehab costs. He did choose some of the more expensive finishes with the idea that he would be able to rent it out easier upon moving out.

Once Rick finished the rehab, he went to refinance the property. The appraisal came in at $260,000 so Rick added $35,000 of value with just $18,000 in rehab. Not a bad return. After he refinanced, Rick's mortgage payment and HOA dues were a combined $1,500 per month, and he was renting one of the rooms for $800. Utilities and a bi-weekly maid service was included in the rent, so he was looking at spending approximately $900 per month out of his own pocket. For Rick to find a comparable place to rent in his area would be $1,500–$1,600 per month. That's $600–$700 per month in savings.

Rick lived there for a few years and in 2019 he saw an identical unit in his condominium complex sell for $345,000. He knew that his could easily sell for that much so rather than sell, he decided to take a line of credit out on the apartment to fund the down payment on his next house hack. Today, Rick is renting out the condo for approximately $2,000 per month with $1,900 in total debt payments (mortgage + HELOC).

Rick's second house hack was a single-family residence that he purchased for $520,000 in early 2019. The property itself did not need a whole lot of work, but because he and his fiancée were going to be living there, he wanted to make it nice. They spent $50,000 to $60,000 in renovations to the actual house. The reason why Rick purchased this place though was because there was a detached garage that could be turned into an accessory dwelling unit (ADU). He spent about $200,000 running plumbing, electrical, and completely redoing the garage into a livable unit.

Once the ADU is complete, he believes he will have increased his home value by $200,000 (same amount he invested) to $720,000. He is then going to refinance his secondary property where the PITI will be about $4,000. Rick will be able to get $1,600 in rent for the ADU so rather than paying $4,000 per month to live in his dream home, he is going to be paying just $2,400.

As you can tell by this story, Rick is not taking the most financially aggressive approach to house hacking. He is taking the approach of building wealth through his living situation while living in the exact situation he wants to. He has a house that he really likes with his fiancée that is close to family and friends. Rick plans to stay in this second house hack for a few years as they save up for the next one.

WHY

"I'm house hacking to have financial stability and the freedom to do what I like in the long term. I love what I do and have no intention of quitting in the short term. But, if I want to travel, I can. If I want to buy my wife something nice, no problem. I no longer want money to be the reason why I can or cannot do things."

ACTION STEPS

❏ If you are doing a short-term rental, create accounts on the major short-term listing sites, such as Airbnb and Vrbo.
❏ If you are doing a long-term rental, research some other listings so that you have an idea of what yours is going to look like once you close on your house hack.
❏ Buy a nice camera and a tripod, or start looking for a photographer.

CHAPTER 10

SCREENING TENANTS/ ROOMMATES

You have heard the horror stories. The phone calls in the middle of the night to fix a running toilet. Drug deals, murders, or prostitution happening in your properties. Do you want to be dealing with this?

I'm going to take a wild guess and say no. If this is what every landlord had to go through, I can guarantee you that you would see fewer landlords. So then why is it that these stories exist? Who are the fools that subject themselves to these awful tenants? Let me tell you. It's the landlords who do not screen their tenants.

Bad tenants, whether they do not pay their rent, destroy the property, or sue you as the landlord, are the number one reason people give up on real estate. One way or the other, headaches are almost always because of the tenant. Unfortunately, there is no way to eliminate all future tenant troubles, but there are ways to drastically reduce them. That process is called "screening" your tenants. This chapter is going to take you through the process of finding the highest quality tenant so that you do not end up part of the retired landlord statistic.

Don't you fret though. There's a reason why I'm writing this book. It is so that you will not need to make the same mistakes that many real estate investors have made when choosing tenants. Before we get into how to screen for a great tenant, let's first define what a great tenant will look like.

Characteristics of a Great Tenant

Can They Afford It?

The most important quality of a good tenant is their ability to afford the rent. Without timely rent payments, you are going to be forced to evict them. Evicting a traditional tenant is bad. Evicting a tenant when they are your roommate or neighbor is even worse. Not only is the process of eviction emotionally painful, but depending on your state, it can be a financial drain as well. In many cases, evictions cost thousands of dollars in lost rent, legal fees, and damages. Evictions really stink. There are plenty of rules of thumb out there when it comes to screening tenants to make sure they are financially responsible. The two that I live by are:

1. Monthly gross income must be 3x the rent payment
2. Credit score must be above 600

Income of at least 3x rent is a rule of thumb in the industry that usually works. If they are a little over or a little under, you can use your best discretion as to whether or not you will accept them. Perhaps if they have a great credit score, you accept them. Otherwise, move on to the next potential tenant.

Similar to how the lender is going to want to see your credit score when approving you of a loan to purchase a property, you should be looking at your tenant's credit score to gauge how responsible they are financially. Although you are not lending them any money, they still are expected to pay you on a monthly basis. If they are unable to make their monthly payments to a bank or they do not care about their credit score; it is likely that they will not be able to make their monthly payments to you, or care about your property.

I've talked to thousands of real estate investors, many of whom have had to evict tenants. In almost every case, the tenants who had to be evicted had a poor credit score, no credit score, or a monthly income below the 3x threshold. If there is any objective metric that you want to hold your tenants to, it would be their income and their credit score.

Can They Pay On Time?

Some landlords do not mind if rent comes in a few days late because then they get to charge a late fee. However, a tenant who pays late is an indicator that they likely will stop paying all together in the near future.

Not only that, but it is really frustrating to ask for the rent check every month. One way that I have combatted this problem is to use a free software called Cozy. I mentioned it back in chapter 1, but let me remind you that with Cozy you can set their monthly rent payments up using autopay, so every month rent gets deducted from their account and deposited into yours. They have no choice but to pay on time. Cozy will alert you when the money is being withdrawn from the tenant's account. If there are insufficient funds, you will be notified and can take appropriate action to make sure that the tenants do make their payment.

Job Stability

What is it that your tenant does for a job? Likely, their job will be the primary way that allows them to pay rent. If they are the type to switch jobs often, or be unemployed for a significant period of time, they are likely not going to be able to consistently pay the rent. This is obviously a problem you will want to avoid.

To ensure that the tenant pays on time, I recommend asking them how long they have been employed at their job. You can do this in normal conversation to make it sound like you are just being friendly. If you are skeptical of their answer, ask them for employer references and the prior year's W-2. If they have a full year's W-2 and are still working at the same place, you can confirm that they have been at their job for as long as they say they have. If they do not have a W-2, ask for employer references and ask: How much do they make? How long have they been working there? Do they have a secure job for the next twelve months?

Cleanliness and Housekeeping

I can't stress this enough. You are going to be living with your tenants, or at least right next to them. You need to make sure that your life for the next twelve months is not going to be miserable. A dirty tenant who does not keep the place orderly will be quite the hassle for you.

Here are some tips on gauging whether the tenants will be clean and orderly. The first is to check out what their car looks like. If there is a layer of McDonald's wrappers, dirty laundry, and filth between your line of vision and the car seats, there is a high probability that their house is in a similar fashion. Secondly, on the application, you are going to ask them to provide their current address. If they are not moving from out of state, go drive by where they currently live. What does the yard look like?

Because that is what your yard is going to look like when they move in. Thirdly, how do they dress? This is not as good of a barometer as the other two, but if the tenant comes dressed in sweats, with barbecue stains on their shirt and look like they haven't showered or done laundry in weeks, there will likely be a problem here.

Are They Involved in Crime or Illegal Activities?

In almost every life scenario, your safety is going to be the important thing. Having a gang member, drug dealer, or heavy drug user living in your home is going to threaten your safety. Not only that, but a person who has no regard for government law will likely have no regard for the rules you set in your property.

You can easily figure out whether someone has a criminal record by simply running a background check. Cozy (same company that does rent payments) offers a way to run a credit and background check for only $40. I usually send the application to the tenant to fill out and pay for the service directly. If you see that there are any blemishes in their background check, you can decline their application.

Are They Cool?

The final quality of a great tenant is something that I call the "cool factor." I can't iterate this enough. *You are going to be spending a lot of time with these people.* They are not just your tenants. They are going to be your neighbor, friend, or roommate. It is unlikely that you will find someone who is 100 percent perfect, so deciding what qualities you value most and choosing someone who meets those qualities is crucial.

If you are renting by the room, the "cool factor" is definitely something you will want to consider. Having a roommate that does not mesh with you or the other roommates is going to be a huge burden on you. Trust me, I have dealt with this issue.

I've lived with two roommates that were at each other's throats for weeks at a time about minor issues. One is 23 years old, relaxed about everything, and slightly immature while the other is 32 and uptight about a lot of things. These are clashing personality types when it comes to keeping a peaceful environment among roommates. For example, while I was traveling to California for a real estate conference, the older roommate threw the younger roommate's box of pizza away. Granted, the pizza was in there for a week! I had to make sure they each saw both sides of the story: The younger one should not have pizza in the refrigerator for a week. On the other hand, the older one should ask before throwing someone else's food away. Thankfully, they talked it out and resolved the issue, but that was a frustrating situation to deal with on my end.

If you are house hacking a two- to four-unit property, you likely will not be running into them all that much so you can relax your standards on the "cool factor." Make sure that they meet all of the other standards, and if you have two applicants, who meet all of your initial criteria, go with the one who has the highest "cool factor." If you are house hacking a single-family residence, then the "cool factor" is of much higher importance. You will be living with this person. If you do not get along or act respectfully around each other, your life will be miserable. No one wants that.

You know what defines an ideal tenant; now it is time to weed through the applicants to make sure you are picking the best possible tenant for your property. This is the most important decision you will make when house hacking, even more than traditional real estate investing. You will need to choose wisely.

The million-dollar question is, how? How do you ensure that you are placing high-quality tenants in your property? That process involves setting standards for each tenant and verifying if the tenant actually meets those standards. The name for that process is called tenant screening. Now, let's go over what tenant screening is and how to do it correctly.

What Is Tenant Screening?

What does it mean when I say that you need to screen tenants? Just like how you did due diligence when purchasing the property, you need to do due diligence when choosing your tenants. Tenant screening involves digging into a potential tenant's background and discovering who they really are. For many people, applying for a place to live is much like applying for a job. They will always put their best foot forward to get in the door, but that behavior is clearly not sustainable over time. You need to verify that the things they are saying and how they are acting will actually hold true for the next month, six months, year, or the duration of your lease.

An application, which we will discuss, will only tell you so much about the person. Besides, manipulating or lying on the application is as easy as telling the truth. Never solely rely on the information that the applicant has provided you. Screening involves taking the information they give you on the application, researching, and determining whether it is true or falsified in some way.

Unfortunately, when dealing with tenants, your "word" does not go far. People lie, cheat, and steal. There are people out there called, "professional tenants" who are leeches to landlords. They move into a property, don't pay rent, destroy the place, and force the landlord to evict them. In some states, the eviction process may take up to nine months. For those nine months, you are giving these "leeches" a place to live as they suck the blood out of your deal. You'll need to avoid these people at all costs. These are the tenants who are really good at putting their best foot forward until they get into the property.

After you have vetted your tenants and confirmed that everything they say on the application is true, then you will have a good idea as to the character of this potential tenant. You will have all of the information you need to accept or decline them.

Alright, let's get into the weeds. What do you have to do in order to screen a tenant? The first step is pre-screening the tenant.

Pre-screening

You have completed your listing and have now published it on all the major platforms. The applicants are starting to pile in. Screening does not involve just completing a background and credit check and calling it a day. It starts with your first interaction. This is the "pre-screening" phase.

Screening is not a process that you should take lightly, and it is not something that can be done in just a few minutes. You will find that in most cases, you will not accept your applicants, and you will likely know at the point of initial contact. If you were to complete the full screening process for each applicant, it would be exhausting. That is why "pre-screening" exists. The pre-screening process is the first part of the tenant screening funnel.

In order to know what you're looking for in a tenant, write down a list of standards you expect from each tenant. If they do not meet your minimum standards, they understand that they will not qualify, and therefore will not apply. Be sure to avoid discriminating language in the application and advertisements. Remember that tenants are protected with fair housing laws. For example, some language that you should not use includes:

- "No kids"

- "What is your religion?"
- "What country are you from?"
- "Family-friendly"
- "Are you married?"
- "When is your baby due?"
- "How many kids do you have?"

If there are any questions that the tenants ask you that raise a red flag, always be sure to remember the standards that you expect from your tenants. For example:

> **Tenant:** *"I just started a new job and need to find a place ASAP. Can we delay the security deposit until I get my first paycheck?"*
>
> **You:** *"I require that a security deposit and first month's rent be given at signing. Unfortunately, I cannot accept first month's rent or security deposit late."*
>
> **Tenant:** *"I don't have any credit. Do you accept people with no credit score?"*
>
> **You:** *"My standards require a minimum credit score of 600. Unfortunately, I cannot accept a no credit score as an answer."*
>
> **Tenant:** *"I work in the restaurant and bar industry. Most of my money is through tips that I do not claim. Although my W-2 and paystubs look small, I take home almost three times what my paycheck shows."*
>
> **You:** *"My standards are that I require proof that income exceeds rent by at least three times. If you cannot show me this on your pay stubs then would you mind sharing your bank statements? I just need proof that you are able to pay the rent on time and with ease each month. Unfortunately, if you cannot prove this to me, I cannot accept you."*

By always referencing your quality of standards, you let your potential tenants know that you are not declining them for personal reasons. It is just that they do not meet your standards. This will make them significantly less likely to report you to any of the fair housing authorities.

Let's get through the pre-screening process. There are three steps in the pre-screening process:

1. Pre-screen through listing
2. Pre-screen through phone call
3. Pre-screen in person

Pre-screen Through Listing

Believe it or not, if you have created your listing, then you have already started the pre-screening process. In the advertisement, you are going to be including as much information that you can about what you want your future tenant to look like. If you write "no smokers," smokers will not apply. If you write "no pets," pet owners will likely not apply. Put down your criteria such as: credit score above 600, no prior evictions, income three times rent, and clean criminal background on the listing. Just by doing this, you will eliminate a significant number of unqualified applicants and save yourself a lot of time in the process.

Pre-screen Through Phone Call

Now that you know the majority of the people who will apply meet your standards, it is time for the next phase of pre-screening, the phone call. It is likely that someone will reach out to you via email, Facebook, or some other online medium. Once they do this, set up a time to chat so they get to learn a little more about the property, and the process. Oftentimes, in these phone conversations, they reveal things that are immediate red flags. Perhaps they smoke or they are out of a job, etc. Do not automatically set up a showing to someone who you already know does not meet your standards.

When you talk to them on the phone, you will get a feeling of the person too. What is their tone of voice? Are they positive or negative? Does this sound like the kind of person you want to live with you? I always start with some small talk, and then let the conversation flow naturally from there. The applicant will likely end up answering many of your questions during this part of the conversation so be sure to take notes.

I'll usually start the conversation as I would if I was on the phone with one of my friends. This helps reduce my nerves and is a normal way to start a conversation. Remember, this person is going to be your roommate or neighbor. They will also want to feel comfortable with you. Here is a sample conversation:

>**House Hacker:** *Hey [Insert Name Here], how are you doing?*

>**Tenant:** *Good, how are you?*

>**House Hacker:** *Good! Thanks for asking.*

Usually, when setting up the call, they will reveal a little bit about themselves or what they are doing. If the time you initially suggested did not work for them, they will likely tell you why, and then suggest another time. Use this reason as a conversation point during the call. In many cases the reasoning has to do with work (a great one!). It's always reassuring to know that your potential tenant has a job.

>**House Hacker:** *You working hard?*

>**Tenant:** *Yeah, we have this crazy project going on right now that is taking up a lot of my time. It's exciting, but, man, can it be draining.*

>**House Hacker:** *Can I ask what this is?*

>**Tenant:** *I'm sorry, but the project is confidential at this time.*

>**House Hacker:** *No worries. Can I ask what it is that you do? Your work seems interesting.*

>**Tenant:** *Yeah, I am a software developer for Apple. We have a new product coming out and I am one of the engineers on the project.*

Boom! You got a crucial piece of information right there. You have learned their occupation. I always recommend figuring out their occupation since it tells a lot about who they are, and more about their friends. I know that they are likely responsible and make a decent paycheck as an engineer for Apple. Two great qualities to have in a tenant.

House Hacker: *Cool! That sounds awesome. Sounds like you're much smarter than me. I'm just a finance guy at this startup.*

Tenant: *Ha! I don't know about that.*

House Hacker: *So, whereabouts do you live now? Why do you want to move?*

Tenant: *Right now I live downtown. But honestly, I am in a tough spot. My roommate situation is horrible. We do not get along at all. They are messy, loud, disrespectful, and I just need to get out.*

You have been given another valuable piece of information here. They're moving because they do not get along with their current roommate. If you are renting by the room and are actually going to live with this person, this would be a red flag. I would recommend trying to gather more information here. If they do not get along with their current roommates, there is a high probability they will not get along with you and your roommates.

House Hacker: *Oof. I'm sorry to hear that. There's nothing worse than bad roommates. What are some examples of things they do that tick you off? I would like to know to make sure my roommates and I do not do them either.*

Tenant: *Well first off, there is always a pile of dirty dishes in the sink. They smoke a lot of marijuana and their paraphernalia is always in the common areas. The bathrooms are disgusting. They always go out on Friday and Saturday nights and are never quiet when they return in the middle of the night. Sorry, I don't mean to rant, but I am just looking forward to renting a place with a group of mature people.*

House Hacker: *Oh man, that does sound rough! Well, I can promise you that we have none of those problems. Most of the roommates keep to themselves. One of our biggest pet peeves is dirty dishes in the sink so that is not something you will* *have to worry about. We rarely go out on Friday and Saturday night. If we do, everyone is always super quiet coming in and out. Our three biggest qualities are being clean, quiet, and respectful. Anyway, what is it that you like to do for fun?*

Tenant: *I am big into the outdoors. When I'm not at work, I enjoy hiking, biking, skiing, and just getting out to enjoy this Colorado weather. I'm originally from the Seattle area so I have not had much exposure to sun.*

House Hacker: *Awesome, sounds like we might get along nicely. I've got a lot of the same interests. Almost every weekend I'm out in the mountains doing something. You're of course more than welcome to come along on any of the trips we do.*

Tenant: *Sweet, thanks!*

If you are renting by the room, you will want to gauge their interests and see if it is likely you will be friends or just roommates. It is not a deal breaker if your tenants have different interests from you. Just as long as you can be clean, respectful, and reasonable.

House Hacker: *Awesome! So, let me tell you about the property and living situation. The property is a five-bedroom, two-bathroom house. The roommates are all aged 25 to 32 and all get along nicely. Occasionally, we all hang out, but we do have different schedules, so we are rarely all home at the same time. Two work nights. The other one and me work a normal schedule. We are all happy to chat whenever, but if you need time to yourself, you can always be in your room, and no one will bother you. Your room will be the upstairs room. It's a typical bedroom that's about 120 square feet with a closet. The rent is $700 per month and we will need a security deposit of $700 upon move-in.*

A lot of this information will already be in the advertisement, but it is likely they are looking at multiple places, so it is always good to remind them.

House Hacker: *What else can I tell you about the property?*

From there the conversation can go in any which direction. They might try to negotiate the rent down, ask about the location, or just try to set up a showing. The questions they ask will be a great indicator as to what kind of tenant they are. If they are asking for help with the security deposit or are unable to pay you until their next paycheck, this is a tenant you will probably not want to accept.

In many cases, they will ask location-based questions. Is it close to downtown? Are there bars and restaurants nearby? What is the closest train stop? Answer all of these honestly.

They will also likely ask you questions that are already answered in your advertisement. Do you allow smokers, pets, etc.? Although these can be frustrating, be nice about answering these questions. Understand that they are likely looking at several properties.

> **Tenant:** *Thank you for all of this information. I really appreciate it. I don't think I have any more questions. Do you have time this week to set up a showing?*
>
> **House Hacker:** *No problem! Yeah, how does Thursday at 6 p.m. work for you?*
>
> **Tenant:** *Works for me.*
>
> **House Hacker:** *Perfect, I'll see you then! I'll text you the address. If you have any questions in the meantime, you have my number. Don't hesitate to reach out.*

If you feel good about the conversation with the potential tenant, you can now set up a showing. This leads us to the final part of the pre-screening process.

Pre-screen in Person

The final step of the pre-screening process is in person. At this point, you would have already talked to them on the phone and believe that there is a high probability this person will be a good fit as your tenant. How do you meet them in person? You are not going to ask them out for drinks.

Things could get weird. You have them come check out your property.

When you meet the potential tenant in person, this is a great time to make some judgement calls before any of the official paperwork is completed and processed. At this point, always reiterate what the tenant is going to need to move in: background/credit check, security deposit, first month's rent, landlord references, and pay stubs. Let's not digress too far here because we will talk about how to show the property after this section. What is it that you should be taking note of?

1. *How are they dressed?* They do not need to show up to your house in a tuxedo (here's hoping that's not the case either), but if they are coming in their pajamas or it looks like they pulled these clothes out of a dumpster, this could be a red flag.

2. *Are they clean?* If they do not look clean and put together, what makes you think they will keep your rental clean and put together?

3. *How is their personality?* Is this someone that you could get along with? If they are rude, loud, obnoxious, or cut you off, then it likely will be tough living with this person. Even if you are doing a strategy where you do not live with your tenant, doing business with this kind of person will take quite the toll on you.

4. *Who did they bring along with them?* When looking for a rental, it is common to bring other people that may live in the property with you. For example, if your tenant brings along his/her significant other, you can bet that they are going to be spending significant time at your property. Are you okay with this?

5. *What does their car look like?* I'm not saying that you should only rent to people who drive Bimmers, Benzes, or Bentleys. The type of car does not matter so much as the actual condition it is in. A car is essentially a four-foot by eight-foot room on wheels. If it is filled with junk, food wrappers, and is falling apart, you can bet their room will look quite similar.

After you make your observations from meeting the potential tenant, this is also the time where the tenant will feel like they trust you more and may reveal some more facts about themselves. Perhaps they let you know that their credit score is lower than your standards, or that they want to own a pet. If one of these questions do come up, you can let them know whether it is a deal breaker or not. It is a good practice to still let them fill out an application to ensure that you do not break any of the fair housing laws.

These suggestions are just a small part of the screening process, hence why it's called, "pre-screening." In addition to pre-screening, you are going to want to have your prospective tenants fill out an application. You want to make sure that the details they complete on the application are consistent with what they told you during the "pre-screening" process.

Setting Your Standards

The standards that your prospective tenants need to meet in order to qualify for your property are extremely important. In almost every "bad tenant" situation that I have heard, the landlord accepted the tenant despite the fact that they did not meet the standards. It is easy to get caught up in the moment. What if you really like the person who came to check out the property? You can make an exception for this person, right? Nope!

To help you stay unbiased, I highly recommend you write down your standards and refer back to them often. In fact, refer back to them as you are reviewing each tenant's application. If you have a stack of applications, hide the name. Fold the top part of the application over (where their name is), and then shuffle the papers. Not only will this help you make an unbiased decision, it will also cover you if you do in fact ever get in trouble with fair housing laws.

Here are some of the standards that I set:

Credit Score Greater Than Requirement

Credit score is a major indicator in whether or not the potential tenant will pay their bills. Since you are going to need someone who will pay their rent on time, as well as pay utilities and other associated expenses, it is not a good idea to accept someone with bad credit. To ensure that you treat everyone the same, please write down the minimum score you are willing to accept on your standards document. As a refresher, here are what the range of credit scores look like:

- Good: 700+
- Decent: 550–699
- Horrible: 300–549

Every time I hear a story about a bad tenant, I always ask the landlord what the tenant's credit score was. The answer? Below 600 or "I don't know." Even if it did not have to do with paying rent on time, credit score is a great indicator of how responsible a person is. A bad credit score means that the prospective tenant has not paid their bills, and has done nothing to remedy the problem. A person who is not responsible with their credit will likely not be responsible with your property.

In some cases, you will run into a person with no credit. Either they are not from the United States or they just have never had any debt. This should not be a deal breaker; someone who does not take on debt could be a very good tenant. You will just need to make up for this lack of information in other places. Call previous landlords, require a co-signer, or require double the security deposit (check your state's landlord-tenant laws) to cover for any potentially lost rent.

At this point, I hope that I have convinced you on the importance of a credit report. I will show you exactly how to run the credit report in the next chapter.

Monthly Income Must Be Three Times Rent

Out of about 250 million adults living in the United States, over 1 million of them file for bankruptcy every year. [8] What does this mean? It means that Americans have this tendency to purchase things that they are unable to afford. Since many Americans do not know what they can (and cannot) afford, you need to be sure that your tenants can afford your rent. For that reason, go by the rule of thumb that landlords and lending institutions have used for years. Gross income needs to be at least three times the monthly rent. This is an important standard if you want to make sure that the rent will be paid every month.

Not all money is good money. As a landlord, you will not only want to make sure that the income is in fact three times the rent, but you need to make sure that the money will come in on a consistent basis. If you are dealing with a prospective tenant who is in sales, and their income is 100 percent commission based, then you will want to take a look at their last year's tax returns to make sure that the numbers they listed are true.

Good References

If you are playing in the stock market, past performance is no guarantee of future results. When finding a tenant, past performance has a very high correlation with future results. This is why you ask for references of previous landlords, employers, or former roommates. Can people

---

8   https://www.uscourts.gov/news/2018/03/07/just-facts-consumer-bankruptcy-filings-2006-2017

change? Sure. Is it likely they will? Probably not. A bad reference from either of these sources will indicate that the person is either irresponsible, hard to live with, or a bad tenant.

Make sure the prospective tenant isn't using family or friends as references. If they do, and you call them, be sure to take any "good references" with a grain of salt and any "bad references" as a huge red flag. A past landlord is my favorite referral source. They have absolutely zero incentive to lie to you, whereas if they are horrible tenants, their current landlord might say they are great tenants just to get them out.

No Evictions

If you have filed for bankruptcy, it is going to be difficult for you to get accepted in an apartment. Same thing goes for evictions. No landlord wants to go through the eviction process. If an applicant has an eviction on their record, it means that they have seriously broken a lease, and done nothing to work with the landlord to remedy the problem. The typical cause of an eviction is not paying rent. Not only do they not pay rent, but when the eviction process is finalized and they need to move out, they trash the place. This will be amplified by the fact that you are house hacking so they are also your roommate or neighbor. Now you and your other tenant's safety may be threatened. A positive eviction record is a hard no.

Luckily, I have not yet been through an eviction (knock on wood). However, I have recently heard a story where a fellow BiggerPockets member accepted someone with an eviction that happened three years ago. Since it was a while ago, they thought that she might have changed. Nope! She consistently paid rent late, threw trash out the window, broke things in the unit, and eventually completely stopped paying rent. They were forced to evict her, and the entire process cost them over $5,000. Learn from this story: If there's an eviction in their past, pass on them.

Background Check

I'm going to go ahead and take a guess that you probably do not want to live with murderers and drug dealers. This is why background checks are so important. A background check is crucial to ensure that you are not accepting a convicted criminal. This becomes even more important when you (and your other tenants) are living under the same roof. I usually use Cozy's background and credit check option. As I mentioned before, it's $40, and the fee gets directly passed on to the tenant. The tenant fills out the form themselves and you see the results instantly.

A thorough background check will include criminal history, judgements/liens, and prior evictions. If any of these come up positive, it's an easy no. When you do get the background check back, be sure to verify that the social security number and address match exactly what they put on their application.

Additional Standards

In addition to the minimum standards mentioned above, there are others that are likely not deal breakers, but can still distinguish between an okay tenant and a great tenant. Some of these standards include:

- **No smokers:** Between the smell and the butts left out on the front porch, cigarettes are a great way to dirty your property. Be especially mindful of this when you are renting to other tenants. The smell of cigarettes bothers a lot of people so you might get stuck if you accept a smoker that you and your other tenants do not like.
- **Pets:** There has never been a scenario where a pet has made a property nicer. They do not clean, fix things, or make extra money to help with the rent. In fact, they do the opposite. While I understand some people love their pets more than they do their kids, they are a hazard to your property. Given the option, it is always best to accept someone without pets. Again, this is not a critical standard. Even I have been suckered into letting tenants with cute dogs occupy my properties. When screening for pets, be sure to remember the fair housing laws. You can only decline someone on the basis of having a pet if the pet is for recreational purposes. In other words, declining someone with an emotional support or a doctor approved animal will get you in trouble.
- **Occupancy limit:** The last thing you want is six people living in a three-bedroom house. Things get cluttered, people start fighting, and it often becomes a messy situation. The more people, the higher the probability that things will go wrong. I like to keep it to a maximum of two people per room and five people per unit (whatever number is less).

I cannot stress enough how important it is to have standards, write them down, and stick to them. Countless times landlords have been accused of discrimination for not having any standards to reference. Having your standards written down holds you accountable to not make any exceptions. Any landlord that has ever had a problem was because they were a little too lenient on their standards. *Don't be that landlord.* The only thing worse than no tenant is a bad tenant. Now you have an idea as to what your standards should be when screening tenants. Now, let's get into showing the property.

Showing the Property

Prospective tenants are always very quick to want to view the available unit. Before you jump right into setting up the time to do a showing, you need to make sure that this person is someone that you would accept. Time is our most valuable resource. It's the only thing we cannot get back. Don't waste it on showing your property to unqualified prospective tenants. Remember the phone pre-screening we just talked about? This is the time to practice what you learned.

Before you schedule a showing ask them the following questions:

- **Ask them what they would like to know about the property:** This should always be the first question. It is open-ended, and can guide the rest of the conversation. Also, if the tenant is looking for something that you do not (or will not) provide, you know it is not a good fit.
- **Confirm the rental terms:** You will be surprised to discover how many people do not read the advertisement you posted. Maybe you can give them the benefit of the doubt and believe that they simply forgot the details. Either way, be sure to confirm the rent, security deposit, lease term, pet policy, and whether utilities are included or not, as well as a brief overview of the property and roommate situation (when applicable).
- **Restate your standards:** While on the phone, be sure to let them know what the next steps would be for the application process. For example, if you are going to have them fill out a background and credit check, be sure to let them know so they understand that you are going to need to see a clean criminal background and a credit score of 600 or better. Run through any other pertinent criteria as well.
- **Let them talk:** Silence is awkward. Especially amongst strangers. Use this to your advantage and do not be afraid of the silent points in the conversation. Make the tenant be responsible for filling these awkward silences, and in doing so, they may reveal something that would cause a red flag.

When doing the showings, it is up to you to decide whether you want to perform each showing as a group, or individually. Personally, I like to do the group showings, but let's outline the pros and cons of each here.

Individual Showings

When you schedule appointments separately, you are able to give one prospective tenant your undivided attention and really get to highlight the parts of the property you think they will like most. Not only that, but it makes it much easier to perform the in-person screening. The downside to individual showings is that you may need to do a bunch of them until you find your ideal tenant. It takes the same amount of time to do an individual showing as it would take to do a group showing. Another thing is what if the tenant never shows up? What if they found a better spot, slept in, forgot, car broke down, or they forgot to feed their cats? Whatever the excuse, they happen. It can be frustrating if you are altering your day to meet a tenant and they bail on you without notifying you. Pre-screening and calling a few hours before the intended time will reduce the number of no-shows. Because of this, many house hackers prefer to do group showings.

Group Showings

Group showings are essentially an open house for your rental. Rather than sitting around for four hours, you have one time to meet with all of your prospective tenants. Because no one is ever on time, they will all show up at different times within ten to thirty minutes of each other. Nonetheless, they can all view the property at the same time. The largest benefit is how much time you save. By knocking out a lot of showings at once, you no longer have to make yourself available for each individual person. Not only that, but by doing a group showing, the tenants see their competition right in front of them. This fosters a competitive atmosphere that creates a sense of urgency for the tenants. They will want to apply right away so they get the spot before anyone else does.

One thing to be cautious of when doing group showings is that it is nearly impossible to keep your eyes on multiple people at the same time. If you are doing the rent-by-room strategy, you will want to be sure that all occupied bedroom doors are shut and locked. Also, be sure to give notice to your current tenants so they can be aware of the showing and secure anything important.

A nice hybrid approach might be to schedule your appointments fifteen minutes apart. Let the prospective tenants know that it is crucial they be on time because someone else is coming to check out the property fifteen minutes after them. This creates a sense of urgency and if they see their competition walk in as they walk out, it will generate that same competitive atmosphere.

Always Confirm Appointments

If this is your first house hack, you will probably be excited to show your property. Before you get too excited understand that there will be times that you run over to your property and discover that your prospective tenant canceled on you or never showed up. I suggest that you call them to confirm before each appointment. By doing this, you will drastically improve the rate at which your tenants show up for the appointments. Sometimes, even after confirming, they don't show up. There is nothing you can really do about this. Take the loss and move onto the next one without thinking twice about it.

Make Sure Property Is in a Good Condition

Before showing your house hack, make sure that the property looks good. Turn on all of the lights, open all of the curtains and blinds, adjust the thermostat temperature, and tidy up. You'll be surprised as to how much better a property looks when it is clean and under sufficient lighting. If you want to go the extra mile, add flowers or a bowl of fruit on the table to make it look extra inviting.

Safety

For a majority of the time, you're not going to need to worry about safety. However, revealing where you live to a complete stranger does put you in a vulnerable position. You do not know their history, their motives, and if you ever watch the news, you know that there are some messed up people out there. For that reason, I recommend doing the following things:
- Hide and lock up all valuables.
- Conduct showings during the day—never at night or at dusk.
- Always let your tenants know the date and time you plan to do the showing. It's best if someone else is home with you.
- Carry pepper spray or some sort of self-defense mechanism on your key chain.
- Be aware of your surroundings.

- Let them know that other people are on their way to check out the property.

This little section was not meant to get you scared, just make you aware. Most people are going to be normal people just like me and you. The point is to be cautious.

The Tour

The tenant has passed all of the pre-screening and it is now time to give them the grand tour of the property. What do you think you should do? Should you let them walk the property alone? Or should you show them around? That certainly depends on the type of house hack you are doing. If you are doing a multifamily that is unfurnished, I would recommend you walk them around once and then wait outside while they take their time deciding. However, if it is a single-family residence with personal items around, I would recommend staying inside with them. While most people are nice, they are still strangers in your house who can easily steal or ruin anything.

I always laugh when people give property tours. They always show you around and say, "This is the living room, this is the kitchen, and this is the bathroom." Most people know what a living room, kitchen, and bathroom look like. You don't need to tell them. Instead, highlight the parts of each room that really sell the place. For example, if there are stainless steel appliances, mention that. Or if the bathroom is custom tiled with two sinks and a large closet, mention that. Maybe the bedroom is in an isolated part of the house so they can retreat to a quiet place if necessary. Don't point out the obvious. Really sell the place!

Showing Units While Occupied

Regardless of whether you are house hacking a single-family or a multifamily residence, there is a high probability that you will be showing the property while current tenants are living there. Make sure to be respectful. No one is happy when their landlord comes in with a random group of strangers to show all of the rooms in their house. However, it is necessary, expected, and should be in the lease. You just need to be a reasonable landlord and give them at least a 24-hour notice. If you or your tenant is in a pinch and you need to show it before that 24-hour time window, call your tenants and confirm that it is okay.

Materials

If you have ever been to an open house, usually on the table, there will be a one-pager with all of the property's information. Amenities, price, some nice pictures, and any other details you choose to feature. You should have something similar when you are showing your property to rent. Give one to every prospective tenant that walks through the door. The one-pager should include:

- **Front side:** A professionally taken picture that really sells the property. Include the location (screenshot from Google Maps), the rent amount, and your contact information.
- **Back side:** A full description of the property. You do not need to re-invent the wheel here. You can just use the same description from your online listing. You will want to include the rent (again), deposit, lease term, utilities, pet policy, and any other lease specifics. You'll also want to include your tenant standards of credit score, monthly income, professional references, etc.

If you want people to start applying right on the spot, attach the rental application to the one-pager. Be sure to have lots of pens handy. That way, they can fill it out right there and you'll be able to build out your applicant pool.

10 Most Commonly Asked Questions by Tenants

Throughout the pre-screening and showing processes, you will find that people are always asking the same questions. Some are easier than others. Whatever you do, be sure to answer them in a nice, respectful tone, and act as if you have never heard the question. You do not want to be the reason why someone does not pick the place. Inspired from Brandon and Heather Turner's *Book on Managing Rental Properties*, here are the ten most commonly asked questions by tenants.

1. *"Can I pay X months up front?"*

While receiving a bulk rent payment up front is enticing and eliminates the risk of not getting paid, there is usually a reason why the tenant needs to offer this. Many times, a tenant who offers to pay rent upfront is compensating for something else. It may mean they have poor credit, a sketchy background, or no income. Paying in advance does not make them more or less risky. They are still going to be living in your property. Besides, what happens when the prepaid rent runs out? At this point, the tenant has not paid rent in X months. They are not in the habit of paying you rent, and I would be willing to guess that they had not been budgeting for it.

Much of real estate is delayed gratification. Do not take the money up front. You will have a huge pain in your rear later. If someone does ask you for this, here is how I would respond: "I'm sorry, I do not accept prepaid rent of any kind. You are more than welcome to proceed with the application. If you meet all of my criteria, we can move forward and get you into the property as soon as possible." If the tenant does have something to hide, this will likely deter them from applying and they will be out of your hair.

2. "Can I move in this weekend?"

Another question I frequently get is, "Can I move in tomorrow? Or this weekend?" This is a red flag to me. In many states and municipalities around the world, a landlord needs to give the tenant at least a thirty-day notice before ending a lease. If they are waiting last minute to find a place and need to move in tomorrow, it likely means they are a huge procrastinator, or someone you do not want as a tenant. Or it means something bad happened in their current living situation that is forcing them to move out immediately. In other words, you are going to be inheriting someone else's problem. No thanks! I usually like for someone to move in one to three weeks after they have been approved.

3. "I know you said you don't allow pets, but would a small dog be okay?"

This question is always funny to me. I do not allow pets on my properties. The reason being is that not everyone loves pets. Some people are allergic, and I do not want a pet being the source of contention between roommates or neighbors. For that reason, no pets. However, prospective tenants will still ask if a small dog is okay. Some will even claim that their dog does not bark. Let me reveal something to you. All dogs bark. There is a high probability that the pet will become a pain for you, and it is not worth the trouble. An easy response to this question would be, "I'm sorry, but this is a pet-free home."

4. "Can I pay my deposit in installments?"

Your prospective tenant will not be able to pay the deposit entirely up front many times. This should be a huge red flag. Not only does this mean that they do not have enough savings for a security deposit, it also means that they might have not received a large portion of their security deposit back from their previous rental. The security deposit is a great way to assess your tenant's financial position and gauge how they might treat the place. If they can't pay the security deposit up front, this is a good indication that you will have trouble later. I would respond to this question like this: "I'm sorry, I do need to have the security deposit paid in full, up front. Do you have family or friends that could lend you money? Or perhaps a deposit being returned to you from a previous rental?" If they can come up with the money, great! It's likely they had it all along anyway and they were just trying to prioritize their spending. If not, then it's time to go back to the application pool.

5. "Can I take possession in two months?"

This question can be tricky. This person will likely be responsible as they are looking for a rental far in advance. However, this is a business you are running, and you want to maximize the amount of money you make with the least possible problems. Are you willing to wait two months for someone to move in? This can depend on your market. If you are in or around a large city where tenant turnover is more common and filling vacancies is easier, I would recommend saying, "I'm sorry, but I'm looking for someone to occupy the property in one to three weeks. If this place is still of interest to you in a month or so, let's chat again and maybe we can figure something out then." However, if you live in a place where it is much more difficult to find tenants, two months may not be that long. In this case, feel free to accept them. With this question, do what makes you feel comfortable. I do not believe you will get yourself into a horrible situation, you just have to make a few extra mortgage payments without the help of that tenant.

6. "Can my rent due date be the 15th?"

"No." This is a huge no. Having the rent be due on the 15th is an indication that the tenant is not responsible with their money. Not only that, but you will get extremely confused as you scale. Accepting different rents may be okay for the first couple units. As you build your business, it will start to get confusing tracking everyone down for their rent. It is industry standard to pay rent on the first of each month. Let's keep it that way.

7. "Are you the owner?"

Although this question seems rather easy, it is up to you on how you respond. In most cases, your potential tenants are just curious as to who owns the property. However, in other cases they want to know who has authority over the house and may use that against you when asking to make certain exceptions for them. Instead of calling yourself the "owner," you can call yourself the "property manager." That avoids a bit of confrontation and if you do in fact need to decline a request, you can blame it on the "owner" since you're just the "property manager."

Answering this question depends on what type of house hack you are doing too. If you are doing a more traditional house hack—renting units in a duplex, triplex, or fourplex—then you can likely get away with saying you are the "property manager." However, if you are renting out the rooms in a single-family residence, you will likely be seeing your tenants every day. Over the course of the year, they will figure out that you are the owner. Now you put yourself in a position where they feel like they have been betrayed or lied to. Good luck trying to get them to re-sign their lease. Personally, I tell my tenants that I am the owner if they ask. Lying (even if you don't perceive it to be) is much more difficult, and far more work than telling the truth.

8. "Will you consider a short-term lease?"

Turnovers and vacancies are often a landlord's biggest expense. This does not even include the time and effort it takes to market and show the property. For this reason, many landlords look for long-term rentals with a minimum of one year. However, if you are finding it difficult to fill your vacancy, you might be able to find a tenant for several months to bridge the gap between longer-term tenants. Before you agree to a short-term lease, I recommend that you pay attention as to when that lease is expiring. In my area, it is extremely difficult to fill vacancies between December and March. There is no way that I would let a lease expire during these months. If the lease expires in June or July, I would be much more open to doing a short-term lease. That way, I can bridge the gap for a few months, and then get the next tenant on a yearlong lease that begins at the best time of the year. If someone does ask this question, but the lease would expire at an inopportune time, I recommend replying, "I'm sorry, I'm looking for people who are willing to commit to stay for a year."

The one caveat to this question is going to be, again, the type of house hack you are doing. If you plan to house hack a small multifamily, I would stick to the one year minimum. However, if your plan is to house hack a single-family residence, it might make sense to start someone on a one or two-month lease. This way, you can have a trial run to see if they get along with the other roommates, but you know that if they do not work out, you are not forced to deal with the headaches for a full year. If they discover that they absolutely hate living there, then you move on after a month to find a new tenant. I've seen it done both ways. The choice is yours.

9. "My boyfriend/mom/sister wants to live with me, but I don't want them on the lease. Is that okay?"

This is a resounding "no." Anyone who is over 18 and occupies your property should be on the lease. What happens if this tenant is the only one on the lease and they decide to leave, but the boyfriend/mom/sister stay? Now you are stuck with a tenant that has no obligation to uphold the lease. Other than this scenario, having someone live with you, but not be on the lease, is a giant red flag. There is a high probability that this person has either a history of eviction, a criminal background, horrible credit, or something wrong that would make you want to decline the tenant's application. I would respond to this question in the following away, "Anyone who is over the age of 18 and lives in this property is required to sign a lease. I apologize, but I'm strict on this rule."

10. "What if I don't meet all of your criteria?"

In many scenarios, if a tenant asks you this question it is because they do not meet your criteria. This is when you need to perform some further due diligence and figure out exactly what part of your criteria that they don't meet. Some reasons are better than others. For example, if they lack rental history or a small misdemeanor from years ago, I will probably give them a shot. If it makes you feel comfortable, you can also ask them for a co-signer or an additional security deposit to help you hedge this risk. In almost all cases, you are going to want to obtain more information. Based on this additional information, you will be able to make your ultimate decision.

What if You Can't Answer the Question?

It is unlikely that you will remember the answer to all of these questions when asked. You might look a bit foolish if someone were to ask you a question and you had to flip through a book to find your answer. You also might get a question that is outside the scope of what has been answered in the previous pages. If any of these scenarios happen to you and you do not know how to answer the question, do not be afraid to say, "That's a good question. Let me think about that for a little bit and I will get back to you as soon as possible." Then you can reference this book, hop onto the BiggerPockets forums, call your mentor, or whatever it takes to determine the best answer before following up with them.

This brings us to the end of the chapter. If the prospective tenant likes the property and checks all of your boxes, it's then time to roll up your sleeves and get dirty with the due diligence. Before I get into that though, let's learn about our house-hacking friend, Brett Fink.

CASE STUDY
BRETT FINK

- **House-hacking strategy:** Rent by room/co-living/dormitory
- **Age at first house hack:** 24
- **Location:** San Francisco, California
- **NWROI:** 1162%

Brett Fink was born and raised in a town called Holbrook in Long Island, New York. His father was a custodian and his mother was a stay-at-home mom, so money was never prevalent in his family. After graduating high school, he attended the University of Scranton for one year and then transferred to Northeastern University in Boston, Massachusetts his sophomore year. When he lived in Boston, he was quick to realize just how expensive it was to live in this area. His initial thoughts were to do what most people do and find the cheapest place to live. He searched and searched and found a room in Mission Hill for just $583 per month in 2011. For those of you who are not familiar with rent in Boston, that is cheap!

After two years of living in Mission Hill he wanted to do better. He wanted to live for free. I know what you are thinking: He probably immediately started house hacking. Nope! Not yet. He became a resident assistant (RA). In other words, he got a free room to himself in one of the Northeastern dormitories while putting events together to strengthen the community of residents while also making sure all of the students followed the rules. He got to live for free AND meet new people. For him, a win-win.

His creative living situations did not end there. Just one year after graduation, Brett moved to San Francisco, one of the most expensive cities in the country (even more expensive than New York)[9]. He was working at 500 Startups, a venture capitalist company that invests in early-stage startups and gives them guidance on how to increase enterprise value by five to ten times in three to five years. While living in San Francisco, Brett was determined to live for free. He searched and searched, but could not come up with any opportunities. But he didn't quit and say, "I can't." He thought hard and persisted while asking himself, "How can I?"

Finally, he came up with an answer—something that no one was doing. He rented a large six-bedroom house in Daly City that was fully furnished, right on the border of San Francisco proper for $6,000 per month and a $6,000 security deposit. For $1,000, he was able to add a seventh bedroom with the landlord's permission and so now had an extra room. You probably know where I'm going with this, but keep reading, there is a twist.

The traditional model is to rent out each room individually. However, there is a void in San Francisco that traditional landlords do not fill. Hundreds of thousands of people move there each year for some entrepreneurial venture and do not have any friends in the city—never mind like-minded ones. Brett saw this void and leveraged his experience both as an RA and as an employee at 500 Startups and he turned the house into a co-living space, or miniature dormitory, and filled the beds with employees of the startup companies in 500 Startups' portfolio. Anytime he had a vacancy and could not get it filled through 500 Startups, he would use Airbnb to fill the spots.

In total, there were one to two bunk beds in each room and sixteen total beds in the house. He charged a minimum of $1,200 per bed and had a vacancy rate of about 10 percent throughout the year. On a monthly basis, he was bringing in $17,280 per month while paying $6,000 in rent to the landlord. He paid his team of two who also lived on

---

9   Thomas C. Frohlich, What It Actually Costs to Live in America's Most Expensive Cities (April 2019), https://www.usatoday.com/story/money/2019/04/04/what-it-actually-costs-to-live-in-americas-most-expensive-cities/37748097/.

the property $3,000 each month and put another $3,000 each month in improvements and buying things for the house. He could have spent less on house improvements, but he wanted to keep both the landlord and the tenants as happy as possible. When all was said and done, Brett pocketed $5,280 per month and lived for free in his own bedroom. Let's value living for free in his own bedroom at $1,500 per month; that would be a total of $6,780 per month in total savings. There were a lot of numbers there. Let's recap:

Security deposit: $6,000

Rent to landlord: $6,000 per month

Startup costs: $1,000

Co-living rent: $1,200 × 16 spots = $19,200 × 0.9 vacancy = $17,280 in monthly rent

Monthly improvement costs: $3,000

Management fee costs: $3,000

Brett's monthly cash flow: $17,280 - $6,000 rent - $3,000 management - $3,000 improvements = $5,280

Brett's monthly cash flow AFTER rent savings = $5,280 + $1,500 = $6,780 per month

Many of Brett's friends thought he was absolutely nuts for running a co-living space/dormitory after graduating college. Brett thought his friends were nuts for *not* doing it. Brett did this for one year and was able to save $81,360 (6,780 × 12). An investment return of $81,360 divided by $7,000 or 1162 percent. Who is crazy now?

Unlike me and many of the people reading this book, Brett's passion is not in real estate. Brett went ahead and invested that money in himself. What do I mean by that? He wanted to have a solid financial basis so that he could go ahead and take risks that will substantially increase his wealth and put him and his family in a position where money will never be a problem. In other words, he is in a position where he is playing to win, rather than playing not to lose.

There you have it. For those who have ever said that you can't house hack in San Francisco, Los Angeles, or New York City, here is a case study of someone who has done it with great success. Sure, you need to get creative. You need to live differently. But is one or two years of sacrifice worth living your dreams for the next forty to fifty years? Heck yeah!

WHY

"I'm house hacking because my passion lies in starting businesses. Since my house hack in San Francisco, I repeated the co-living house hack in Chicago and am now living in Los Angeles starting a cannabis company called Old Pal. I'm employee No. 2 there (after the founder), and already have equity in the company. Upon an exit (sale or IPO), I will likely cash out and move on to the next business. I lived with 16 other people in San Francisco so I could pursue my passions of building wealth through starting businesses so that money will never be a problem again for me and my family."

ACTION STEPS

❏ Create an application that is easy for your tenants to fill out.
❏ Confirm that the application addresses your minimum criteria.
❏ Get familiar with the credit and background check companies. Know which one you plan to use.
❏ Decide whether you want to do individual or group showings.
❏ Get your property cleaned and ready to show.

CHAPTER 11

TENANT DUE DILIGENCE

You have now completed the pre-screening and showing the unit parts of tenant screening. You have a few applicants that meet all of your criteria; now it is time to dig deep to actually verify the validity of what the tenants have told you up to now. This all starts with the application.

The rental application is what you will give to your tenants to complete. Once they are finished, you will have everything you need to know about the tenant—all on one piece of paper. However, you are certainly not done. Lying on a rental application is as easy as cheating on a test with no teacher in the room. You will need to verify all of its information. It is during this in-depth process when you might find an eviction, negative landlord references, lower income than previously stated, or an invalid social security number. In many cases, the tenant is truthful. However, in a few others, you will find that there are some inconsistencies on the application from what is actually true. You can be the one to choose whether you want to dismiss the prospective tenant all together or contact them to ask for further clarification.

When creating the application and accepting tenants, here are a few things that you will want to keep in mind:

- Make sure the applications include all of the information you need to conduct your full screening. Do not make it too cumbersome. It should easily fit on one piece of paper (front and back), and be clear.
- Include your contact information and information about the ap-

plication process. Reiterate your standards in the application so unqualified tenants will not apply.

- Be sure that the tenant fills out the application in full. In many cases, the tenant will pick and choose which information they want to fill out. This is likely because they know that whatever their actual information is will not be accepted by you. Mention that an incomplete application will not be accepted.
- In many cases, you may have a couple moving in or perhaps even a family. Make sure that a separate application is filed for each individual over the age of 18.
- Ensure that your application upholds to all of the fair housing law standards. Be sure not to ask anything based on race, sex, color, national origin, religion, familial status (pregnant), or any disabilities. Having any of this on your application will get you in a lawsuit very quickly.
- Never take the rental off the market until you have an approved application and a security deposit in hand. In many cases, your prospective tenants will have a sudden change of heart and decide to not go with your place. If you do take the rental off the market and your prospective tenant backs out, you will have indirectly turned away many would-be renters.

The Application Itself

Let's get into actually creating your application. The application does not need to look like a legal document. It just needs to be thorough and have enough space for the prospective tenant to fill out all of the necessary information. Luckily, you do not need to create this application from scratch. There are tons of resources online. More specifically, a rental application is included in the suite of landlord forms that BiggerPockets offers for each state. Lawyers have reviewed these applications, and are 100 percent compliant with all fair housing laws. We try to make it as thorough as possible, but if there is something we are missing, or if you do not like the formatting, you can adjust it as you deem necessary. Let's just go into what should be on every application.

Personal Information

First off, you are going to need to know who your applicant is. At a minimum you will need to gather their name, date of birth, and contact information including email address and cellphone number. In many cases, landlords will ask for their social security number and driver's license number, but people can be very hesitant about volunteering this information. Rather than request their social security number, I send them the link to fill out (and pay for) their credit and background check. They put in their own social security number and other personal information. I get the report and everyone is happy. In summary, the personal information you will want to gather is:

- Full name
- Social security number (optional)
- Driver's license number (optional)
- Contact information
- Name of all occupants

The last question is extremely important, especially when you are house hacking. You are going to want to know exactly who is going to be living with you, or next to you. You do need to be careful in that you cannot ask for the exact ages of the applicants, their children, or their relationship to people in this section, but they may volunteer this information.

Rental History

When it comes to tenant screening, past performance is a useful indicator of future results. How do you gain this information? You need to ask their past landlords. How do you ask their past landlords? You'll have to request this information on the application. I recommend leaving space for at least three prior landlords. Any more than three can get overwhelming. Any less can be insufficient information. If they do not fill out all three, this is not a huge deal, just proceed with caution. If your applicant has no rental history, but everything else on them checks out, you may still feel comfortable renting to them. You may just need to require additional securities such as a co-signer or an additional deposit.

You will also want to look into the reasons that they do not have a rental history. Are they young and just moved out? Or are they older and have been living with family and friends for the past few years? I would be much more willing to accept a motivated younger renter rather than a lazy one who has been bumming around for the past couple of years not attempting to save up. Here is what you will want to put in the rental history section of the application:

- Current address
- Move-in date
- Landlord's name
- Landlord's phone number
- Monthly rent
- Reason for moving
- Previous address (x2)
- Move-in date
- Move-out date
- Landlord's name
- Landlord's phone number
- Monthly rent
- Reason for moving

Employment Information

If the applicant is employed, you will need to verify their job stability and income. If they are self-employed, you will still want to verify that information as well. Regardless of the scenario, you will want to ask for their last two pay stubs and last year's tax returns at a minimum. If you want to go the extra mile, I would recommend requesting that they show you their last two months' worth of bank statements as well. What you will want to include on the application is:

- Current employer
- Position
- Employer contact information
- Supervisor's name
- Annual salary or gross wages per month
- Hire date

Other Sources of Income

In 2019, the sharing economy has truly taken off. More and more people are renting their properties out on Airbnb, driving for Uber and Lyft, or going grocery shopping for people on Instacart. Believe it or not, in some instances, your tenants may have a rental property out of state and are just choosing to rent right now. You will want to capture this information. If they drive for Uber or Lyft and bring in an extra $500 to $1,000 a month, this could be significant. When asking for other types of income, you will want to include:

- Other sources of income
- Average amount per month
- Explanation of income

Other Questions That Should Be Asked

I highly recommend that you put these questions on your application, but you can also ask them on the phone, or during the pre-screening process. Either way, it is information that you should know.

"HOW LONG DO YOU PLAN ON LIVING HERE?"

In many cases, a landlord's largest cost is going to be vacancy. You drastically increase your odds of vacancy if the person you are renting to only wants to be there for a couple of months. However, in the event that you are renting by the room, you may want to do a month to month. What happens if one of the tenants does not get along with the others? It's much easier to just tell them you will not be renewing the lease rather than waiting it out the full year.

"HOW MANY EVICTIONS HAVE YOU HAD?"

Do not ask, "Have you ever been evicted?" It is much easier to just say, "no." Phrasing it this way will require them to think a little longer than just habitually writing, "no." In almost all cases, you should try to avoid "yes" or "no" questions. It is too easy to lie in these situations.

"HOW MANY FELONIES DO YOU HAVE?"

This is the same idea. Rather than asking them if they have committed a felony, ask them how many they have had. This will show up in their background check, but it is always good to ask to see how they answer. That way they are not wasting their time and money filling out the background check when it is unnecessary.

"HAVE YOU EVER BROKEN A LEASE?"

This question will be answered once you call the previous landlords but is a good way to test their honesty. If they say that they have broken a lease and do not give you a valid reason, it will save you time in calling the previous landlords. You will know that you will decline them.

"DO YOU SMOKE?"

I apologize in advance for anyone who is a smoker, and is reading this. In most cases, smokers do not make for great tenants. Smoke gets everywhere. If they smoke in the property, the smell will get into the walls, the floors, everywhere! It will be extremely difficult to rent to the next person without the added expense of repainting and redoing all of the floors. This will not be a cheap task. An extra month of vacancy is well worth ensuring that you find a tenant that does not smoke.

"HOW MANY VEHICLES DO YOU OWN?"

In almost all living scenarios, parking is a point of contention. If you have someone with more than one car (per applicant), they are likely going to cause more problems than you will want to handle. If the property has plentiful parking, you do not need to worry about this. Though, you might want to charge an extra fee each month for additional parking.

"DO YOU HAVE THE SECURITY DEPOSIT AND RENT AVAILABLE NOW?"

Most people like to live in the best possible place they can afford. For that reason, if you are doing a rent-by-room strategy, you are likely going to get people who are unable to afford a place by themselves. Many of your prospective tenants are going to be living paycheck to paycheck. You will want to do your best to avoid these types of tenants as they will be out of luck with just one hiccup in their finances, or if they lose their job. And so will you.

"WHEN WOULD YOU LIKE TO MOVE IN?"

If the applicant answers, "ASAP," then be extra careful. A tenant wanting to move quickly could mean a few things: 1) They are being evicted, 2) their landlord is asking them to leave, 3) they have horrible planning skills, 4) they are currently homeless, 5) there are probably fifty other reasons, all of which will put you in a bad position. On the other hand, if you have someone looking to move in three or four months from now, that is also a bad sign. You will not want your place to be vacant for that long. The best answer to this question is to rent to anyone who is willing to move in anywhere from one to three weeks from when they apply.

"HOW DID YOU HEAR ABOUT THIS?"

If you do not already know where they found your home, ask them! It's always good to find out what marketing strategy is working.

"WHO IS YOUR EMERGENCY CONTACT?"

You will want this information for when you move out. What happens when they are late on rent and not answering any of your phone calls or messages? This is when you get in touch with their emergency contact and ask them if anything is wrong. Let them know that you have not heard from your tenant in the past few days and they are late on rent. God forbid if something tragic happens, you now know that you will need to send your regards and find another tenant quickly. In most cases, everything is okay and they are just trying to avoid paying rent. This is when you either need to hunt them down or start the eviction process.

Legal

This is where a lawyer comes into play and why I highly suggest going to www.BiggerPockets.com and downloading the landlord forms for your state. The legal text in the application should include:

- **Assurance:** This states that the applicant agrees that all of the information on the application is true to the best of their knowledge. Any information that is incomplete or discovered to be false can be a reason for you to decline.
- **Application fee:** For me, the application fee is the cost of the background and credit check. I usually send them a report to fill out via Cozy and they will pay Cozy directly through the site rather than to me. No one is going to want to pay an application fee and a fee for the background and credit check. Depending on whether you are charging the fee or they are paying for it themselves, this portion can be removed from the application. If you do require the application fee, make sure you state clearly that if accepted, it will be deducted from the security deposit owed, first month's rent, or whatever you deem necessary.
- **Permission to contact:** This tells the tenant that you will be contacting their references and gives you permission to do so.
- **Initial and signature:** Make sure there is a line at the bottom of each page on the lease where they can initial as well as a line at the end of the lease for an official signature.

Reviewing the Application

Once the applicant has completed the application, it's time for you to review. Before you take the application and run back to your lair to analyze, confirm that it is completely filled out. If not, ask the tenant to please complete the form and send it back to you when it is done. Next, you will want to look it over and check for any red flags such as gaps in rental or employment history, lack of income, criminal history, eviction, poor credit score, and broken leases.

If there are any obvious issues that disqualify the potential tenant, you can tell them right on the spot. If everything seems to check out nicely, you can move forward into the real due diligence. This part may seem trivial because you have the answers right in front of you. Do not rush this part. It is exciting to get your first tenant and you will want to accept them right away because you want to get it over with. Do not do this. You will be sorry after a couple of months. The worst-case scenario is that you will be stuck with a tenant you do not like who lied on their application. When processing an application, there are four main things you are going to want to confirm:

1. Verify income
2. Order a background check
3. Order a credit check
4. Get references of previous landlords

There are additional items you can confirm with the application, but if you can verify these four things, there is a high probability that this applicant will be a good tenant.

Verifying Income

Your applicant will likely have income from a job or be self-employed. Regardless of what type of income they earn, you will need to verify that it is in fact accurate. I recommend asking them to send you their last two pay stubs. If they are moving here for a job and have not yet earned a paycheck, ask for their offer letter that confirms how much money they will be earning.

While getting the pay stubs is a great form of verification, you will be surprised at the swindlers out there. It is very easy to create a fake pay stub and submit it as a real one. The best way to verify whether their income is sufficient and stable is to call their place of employment. The employer may not be willing to reveal their pay, but you can confirm that they do in fact work where they claim they work and whether or not their job is stable or not. The questions you will want to cover with the employer include:

- Position title?
- Rate of pay (if possible)?
- Average hours per week?
- How long have they been with the company?
- How long do you expect them to be hired?
- Any additional thoughts?

Background and Credit Check

When house hacking, a background and credit check are some of the most important pieces of information you can obtain. Not only does it reveal any criminal background or financial blunders that the applicant may have, but it also confirms that the person is who they say they are. I have heard stories of applicants putting in social security numbers of dead people, or those who have been convicted of rape and murder. You can bet they were denied.

You can either run the background and credit check yourself or send the prospective tenant the form to fill out. If you wish to do it yourself, be sure that they have paid you the application fee and that their name and social security number are on the application. Once you have this information, you can go to one of many background and credit checking sites. One that I recommend is called www.RentPrep.com. RentPrep has three services, which include basic, pro, and platinum ranging from $20 to $40. The pro package usually suffices which includes:
- Social security verification
- Address history
- Eviction history
- Bankruptcy search
- Judgement and lien search
- U.S. criminal search
- U.S. sex offender search
- Global Homeland Security search

If you decide to have the tenant do the application themselves, then I would recommend www.Cozy.co (as I have mentioned). Full disclosure. I do not get paid a dime for mentioning Cozy in this book. It is just a piece of software that I truly love. When logging into www.Cozy.co, click on "screening" then click "request reports." You will enter in your applicant's first and last names as well as their email address. The form to fill out will be sent to your applicant. It will take them a minute to complete, and you will get the report sent to you instantly.

What To Do with Background and Credit Check
Once you get the results from the background and credit check, you will want to look through both. Is there anything that stands out? You are going to want to:

- **Confirm they are who they say.** If a different name shows up this is something you will want to follow up with. Sometimes people go by different names than what their original birth name is, so don't dismiss it without bringing it up with the potential tenant.
- **Look for any criminal history.** Not all crimes are created equal. If someone has a murder, rape, assault and battery, or any type of violet criminal history, you can bet they are an automatic "no." Personally, I would be a little more lenient on a one-time driving under the influence because people make mistakes, as long as no one was hurt. Obviously, it's better to have a 100 percent clean history, but if a person passes the screening with flying colors and the only blemish is a DUI, I would likely still accept them.
- **Look at their credit report.** First off, what is their credit score? Remember the standards that you established. Anything below 600 is an automatic refusal. If their credit score is on the lower end of your standards (below 650), you might want to dig a little bit deeper to determine the cause. If it's because of a medical bill from five years ago, it's likely they forgot about it. However, if they have outstanding credit card balances in the tens of thousands of dollars, as well as a car loan, and all these other debt vehicles, you might want to be careful with proceeding.

References from Previous Landlords
If there is any phone inquiries you are going to make during this entire process, please have it be these calls. A lousy tenant can be nice in person and over the phone, but they cannot hide the scars they have left on previous landlords. Remember, past performance is indicative of future results when it comes to accepting tenants.

When you call the previous landlord(s), it is entirely possible for the tenant to give you their friend's information. The way to combat this is to ask the landlord to verify the address that your prospective tenant occupied. If it matches the details on their application, it is likely you are talking to the correct person. Before you start asking questions, do not be afraid to engage in some friendly real estate small talk. They are in the business and will like it just as much as you. Ask them if they are the landlord or just the property manager. What is their vacancy like in that area? And other fairly easy questions that a landlord could answer and a friend could not. If this conversation goes over smoothly, then you can be sure that the person you are talking to is in fact their previous landlord.

After a few minutes of getting comfortable with each other, now it is time to ask the questions you called to ask. I would recommend having these written down so you don't forget. If you are calling multiple landlords, you are going to want to ask the same exact questions so you can compare. Here are some questions that I would suggest asking:

- What was the monthly rent?
- How long did the tenant stay? Did they carry out the terms of the lease?
- Did the renter always pay on time and in full?
- Were utilities paid on time?
- Did you find that the tenant had frequent guests?
- Did you ever have to give the tenant any legal notices (late rent, noise, unauthorized occupants, or notice to vacate)?
- Were there any pets?
- Did the tenant maintain the home and keep it in good condition?
- Did the tenant give proper notice before vacating?
- How much of the deposit did you give back? If they did not give back the entire deposit, ask about the repairs needed.
- Would you rent to this tenant again?

Getting the answers to these questions will give you a lot of information about your tenant. If an answer to any of these questions makes you feel uncomfortable, you have the right to decline their application. At the end of the conversation, always be sure to ask the previous landlord if there is anything they would like to add.

Remember to always get at least two recommendations so you can compare and contrast for consistency. You will also want to be sure that you do not only contact the applicant's current landlord. If the person is a really bad tenant, the landlord may just want him out so he will be incentivized to lie and tell you he is a great tenant. A previous landlord from a couple of years ago will have no incentive to tell you one way or the other.

While it can be scary to pick up the phone and talk to previous land-lords, it is one thing that is absolutely necessary when house hacking or investing in real estate in general. A bad tenant can cost you a lot of money. These phone calls can thereby save you a lot of money and headache.

Other Ways to Screen Tenants

Thus far, I have talked about how to verify income, check background and credit reports, and call previous landlords for references. These are all the official, old school ways to screen your tenants. It is no secret that we have access to almost any type of information and can access it in a matter of seconds today. This comes in handy when tenant screening. Anyone can lie on an application. However, it is unlikely someone will try to appease their future landlords on their social media pages.

Social Media

Looking at your prospective tenant's social media page is a must when house hacking. People put a lot of information on social media. Much more than they should. You can gather a whole lot about your prospective tenants just by looking at their recent Facebook, Instagram, or Twitter posts. Information that their own mother may not know about them. Looking at the social media pages is especially important when you are house hacking.

For example, I had a tenant interested in renting one of my properties. I looked at his profile page and his posts were filled with expletives, violent threats, negativity, and photos of weapons. Is this someone I want living with me or next to me? Absolutely not! No need to even give this person an application.

While that may have been an extreme example, another one might be someone complaining about how they just got fired or how they just got a new puppy or maybe a picture with a cigarette in their mouth. All are red flags and something you will either want to bring up to them or completely avoid.

Google

Everything you have ever done publicly in your life is archived on Google somewhere in today's world. A quick search of the person's name will give you some little-known facts about the person's life. In many cases, typing in the person's name will not be enough. You might have to search their location or something else about them as well. To be sure that you are getting someone's exact name try searching their name in quotation marks. For example, if you try to type in Jennifer Lawrence, you might get people with the first and last name Lawrence. However, if you type in "Jennifer Lawrence" you will be sure to find only people who have the first name Jennifer and last name Lawrence. (Just make sure you have the right Jennifer Lawrence. Chances are you aren't screening the famous Jennifer.)

Unexpected Visit

Are you curious as to how your prospective tenant will care for your place? Driving by their current residence should give you a good idea. I would not go knocking on their door, but driving by to see how the property looks on the outside will show you how much they care. Is there overgrown grass? Random cars parked in the lawn? Ripped up furniture and old kid's toys on the porch? If this is what their property looks like, you might want to think twice about accepting them. However, not all tenants are responsible for lawn maintenance—sometimes the landlord takes care of that. It will be beneficial to ask the current landlord who is in charge of taking care of the yard.

Denying a Tenant

If you are renting out an entire unit of a duplex, triplex, or fourplex, you will need to make sure that you have a logical business reason for denying a tenant. Otherwise, you might run into violating fair housing laws. You will need to be able to show proof that your decision was based on legitimate, fair business reasons outlined in your minimum standards that you have written down or because of the background and credit checks. For this reason, you will want to keep notes on all of your screening materials, including the reason that an applicant is being denied. In many cases, you might have two great tenants. Both of whom meet your standards, but one is slightly better than the other. Make sure that you tell the one you are declining that there is someone who is just slightly more qualified and that you will be in touch if something with your first choice falls through.

If you are house hacking a single-family home—in other words, you are living in one room and renting out the others—the fair housing laws are a little bit more relaxed. However, I highly recommend you adhere to the laws as best as you can by doing what is mentioned above. You do not want to get into bad habits or get into any unnecessary legal trouble. Even if you win, lawsuits are a pain in the neck.

Accepting a Tenant and Next Steps

This is much more exciting. You have done all of this work and it is now time to welcome your new tenant (or roommate)! However, once you approve a new tenant, you are not yet done. There are a few more things you need to do before they move in.

1. Decide on a Move-in Date

Once approved, you and the tenant will need to confirm the move-in date. During the pre-screening process, you should have discussed and have an idea as to whether they wanted to move in next week or next month. Now it is time to lock down the exact day. This is important because this is when you are going to start the lease. If that day is not the first of the month, you are going to want to pro-rate first month's rent accordingly.

If you run into a situation where the date the tenant wants to move in is not in your desired date range (i.e., too soon or too long), then it is not too late to decline the tenant. That is why you need to figure all of this stuff out before signing the lease.

2. Collect the "Deposit to Hold"

After you have approved the tenant, you will want to collect the deposit to hold the unit/room. This assures you that you can take the property off the market and hold it exclusively for your approved tenant(s). You call it the deposit to hold because if something happens between the time that you collect this deposit and when the lease is signed, it covers you for the vacancy they have caused. After all, they made you take the listing off the market so you could have lost out on potential new tenants. Once the lease is signed and you have received all of the move-in funds, then the deposit to hold converts over to their security deposit.

Be sure to explain this to your tenants carefully and make certain they are aware that they are not paying both a deposit to hold and a security deposit. Let them know that it just highly disincentivizes the tenant from walking away after you have taken the listing down.

3. Next Steps

After you have settled on the move-in date and you have received the deposit to hold, it is time to sign the lease and set up rent payment. You can find state-specific leases that have been looked at by lawyers in each state at wwww.BiggerPockets.com/Forms or free, generic forms if you Google your state and "residential lease." Be sure to fill in all of the blanks and if need be add or remove clauses as you see fit. Once the lease is customized to your liking, send it over to the tenant to sign.

When filling out any of these documents, always make sure that you are the LAST one to sign the document. Otherwise, the tenant can change some things to the document that you have already signed. Believe it or not, it happens.

I'm a millennial, and I like to do things from behind my computer screen. However, if you are a bit of an old soul and like to do things in person, print out the lease, fill it out with a pen, and set up a date and time that works for you and the tenant to sign the lease. A good place is usually at the property. If that will not work, a local coffee shop will be fine.

Here I go, plugging Cozy again. I do all of my rent collection through www.Cozy.co. You can easily enter the terms of the lease (rent amount, late fees, date due, and term of lease) into Cozy's system. The tenant then sets up an account on Cozy, enters in their banking information, and the rent gets deposited into your bank account every month. For free!

The only downside is that it does take five days to go from their bank account to yours. You can combat this by having rent be due in Cozy on the 25th so that it hits your bank account by the 1st day of the month. If you'd rather have rent be due on the 1st, make sure you have enough money to make your mortgage payment on that day since you will be reimbursed by your tenants a few days later.

Phew! This chapter was a doozy. I will congratulate you both on making it through the entire thing, as well as now learning how to screen and accept tenants for your house hack. I mentioned earlier Brandon and Heather Turner's book, *The Book on Managing Rental Properties*. If any of your tenant management questions have gone unanswered, I highly recommend picking up a copy of that book.

CASE STUDY
ALEXANDRA HUGHES

- **House-hacking strategy:** Rent by room
- **Age at first house hack:** 25
- **Location:** Denver, Colorado
- **NWROI:** 304%

Let's visit our friend Alexandra (Alex) in Denver. Alex first learned about the concept of house hacking through BiggerPockets and knew it was something that she really wanted to do as it could have a positive impact on her financial strategy. As she started talking about her goals of purchasing a house and the concept of house hacking to her friends and family, for the most part, they were extremely hesitant. They were always reminding her of the "what-if" scenarios (and how *"hard"* life would be without a landlord or property manager to come running when something breaks). What if you can't find a tenant? What if your tenants don't pay? What if the toilet breaks in the middle of the night? What if you can't pay your mortgage? What if you need to replace the dishwasher? Naturally, this caused her plenty of hesitation and she started to second-guess if she was indeed ready to take the plunge into homeownership. So, she waited. It was nearly a year later when something clicked—she knew she was competent enough to effectively manage all of the "what-if" scenarios that were holding her back, so she decided it was time to do what was best for her and what would help her reach her financial goals. Within thirty days of taking the first step, she was under contract.

The search for the property began in January 2018. Inventory was at its lowest, and she could not find anything that met her criteria that was also within her price range: three bedrooms, two bathrooms, and a garage in a decent neighborhood. Alex quickly lowered her criteria but made sure that the numbers still worked in her favor. Ultimately, she found a property: a cozy three-bedroom, one-bathroom bungalow in an up-and-coming Denver neighborhood for $333,000. Even though this option did not have all that she originally wanted, the neighborhood was safer than others she had considered, and she saw the potential that this house had with only a few minor updates, which meant the numbers worked nicely. This was the third offer she put in on a house and—third time's a charm! It was accepted.

Alex financed the loan with a 3 percent conventional mortgage. Her total costs to purchase the home were $11,500. There were small repairs and maintenance that she wanted to do to improve the appearance of the house: new paint, ripping up carpet, refinishing hardwood, replacing outdated light fixtures, and some landscaping. She did much of this work herself and put in a total of $3,500 in rehab expenses. For $15,000 she had purchased the property and it was ready to go. The PITI was $2,150 and she found two housemates through a mutual friend who each pay $900 ($1,800). The three of them have since become friends and the living situation could not have worked out better.

After receiving a total of $1,800 in monthly rent, Alex sets aside $300 for utilities and reserves. In total, Alex is paying only $650 to live in her home, as opposed to her previous apartment which was $950 for a 300-square-foot apartment in a converted historic home that lacked any comfortable amenities. Her total monthly savings for the difference in cost for housing is $300 per month or $3,600 annually. Her loan pay-down (assuming minimum monthly payments) is about $5,000 and her property is worth an estimated $370,000 one year later. After that first year, she has generated $45,600 of net worth after investing just $15,000. That is a net worth return on investment of 304 percent.

Alex has fulfilled her obligation to live in the property for a year so she is now looking ahead to what is next. As she is planning to move in with her significant other, who is also a homeowner in the area, she has already taken the next steps. A new tenant has signed a lease at a total of $2,490, while the mortgage payment remains at $2,150. After setting aside $200 to $300 of reserves, she will be cash flowing about $100 per month in an area that has a likelihood of appreciating.

With all of the money she has saved, Alex is realizing that she may be priced out of the Denver market. For that reason, she is going to start looking to invest in rental property outside the state of Colorado. Now that she has one year of house hacking under her belt, she feels confident enough to take her investing to the next level: out of state.

WHY

"I'm house hacking because, along with financial freedom, I'm seeking personal flexibility. I want to have the capability to spend quality time with my future family and not have to make the sacrifices that many young families do. Instead, I'm making small sacrifices now by house hacking so that I can be in a comfortable financial position. I will very soon be able to dedicate the majority of my time with the ones that I love rather than being bound to a 9 to 5 job."

ACTION STEPS

❏ Create an application that is easy for your tenants to complete.

❏ Get familiar with the credit and background check companies. Know which one you plan to use.

❏ Call on any professional reference your applicant has given.

❏ Confirm that the application checks all of your boxes.

❏ Set up rent collection, security deposit, and other payment systems.

CHAPTER 12

MANAGING THE HOUSE HACK

You are doing an owner-occupied loan; so remember that you are required to live in this property for at least one year. Disobeying this rule can get you in a lot of trouble. It is not just a slap on the wrist and being sent to your room. This is called mortgage fraud, which means jail time. Serious jail time. Jail time of five years or more. I'm not advocating that you go to jail, but if you do, I suspect you will want a better story to tell the inmates than "I moved out of my house after less than a year." Let's agree that going to jail for mortgage fraud will not be a good situation.

Believe it or not, this owner-occupied requirement is actually going to be more of a blessing than it is a curse. Since you are living in the property, you are going to be able to manage it, saving hundreds of dollars a month on property management. This is not to say that you can't manage properties you do not live in, but it just gets more time consuming. When you live in the property and something needs to be fixed, you just come home and fix it. If a tenant is not paying you rent, you can confront them in person. It's much more difficult to walk by someone every day knowing that you owe him/her hundreds or thousands of dollars even if they are your "friend."

This transitions us into our next section. By living in the property, you are going to be both a landlord and a roommate/neighbor. How do you handle this?

Being a Landlord

Think about some of the people closest to you. Perhaps your parents? Your parents likely play a lot of roles in your life. They are, of course, your parents. But as you grow older, they also become your friends, and your mentors. However, even though your parents are your friends, they are still first and foremost your parents. You can't talk to your parents like you talk to your friends. There is a certain level of respect that they demand, and that you should want to give them. Same thing goes for you and your house hack. You play different roles in your tenants' lives and you need to make sure they know which role you are playing at all times. First and foremost, you are the landlord. Secondly, you are friends.

What the heck does that mean? It means that you need to be sure that your tenants are paying their rent on time as well as being respectful of each other and your property. You can like them as people, but if they don't pay you rent on time, there is going to be a problem. If this discussion ever occurs, you will need to sit them down and tell them that you are putting on your "landlord hat." Tell them that this is nothing personal, but you need to be sure they pay the rent on time. Let me give you an example of a time I had to deal with this situation between me and one of my roommates.

As a pretext, I really liked this roommate. We had a lot in common. We liked to travel, listen to country music, and loved playing cribbage. It's hard to find millennial cribbage players. We often did these things together, but before her lease ended she was forced to move. Unfortunately, it was in the worst time of year, January. She sat me down and we had a conversation that went something like this. For anonymity I'll call her Kate:

> **Kate:** *Hey Craig, can we talk?* (Never a good way to start a conversation.)
>
> **Craig:** *Sure, what's up?*
>
> **Kate:** *So, there has been a lot of stuff that's been happening recently. I don't want to get into all of the details, but*

the main thing is that with my new job in South Denver, my commute is over ninety minutes long and I just need to move. I will be out of here next week and I will not be paying rent for February. I'm really sorry to do this, but it is something that I have to do.

Craig: *Oh, wow! Kate, I'm really sorry to hear about your situation. You certainly don't have to go into any more detail, but I'm happy to listen if you need someone. I understand your situation is serious and I want to help you out in any way I can, but you have signed a lease that says you are obligated to pay rent until August. Not paying this would be very unwise.*

Kate: *Why do you say that?*

Craig: *It will put me in a situation where I would be forced to take action against you. I would have to report the lost rent to a collection agency, which would negatively impact your credit score, which will 100 percent impact you down the line. I really do not want to do this because I do like you, but this is "landlord Craig" talking. It's not personal, it is business. I need to treat you just like I would anyone else.*

Kate: *Really? Okay. . . .*

Craig: *Kate, that is not to say I will not do my best to help you. I'm not in the business of screwing people over. I am also not in the business of getting screwed over. So, let's relist your room and start finding people. I will help you create the listing, but it is going to be your responsibility to find the tenant that I approve of to replace you.*

Sound good?

Kate: *Sure, thanks Craig.*

You can handle that conversation in the way that is best for you. Although it was not my problem, it did hurt me quite a bit and I wanted to help. Again, it's the idea of not wanting to screw people over, but not getting screwed over. I could have just said, "No, you need to stay here for the remainder of the lease." That would have created misery for the both of us. I could have said, "Yes, feel free to go." That would have put me in a very tough position with an unexpected vacancy. I feel like what I did was a fair compromise. A firm, but fair approach.

As of today, we are still friends. She has found a replacement and we frequently get together to play cribbage. Win. Win.

Fixing Things

There is likely an entire book on how to handle contractors. I'm not going to dive too deep into this here, but there are going to be times when things break at the property. Many times, it will be little things like a closet rack breaking, the pipe under the sink coming loose, or the toilet paper rack falling off. As the landlord, you are responsible for fixing these things. The quicker and more attentive you are, the better. If you consider yourself handy, then by all means go in there and do it yourself. You are going to be home anyway, so it is hardly any time taken out of your day if you know how to fix it.

If you are anything like me and you try to hammer a screw and screw in a nail, even the little things might be worth calling someone to fix. I know if I fix something, it is going to be janky and likely break again in a few days. I'll save myself the hassle and call in the maintenance crew.

If you are somewhere in the middle, there is actually a formula you can use to see whether it is worthwhile to call someone or to just do it yourself. It's:

$$Your\ dollar\ per\ hour\ wage \times hours\ worked > cost\ of\ handyman$$

The formula itself should be easy to remember. The hard part is filling in the variables. Your dollar per hour wage should be easy. How much do you make at your W-2 job? If you don't have a W-2 job, then take your last year's earnings and divide it by 2,080 (working hours in a year). The next part is where it gets tricky. How long will it take you to complete the job at the same level, or better than the maintenance crew? This includes running to Home Depot if needed, replacing the broken apparatus, and throwing away the old one. If the left side of the above equation is greater than the right, hire it out. If it's not, then do it yourself. As you begin to build wealth and advance in your career, you will notice that your time becomes more and more valuable. At some point, you will be hiring-out all of these activities.

Don't have a maintenance crew? There is this app out there called Task-Rabbit, which is where you can find people to do these random chores. It is not limited to home repair, but many of the taskers are handy individuals looking to make some extra money on the side. These folks are much cheaper than a plumber, electrician, contractor, or even someone with a full-time house maintenance business. For those little things that take less than an hour or two to complete, I highly recommend TaskRabbit.

Being a Roommate/Neighbor

Do you tell your roommates or tenants that you are the owner? That is a decision that is completely up to you. Personally, I do not like the idea of lying to your tenants right from the start. Even if it's not technically lying because you do in fact manage the property. To them, it will feel as though you are if they ask you, "Do you just manage the property?" And you respond with, "yes."

Keeping this from your roommates will be difficult. You will see them almost every day and if they figure out you are the "owner" rather than just the "property manager," they will feel as though you lied to them, and perhaps cannot be trusted. You do not want any animosity between you and your tenants.

If you are house hacking a two- to four-unit complex, it will be easier to hide the fact that you are the owner since you will likely only see them a couple times a month in passing. My recommendation is always to be truthful. However, if you really feel uncomfortable revealing to your tenants that you are the owner, only do so if your tenants do not live in the same unit with you.

Now that we got that question out of the way, how do you go about being a good roommate or neighbor? You do not want to be the reason why someone moves out. You should already know how to be a good roommate or neighbor. In case you are not sure, I'll go through it briefly.

If you are house hacking a single-family home, you will be roommates with your tenants. To be a good roommate, you do not need to be best friends with them. You just need to be clean, quiet, and respectful. Make sure the common areas are kept clean, the dishes are washed, the trash gets taken out, and common supplies (paper towels, toilet paper, and soap) are always stocked. If you can, create a system that works to allow all of you to take turns purchasing common household items. If you can't get the system to work, just go buy the toilet paper. Pick your battles. It makes no sense to create hostility in your house over a $5 item. Remember how much you are saving?!

This goes without saying, but if you are planning to have a party or friends over, be sure to let the roommates know. No one likes to come home after a hard week's work on Friday expecting to relax and instead find a house full of people drinking, and listening to loud music. What it all boils down to is the golden rule: "Do unto others as you would have them do unto you." In plain English, "Treat others the way you would like to be treated." If you always have this philosophy in the back of your mind, you will have much greater success in establishing a well-maintained household.

What if you are renting out separate units of a duplex, triplex, or four-plex? It is definitely more difficult to be a good roommate than it is to be a good neighbor. To be a good neighbor, you just have to be friendly when walking by and respectful of the quiet hours. Throwing ragers, practicing the drums, or making loud noises is probably not the best idea. If you want to go above and beyond, as a great neighbor, I would suggest doing some of the little things. If you share a walkway, shovel it when it snows. Mow the lawn in the summer. Whatever it is, these little things can go a long way.

Managing Finances

When you watch your favorite sports team play, you want them to win, right? How can you tell if they win? They score more points than the other team. How do you know if they score more points than the other team? There is a scoreboard that tracks this for you. Along with the score, there are millions of other statistics that are tracked. Why? Because they are of interest to the fans, and they help the teams know where they need to improve so that they have a higher probability of winning. What happens if nothing was tracked? It would ruin the entire purpose of the game. It would not be clear who won or lost, the teams would not have a full understanding of what they needed to work on, and the sport itself would be disorganized and eventually crumble to pieces.

That sport could be your personal finances or business if you do not track the important numbers. By tracking your finances, it will unveil ways that you can improve by showing that you could charge more rent, or if you are spending too much on maintenance. It will also help you at the end of the year when it comes to doing your taxes. One of the added benefits that I allude to throughout this book are the tax savings. There have been multiple books written on how the tax code can help real estate investors, and it is out of the scope of this book. Just know that by accurately tracking your finances, you can avoid trouble by the Internal Revenue Service (IRS) while also likely saving thousands of dollars in your taxes.

Getting Started

Once you have closed on your property, the first thing you should do is open up a new bank account for your house-hacking business. It is extremely important to keep personal and business expenses separate. By mixing the two, not only will you have an unclear picture of how your business is operating, but you will also have a terrible time trying to do your taxes at the end of the year.

If you are responsible and know a thing or two about credit cards, I highly suggest you open up a new credit card as well. Be careful though! You need to do this *after* you close. If you do it before, it may change your credit score or your debt-to-income ratio such that you become an unqualified borrower to your lender. The deal will not go through. So be safe and do not open a credit card until you have closed on the property.

Between rehabbing, furnishing, and maintaining the property, you are likely going to have lots of up-front expenses when you first purchase the property. For that reason, if you do decide to open a credit card check out what offers they have. If you are able to pay off your credit card in full each month and you like to travel, look for a credit card that benefits traveling. Take me for instance. I am a huge traveler. Every time I purchase a property, I open up a new credit card that has a 50,000-plus point bonus for travel if I spend a certain amount in three months. Usually that amount is $3,000 to $5,000 so that is no problem. These are expenses that I would incur anyway, so I might as well get free travel perks out of it. I have not purchased a flight in years because of this strategy. Another example is my friend, Connor. He opened up an eighteen-month interest free credit card. This allowed him to borrow money (for free) so that he could rehab his property. Now, he is responsible and knows he can pay that back before the eighteen months expire and the interest rate balloons.

Credit cards can be invaluable tools if used correctly. I cannot emphasize the point enough. YOU NEED TO PAY THEM OFF EACH MONTH. If you do not, you are going to be paying exorbitant rates and you will end up losing lots of money.

The two critical points you need to take away from this section of the book are to:

1. Always keep your personal and business expenses separate.
2. Always pay off your credit cards in full.

Now that you have your personal and business accounts opened and separated, let's move on to the importance of tracking, and the tools that will help you do it.

Software Tools

I hope you understand how important it is to keep track of your finances. There is no standard method when it comes to tracking your finances. Some people prefer to use a software program like QuickBooks or Xero, while others prefer to just use an Excel spreadsheet. It really depends on where you are in your business. If you have just one house hack and you do not have an insane amount of business expenses, then using an Excel spreadsheet will likely be just fine. However, as your business scales and grows, you will find that using an Excel spreadsheet will be cumbersome. There are tons of inexpensive software programs out there that will help you keep track of your finances, which can scale with you as you grow. Here is a recap of some of the most popular:

1. **Microsoft Excel:** As a finance guy in general, Microsoft Excel is a wonderful tool if you know how to use it. Any bank will allow you to export transactions into an Excel spreadsheet so that you allocate them into their appropriate buckets. If you have purchased Microsoft Office, Excel is included. If you have not already purchased Microsoft Office, there is an annual fee of $95. However, if you have no interest in learning Excel, then one of the other options might be a better fit.

2. **Wave:** Wave is a newer tool that allows you to import bank statements and track your finances for free. You can link your bank accounts and get real-time transaction data in Wave. It also lets you view reports such as income statements, balance sheets, etc. It's a great service if you are not comfortable with Excel and you

are just on your first or second property. From my experience, it is quite glitchy, hard to use, and the user interface is not great. But, it's free! So, if you are not proficient in Excel, Wave will be a good start.

3. **QuickBooks:** QuickBooks is a paid accounting software by Intuit, and is the most popular for small businesses. It will help you with bank reconciliation, tracking expenses, and showing your financials. QuickBooks is a more generalized solution that can be applied to almost all businesses. The user interface is intuitive and is easy to use.

4. **FreshBooks:** FreshBooks is a competitor of QuickBooks and has many of the same features. It will also help with bank reconciliations, tracking expenses, and viewing financial reports so you can see how you do on a month-to-month or year-over-year basis. Many people think that QuickBooks's interface is much easier to use, but it's all a personal preference. QuickBooks has been around much longer so people tend to think their interface is easier to use because they're accustomed to it. People don't like change.

5. **Xero:** Xero is another type of accounting software that is similar to FreshBooks and QuickBooks. For a small monthly fee, you are able to do all of your bank reconciliations, track expenses, and view your income statement and balance sheets. Similar to QuickBooks and FreshBooks, the user interface is well designed, but whether it's comfortable or not depends on the user. Personally, I use Xero as my accounting software, but that's because I am comfortable with it.

	Excel	Wave	QuickBooks	FreshBooks	Xero
Price	Included in Microsoft Office	Free	$10 to $60 per month	$15 to $50 per month	$9 to $180 per month
Ease of Setup	No formal setup	Easy, but cumbersome	Semi-complex	Clear, friendly walkthroughs	More to set up, but clear walkthroughs
Expenses	Cannot link bank	Cannot link bank	Can link bank	Can link bank	Can link bank
Reporting	No reporting	Cumbersome reporting	Standard	Basic reporting	Advanced
User Interface	Need to learn	Okay	Great	Great	Great

Ultimately, the decision you make on what accounting software you want to use is up to you. Remember that all of these software programs are made for businesses that involve invoicing, accepting payments, and keeping track of inventory. You won't need many of the functions. For that reason, what distinguishes each of these software programs is not relevant to the house hacker. You are likely collecting your rent outside of this program, but you need something to track the rent coming in, and the expenses going out. Given that we need limited functionality, any solution will work. I suggest doing a free trial and see which one you like, pick one, and then run with it.

Tracking Finances

You have separate bank accounts; you have figured out what software you want to use; and you have gone through the process of linking your bank accounts and setting it all up. Now, it's time for the fun stuff, which is actually seeing the score and measuring how you are doing on a month-to-month basis. Don't worry, this part is super easy.

For the purposes of this section, I am going to assume that you are using one of the accounting software services rather than Excel. If you decide to use Excel, that means you are comfortable and likely already know what to do after importing the transactions. For the non-Excel wizards, one of the software services will be best.

Regardless of the service you end up using, you should be logging in once per week to review your transactions and categorize them appropriately. What do I mean by that? When you look at your profit and loss statement, it will look something like this:

Income Statement
Coupler Realty LLC
For the month ended 30 June 2019

	Jun-19	May-19	Apr-19	Mar-19	Feb-19	Jan-19	YTD
Revenue							
▮▮▮ Income	0.00	0.00	0.00	0.00	0.00	3,251.44	3,251.44
▮▮▮ Income	4,507.59	4,496.56	4,492.07	3,877.09	3,539.97	3,522.91	24,436.19
▮▮▮ Rent	1,900.00	2,990.00	1,450.00	3,550.00	2,150.00	3,583.00	15,623.00
Other Revenue	0.00	873.60	0.00	2.86	0.00	0.00	876.46
Total Revenue	**6,407.59**	**8,360.16**	**5,942.07**	**7,429.95**	**5,689.97**	**10,357.35**	**44,187.09**
Gross Profit	**6,407.59**	**8,360.16**	**5,942.07**	**7,429.95**	**5,689.97**	**10,357.35**	**44,187.09**
Operating Income / (Loss)	**6,407.59**	**8,360.16**	**5,942.07**	**7,429.95**	**5,689.97**	**10,357.35**	**44,187.09**
Other Income and Expense							
▮▮▮ Profit Share	0.00	0.00	0.00	0.00	(2.03)	0.00	(2.03)
▮▮▮ Cleaning Expenses	0.00	0.00	0.00	0.00	(110.00)	(405.00)	(515.00)
▮▮▮ Furnishings	0.00	0.00	0.00	0.00	0.00	178.02	178.02
▮▮▮ Street Repairs	0.00	0.00	0.00	0.00	0.00	(168.62)	(168.62)
▮▮▮ Utilities	0.00	0.00	0.00	0.00	(202.21)	(143.98)	(346.19)
▮▮▮ Cleaning Expenses	(827.18)	(675.38)	(1,341.00)	(776.59)	(747.89)	(675.00)	(5,043.04)
▮▮▮ Furnishings	(10.33)	(28.88)	0.00	118.77	(140.53)	(195.52)	(256.49)
▮▮▮ Mortgage	(2,048.38)	(2,048.38)	(2,048.38)	(2,048.38)	(2,048.38)	(2,048.38)	(12,290.28)
▮▮▮ Repairs	(130.72)	0.00	(336.22)	0.00	(20.00)	(20.60)	(507.54)
▮▮▮ Utilities	(231.51)	(239.68)	(126.25)	(262.28)	(221.40)	(279.86)	(1,360.98)
▮▮▮ Startup Expenses	(530.00)	0.00	0.00	0.00	0.00	0.00	(530.00)
▮▮▮ Furnishing	(242.67)	(32.42)	(61.72)	0.00	0.00	(74.54)	(411.35)
▮▮▮ Mortgage	(2,063.71)	(2,031.16)	(2,031.16)	(2,031.16)	(2,031.16)	(2,031.16)	(12,219.51)
▮▮▮ Repairs	(4,275.92)	0.00	(118.59)	(70.24)	(43.98)	(162.54)	(4,671.27)

Do you see how I have an expense line for my mortgage payments, repairs, startup expenses, cleaning expenses, and utilities? In order to get numbers to appear next to these expense lines, I go in and categorize the transactions appropriately.

When you login, you are going to see that you have a handful of uncategorized transactions. Is that Amazon expense a piece of furniture and to be categorized as "furnishings?" Or is it a material that you used as part of your rehab to be categorized as "rehab expense?" Sure, this is something that you know, but the software may not. At least, not at first. Over time, the software will begin to link certain vendors to certain categories, but you will still need to go into the program and approve them. I recommend that you do this every week. Why? Because over the course of a month, it might be difficult to remember how you spent $40 at Amazon. Over the course of a week? It's much easier.

At the end of the month, you will have to do a bank reconciliation. That sounds much more difficult than it actually is. All that means is that the transactions that line up in your accounting software need to match your bank statement exactly. Since your bank statements are linked, these should match up automatically so it will be a quick exercise.

In the event that you have different amounts on your bank statement and in your accounting software, you will have to go through and find the discrepancy. My first check is to make sure that the dates in the accounting software line up to the dates on the bank statement. If they do, and they still do not match, there is likely a duplicate entry or missing entry in the accounting software. Go through line by line on your bank statement to find what the problem is. Once you figure it out, remedy the problem and reconfirm that the bank statement and the transactions in your accounting software match.

Once the bank statements have been reconciled, you know your financials are correct and you can then look at the profit and loss statement and see how much money you made or lost. Was that a cash-flowing month for you? Or did you have a large expense that may have set you back? How did this month compare with last month? Either way, you will be able to see your financial performance in a nice format and can assess the performance of your business.

At the end of the year, you will take the profit and loss for the year and submit it to your accountant. This will be invaluable to them as they complete your tax return.

This is getting exciting, right? You've got your tenants situated at the property. You are officially house hacking. You can see, right there on your computer screen, how much money you are making each month. You can track it month over month. As your business starts to grow, you will continue to add line items as you deem necessary. Before we officially close out this chapter and move on to some frequently asked questions, let's take a look at another case study.

CASE STUDY
MATT DROUIN

- **House-hacking strategy:** Traditional
- **Age at first house hack:** 22
- **Location:** Rochester, New York
- **NWROI:** 213%

Meet Matt Drouin. Matt graduated with a bachelor's degree in business administration with a finance concentration from State University of New York (SUNY) Geneseo in 2006. His intentions were to be an investment banker on Wall Street. You know, the Gordon Gekko type. Little did he know at the time, the big firms on Wall Street were not interested in someone with a finance degree from a liberal arts college, so getting his "dream job" was nearly impossible. Instead, Matt resorted to be a bank teller.

It was not long before Matt came to the conclusion that he hated being a bank teller. He was telling his father that he did not enjoy his work one day, and his dad suggested that he get his real estate license and work under him as a licensed realtor in the state of New York. He gave it a shot.

Being a realtor is a 100 percent commission job. If you close deals, you get paid. If you don't, then you receive nothing. In the early days, Matt's deal flow was slow and he had very little reserves, so he worked part time at a liquor store to supplement his income. Luckily, his father let Matt live with him to keep his life expenses down. Over the course of six months, Matt was able to close a few deals and save $16,000.

With $16,000 in the bank and six months of realtor experience under his belt, his father told him that it was about time he purchased a property. Both he and his father had an ethical problem with advising people on how to buy a home when he had never bought one himself. Thanks to this push, Matt was now in the market for a property. His goal was to purchase a small multifamily property, live in one unit, and rent the others. There was only one problem. Nothing on the MLS made any sense. What did he do? With his father's advice, rather than solely looking on the MLS, he started driving for dollars. He started going up and down the streets, finding beat-up houses, and calling on the owners to see if they were interested in selling.

Through driving for dollars and scouring the MLS, Matt stumbled upon an expired listing: a fourplex for $165,000 that was in decent shape. Each unit had one bedroom and one bathroom, and all were paying below market rent of $625 to $650 per month. In order to finance the deal, Matt used a 10 percent owner-occupied conventional loan. He negotiated it such that the seller paid closing costs, so he purchased the property for $16,000 down, or all of the cash he had.

Matt moved into the unit with attic access so that he could live in the attic and get a roommate for the bottom level. Between the other three units and his roommate, Matt was making $2,325 in rent while his monthly mortgage payments (PITI) were $1,800. After setting aside $300 for reserves, Matt was making $225 per month, and he was living for free. If he had not started to house hack, he would likely be paying about $700 for a one-bedroom apartment. That's a total savings of $925 per month had he decided not to house hack.

After two years of living in this property, Matt had saved enough for the next property. This time he was confident enough to tackle a much larger project. He found another fourplex just down the road that needed a significant rehab. He purchased it for $80,000 and invested an additional $60,000 for rehab costs. It needed a roof, exterior paint, the porch was falling off the front, and there was a large beehive in the house. It was so bad that a conventional lender would not finance it. He resorted to purchasing it with hard money. He renovated one unit, leased the other three, and refinanced it. The fully rehabbed property appraised for $180,000 and the monthly payment was $1,800 per month. He charged a total of $2,350 for the other three units while he lived in the fourth unit himself. Matt was *still* living for free while cash flowing on both his first and second properties.

That's how the snowball starts to accumulate.

After the second house hack, Matt got married and moved into a house where he and his wife lived alone. Since moving out of his second house hack, he has been slowly growing his real estate portfolio over time with residential, multifamily, and commercial buildings. At this point, he wishes that he did not have the limiting belief of having to start off small with the two fourplexes and wishes he jumped right into syndication. However, house hacking did provide him the foundation and confidence to start tackling these larger deals.

Through less than ten years, Matt is financially independent and now a full-time real estate investor.

WHY

"I house hack for different reasons and the reasons change. First, my why was just so I could be a credible real estate investor and move out of my father's house. Then it became achieving financial independence by 40 years old. I was a few years early on that goal and now my goal is to be the largest owner of commercial real estate in Rochester, New York. Why? It's not just so I can have loads of wealth. It's because the owners of commercial real estate have a lot of influence in the future planning of the city of Rochester. I want to have an influence to ensure the city that I love will remain a quality city."

ACTION STEPS

❏ Determine the difference and establish the line of being a landlord and a roommate.

❏ Lay the ground rules with your tenants or roommates. Be nice, but stern.

❏ When a maintenance request comes in, determine whether it makes sense to hire it out, or complete the task yourself.

❏ Open a separate bank account and credit card for your real estate business.

❏ Choose an accounting software and set it up!

CHAPTER 13

FREQUENTLY ASKED QUESTIONS

You have made it this far, and should have a deep understanding of what house hacking is, and how to do it. I've been in your shoes before. There are always additional questions. We polled the BiggerPockets community and tried to get an idea of some of the most popular questions asked as it relates to house hacking. In this chapter, I make my best efforts to answer these questions.

Do you need an LLC to house hack?

This is by far the most popular question I get when asked about house hacking. I am not an attorney or a CPA so I cannot legally give legal or tax advice. However, I can promise you that you do not need to set up an LLC to purchase a house hack. I do not have one for my house hacks and neither do many of the house hackers featured in the case studies.

Since you don't have an LLC, you do not need to worry about tracking your finances, right? Wrong! You are still going to have to report rental income on a Schedule E (for passive real estate) if you are doing a traditional house hack and a Schedule C (for active real estate) if you are doing short term. For that reason, you will want to deduct as much as possible to keep your tax liability low.

That's where I am going to end this answer so it does not get me in trouble. In summary, no, you do not need an LLC and, yes, you should 100 percent track all of your expenses.

Do you tell tenants that you're the landlord?

This can be a tricky one and there is certainly more than one answer. It really depends on the strategy you use and how comfortable you are with flirting around the truth. If you are doing the traditional house-hacking strategy where you purchase a multifamily property, live in one unit, and rent the others, you can call yourself the property manager and probably get away with it. Since the property manager can sign leases and address any maintenance issue, the tenant won't know you're the landlord. You will likely not run into your neighbors enough for them to realize that you are the actual owner.

If you are pursuing the rent-by-room strategy, this is going to be tough to hide. You will be around your roommates and tenants for a significant period of time, and they will likely find out that you are the owner before your year at the property comes to an end. At some point, they will be genuinely curious and ask about the owner of the property. Lying to your roommates will make living together awkward, and will make your tenants lose trust in you. As in all walks of life, I highly recommend not lying to your tenants or roommates here. It will come back to bite you.

Is a multifamily the best property to house hack?

There is no "best" property for house hacking. It all depends on what strategy is the best fit for you. The traditional way of house hacking is to purchase a two- to four-unit property, live in one unit, and rent the others. However, times and markets change. In many markets in 2019, finding a two- to four-unit property that will cash flow you enough to cover your mortgage is often difficult to find.

With that being said, you need to be flexible. If there are no multifamily properties that work in your area, you might have to find a single-family property and rent it by the room. In almost all scenarios, the rent-by-room strategy will net you more than renting out entire units. It is going to be more work, but the additional cash flow may be worth it for you.

For example, I have a property that is a five-bedroom, two-bathroom unit that I rent by the room while living there. When I move out, I have the option to rent it out as a full unit or to continue renting it by the room. After researching the area and the specs of the house, I know that I can get $3,500 if I rent by the room ($700 per room) or I can get $2,300 if I rent it out as a full unit. In the early stages, while I am still in the accumulation phase, I will absolutely take the additional $1,200 per month. As the nest egg grows and that $1,200 becomes less and less significant in my overall portfolio, I may elect to rent it out as a full unit to relieve myself of the extra work. As you have read in this book, we have shown you five (or really six) house-hacking strategies. Only one of them involves purchasing a multifamily unit.

If you are adamant about getting at least a duplex for your first property, I would think again. Do what makes the most financial sense. Do not worry about what other people think. If your goal was to purchase a multifamily property, you may need to rethink your strategy. Was the goal to purchase a multifamily property, or was it to buy a house hack so you can live there and eliminate your housing expense? In many cases, the latter is the underlying goal. So, put the ego aside and purchase that single-family if need be. I did. If you want the highest possible return, I would recommend renting by the room or doing the trailer hack. Though, as you can imagine, that might impede on how you want to live. If you would prefer to have some privacy or have a family, doing that strategy for a short term would be best.

How do you get to the second house hack?

From a financing perspective, the second house hack is typically the most difficult. Why? Because you can't use your newfound landlord income until you have been a landlord for at least two years. You will have to prove to a bank that you can cover both mortgages with your W-2 (or self-employed) income. This likely will make your debt-to-income ratio way too high. Like anything though, there is a loophole.

If you can prove to the lender that you have a tenant ready to move in to this next property with a signed lease and a corresponding security deposit, they will use that income against your debt and you will likely be able to qualify for the next property. Your first order of business when looking for your next house hack is going to be finding someone to fill your current place.

If you purchased the first house hack with an FHA loan and you are looking to use it again, you may need to refinance into a conventional mortgage. The caveat here is that you will need at least 20 percent equity in the property to get a non-owner-occupied loan. Unless you got a screaming deal, or did a significant rehab, the likelihood of you having 20 percent or more equity in a property after a year is very low.

One thing about real estate investing is you can never say, "I can't." There are always ways around a roadblock. You need to replace the "I can't" with the "How can I?" As of this writing, lenders are offering 3 to 5 percent down conventional mortgages on single-family homes. If you did a multifamily on your first house hack, you may want to consider a single-family on the next one.

As of the beginning of 2019, lenders are starting to offer 5 percent down on multifamily units, as well as through the Freddie Mac offered Home Possible. You do not need to be a first-time homebuyer for this product in particular. I am not sure how long this will last so be sure to talk to multiple lenders to see what they can offer.

Now that the financing is all settled, you should have enough savings from your first house hack for a down payment on the second one. The rest of the process is just a repeat of what you did on the first. Locating the property, analyzing, negotiating, rehabbing (if necessary), and finding tenants. Overall, the process of house hacking should get easier and easier as you go—especially after the first and second properties.

How do you keep track of expenses while house hacking?

At the end of the year, you or your accountant is going to need to do your taxes. In order to pay the least amount in taxes, you need to have the highest amount of expenses possible associated with your business. This is not to say spend needlessly on things, but instead purchase whatever you would normally purchase, but be sure to keep the receipts and write it off as a business expense.

There are tons of software programs out there that do this for you. If you don't mind paying a small monthly subscription fee, I would recommend Xero, QuickBooks, or FreshBooks. If you prefer to do it yourself, but are okay with spending a few hours each month sorting through and allocating expenses, you can use Microsoft Excel. Make sure to go online and look at the Schedule C form, which you will need to complete before submitting your taxes at the end of the year. Bucket all of your expenses into these categories—that way at the end of the year, you only have to copy and paste them into your tax form.

Personally, I use Xero to track all of my expenses. Once I got to a point of managing several properties, Excel was getting far too cumbersome for me and I needed to streamline the process. But do what works best for you considering the circumstances.

How do you set up rents for college house hacking?

In most colleges, school is in session from September through May so what do you do for the summer months when all of the students go home? You treat them exactly like any normal tenant: You make them sign a twelve-month lease. Whether they occupy or want access to the apartment over the summer is up to them. Perhaps, you let them find someone that you approve of to sublease for the summer. Either way, the tenant who is on the lease would be responsible for paying rent every month, including the summer months.

Is there a benefit to paying cash vs. financing a house hack?

Whether you pay cash or finance a house hack is completely up to you, depending on what makes you comfortable. If you pay cash on a house hack, you are removing almost all of the risk from the deal, but you are also getting the lowest possible return on your money. The real power of house hacking and how you are able to get those returns in full after the first year is due to generating similar returns with lower money down.

Let's look at the NWROI equation again. By decreasing the initial payment, you can drastically increase your NWROI.

$$NWROI = (cash\ flow + mortgage\ paydown + appreciation)\ /\ initial\ investment$$

If you do not care about the percentage of your return and are just looking for a large amount of consistent cash flow, then cash financing makes the most sense. Otherwise, I would recommend leveraging to the point where you can still comfortably cash flow on the property.

Does the 1 percent rule apply for house hacking?

The 1 percent rule, 2 percent rule, and 50 percent rules are not rules at all. More so, they are rules of thumb. That means when doing a quick calculation, if the property satisfies these rules, there is a high probability that it will be a good deal. However, nothing is guaranteed. You need to be sure to do your due diligence on the property, but be careful with over analyzing and never actually taking action. As I mentioned in this book, my favorite way to analyze a property is to determine three things:

1. Expected rental income
2. Monthly mortgage payment including principal, interest, taxes, and insurance (PITI)
3. Expected reserves

Once you have these three numbers, you can take the expected rental income and subtract the monthly mortgage and expected reserves. If the difference is equal to or greater than the profit you would like to make, you put in an offer. If not, then move on to analyzing the next deal. Before you move so quickly though, remember that almost every property has a price that could work. If the deal does not work for you at the current listing price, put an offer in with a final price that would work for you. For example, if the price of a property you are looking at is $350,000, but the monthly payments and reserve total $100 more than what you would receive in rent, then this $350,000 price point may not work for you. Offer $300,000 instead. Sure, it may not get accepted, but you never know. It's worth a shot if you like the house.

Remember, since you are going to be living at the property, it is okay for that number to be less than zero. If it is less than zero, that means you are going to be paying a certain amount to live there. This is fine, but make sure that the final number is greater than or equal to the amount you would be paying in rent. Also, make sure that when you move out, the rent that you receive for your room exceeds the mortgage and reserve amount.

Should I bother house hacking if I live in an expensive city?

Living in an expensive city such as New York, San Francisco, Los Angeles, or Boston makes it difficult to house hack. There is always the option of moving just outside the city or moving to another city for a fresh start. Though I know that's not an option for most people, it certainly is the easiest.

If you do decide you want to live in one of these expensive cities for the long haul, you are still able to purchase a property using an FHA or other low down payment loan. Although it will be difficult to live for free in these cities, you can certainly offset some of the mortgage costs through house hacking. This might allow you to save a little bit on rent savings.

In these expensive cities, you will see a lot of volatility through the ebbs and flows of the real estate cycle. However, properties in these large cities have a high probability of appreciating at a higher rate than those in less desirable cities or in small towns over time.

In short, it's certainly not a bad idea when investing in a house hack in these large cities. You will likely still be able to offset some of your living expenses and grow the equity in the property as it appreciates over time. The largest problem the average person may encounter is having enough liquid cash for a down payment in one of these expensive cities. If that's the case, you will need to wait a little longer until you can save the appropriate amount, or ask friends and family for a loan so you can make the down payment. Ultimately, a house hack can be done anywhere. It just depends on how lucrative you want it to be and how much risk you are willing to take.

Do I have to live in the property or is there a way around this?

If you are house hacking and you are using an owner-occupied loan (most are), then you are required to live there for one year. Okay, maybe you aren't "required" to live there for one year, but you need to "intend" to live there for a year. There are many interpretations of this, but unless a big-time life event happens, I would recommend staying in the property for at least one year.

A big-time life event is not clearly defined anywhere, but you would have to use your best judgment. If your job forces you to unexpectedly relocate over the course of a year, this would be a significant life event. Another example would be if a relative got really sick and you needed to go home to care for them. All of these situations could not have been forecasted when first purchasing the property, so the lenders will typically let them slide.

I would recommend doing everything in your power to live in the property for at least a year. Otherwise, you could be tried for mortgage fraud, which could be one to up to ten years of prison time depending on your state. Don't go to prison for something as silly as not being able to wait a year to move to your next desired location.

CASE STUDY
DAVID THOMPSON

- **House-hacking strategy:** Airbnb
- **Age at first house hack:** 27
- **Location:** Harrison, Arkansas
- **NWROI:** 230%

Let's visit our friend, David Thompson. By trade, David is a firefighter that resides in a small town of about 13,000 people called Harrison, Arkansas. He has always earned about $30,000 per year while his wife has been living out her dreams of owning a dance studio. She purchased the studio from the woman who had taught her how to dance, and has turned that into a school of her own.

But shortly after purchasing the business, the landlord decided that she wanted to sell the entire plot of land including the building where the dance studio was located and a commercial office space across the lot. If David and his wife had not purchased the property, it would have been sold to the landlord's nephew and turned into an auto parts store. Rather than lose their business (and the building), they were left with no choice but to purchase the plot. They were now accidental landlords and were gaining additional real estate experience.

A couple of years later, David and his wife decided to take a vacation to Boulder, Colorado to do some rock climbing. The hotels in Boulder were outrageously priced (surprise, surprise!) so they decided to try this up-and-coming site called Airbnb. Being fairly conservative, they were late adopters to Airbnb, but again, they did not have much of an option in their eyes. They found a place in Boulder for $100 per night, and had a magnificent experience. After talking to the owner and figuring out the numbers, they were inspired and decided that they wanted to do this on their own back in Arkansas.

A few months after their vacation in September 2015, they found a property right near the Buffalo River. It had a pool with a guest house that was completely dilapidated. Their thoughts? Let's fix up the guest house and rent it out on Airbnb. They still get their privacy by living in the primary home while they can still cover most (or all) of their mortgage.

They purchased this property for $120,000 with a 20 percent down conventional loan. They financed the $24,000 down payment through the equity they had built up in their current primary residence. After $10,000 of rehab costs, in March 2016 the guesthouse was ready to be listed on Airbnb. They immediately started booking guests and made an average of $1,750 per month in gross revenue on Airbnb. After operating costs like utilities, supplies, and cleaning they were making about $1,500 per month. David's mortgage payment (including PITI) is $700 and he was setting aside about $300 per month in reserves. By using the Airbnb house-hacking strategy, he is cash flowing $1,500 - $700 - $300, or $500 per month while also living in the larger house for free—a value of about $800. If you add the cash flow and rent savings, David's net worth is increasing by $1,300 per month. I know that reading numbers in paragraph form can be confusing. Let's recap:

Purchase price: $120,000

Down payment: $24,000

Rehab costs: $10,000

Rental income: $1,750

Mortgage payment: $700

Airbnb expenses: $250

Reserves: $300

Rental income ($1,750) – mortgage ($700) – Airbnb expenses ($250) – reserves ($300) = $500 per month!

Rent savings: $800 (if living in a similar home elsewhere)

Cash flow ($500) + rent savings ($800) = $1,300 in total savings per month!

David clearly got himself a good deal here. But one major component is still missing: the appreciation on the property. David spent $10,000 in fixing up the guesthouse. When it was all said and done, the property was worth $180,000 after the first year, and he had paid his loan down by about $2,500. With the $62,500 of equity he gained from the property in the first year, let's calculate his NWROI:

Cash flow & rent savings: $1,300 × 12 = $15,600

Appreciation: $60,000

Loan paydown: $2,500

Total net worth gain: $15,600 + $60,000 + $2,500 = $78,100 net worth change

Total invested: $24,000 down payment + $10,000 rehab = $34,000

$78,100 / $34,000 = 230% return

David realized a 230 percent increase on his net worth based on the original $34,000 invested, all while living in the larger home on the property. In David's scenario, there are very few sacrifices outside of the initial work that went into rehabbing the property. I would say a little work is worth a 230 percent return though.

This first house hack has propelled David into real estate investing. It gave him the capital and knowledge necessary to start purchasing buy-and-hold properties all over that area in the United States. He has two properties in the town of Harrison (where he lives now), one duplex in Wichita, Kansas and a few more in Missouri. David and his wife are well on their way toward financial independence while working on firefighter and dance teacher salaries.

WHY

"I house hack because I was raised in a poor family. My mom and dad worked two jobs and never truly saw the fruits of their labor. They were rarely home, yet were still hardly able to provide for the family. I saw this struggle and did not want to be like that myself. I wanted to be able to easily provide for my family so that I could spend time with them doing the things they loved, rock climbing in particular. Outside of rock climbing, I also want to be able to give back to my parents, brothers, and sisters by helping them live a life of their dreams too."

CHAPTER 14

CONCLUSION: DO IT AGAIN

Congratulations! You made it through this entire book. You are ready for your first investment!

Throughout this book, there have been about a dozen case studies of people who are using house hacking to pursue financial independence. Before I completely conclude this book, I want to take you through an example of someone who has totally completed the journey toward financial independence with house hacking. Note that this is just one example. There are many ways to do it and if this strategy does not work for you, then take another route. Let's get into it.

Who is this person? Her name is Jessica. She is in her mid-twenties and graduated from an expensive university. She works as a consultant at a top firm making $65,000 per year, but has a seemingly insurmountable amount of student loan debt; $95,000 to be exact. She has $5,000 in savings that is invested in index funds generating a 7 percent return each year. She has no mortgages (yet!), no car loan, and no credit card debt. Given the $5,000 in assets and $95,000 in student loan debt, her net worth is a negative $90,000. Here is an overview of Jessica's financial position:

Assets: $5,000 in index funds

Liabilities: $95,000 in student loans

Net worth: -$90,000

After two years of working at the consulting company, Jessica was starting to dislike it. She did not believe in the values of the company and found it very difficult to stay motivated to go to work. The thought of having to go into an office every single day for the next forty-plus years weighed heavily on her. She knew there had to be a better way. With a simple Google search of, "How do I retire early," she came across a well-known blogger by the name of Mr. Money Mustache (MMM), an ex-engineer who retired at the age of thirty. After reading many of his blog posts, she started going down the rabbit hole and soaking up as much information as possible. She was well versed in the idea of financial independence: Rather than spend your money, invest in assets that provide a return. That return is what is known as passive income. When your passive income exceeds your expenses, work becomes *optional.*

Assets × return (%) = passive income

Passive income > expenses = financial independence

She then would be able to do what she was truly passionate about: traveling, spending time with family and friends, and volunteering. This is her breaking free from the rat race, and unlocking her life!

After being sold on the concept of financial independence, she continued learning and finding the most efficient ways to obtain it. She found that many people who have achieved financial independence do it through the method of penny pinching for seven to ten years, paying down all debt, and putting all of their savings into an index fund that generates them four to seven percent annually. Once they hit $1 million of savings, their money will be making a return of $40,000–$70,000 per year. More than enough to live off of with ease. The quickest pursuers of this index fund strategy tend to achieve their goal of financial independence in about ten years. Jessica realized that this is much better than retiring in forty years in a career she felt burdened by every day.

While going deeper down the rabbit hole of financial independence, she stumbled upon the idea of house hacking: eliminating your housing expense by purchasing a property, living in one part, and renting the other parts out such that the rent either offsets or completely covers the mortgage. By house hacking, Jessica realized that she could work both sides of the financial independence equation. She would be able to reduce or eliminate her largest expense in rent, while also increasing her passive income.

Not only that, but she recognized that the barriers to entry were not very high. In her area, the average cost of a house is $300,000. With the owner-occupied, low percentage down loans, she could buy a property for as little as $10,000. Given that the down payment is so low, she was confident that her returns from house hacking—after cash flow, mortgage paydown, and appreciation—would likely be well over 100 percent for the first year and likely even more as rents increase, and more of her mortgage payment is applied to the principal over time. She figured that the returns of house hacking would dwarf that of the stock market. She determined that she could achieve financial independence in five years or less. Sure, there will be more work involved, but certainly not five years of penny-pinching work.

In fact, after she has a few house hacks under her belt she will be saving so much money in rent that she will not even need to worry about the little expenses. Want to grab a drink? Go for it. Want to attend a concert? Do it. As long as she is mindful of what she is spending and does not overdo it. Spending $100 here and there will not destroy her financial position. House hacking will allow her to spend money on the things she truly enjoys without falling too far behind. She can live her life and still advance rapidly toward financial independence.

Okay, Jessica has been sold on the idea of house hacking and believes this should be her next large step in pursuit of financial independence. Paying down her student loans would give her a guaranteed return of 7 percent by saving on the interest, the stock market will give her an average return of 7 percent, but house hacking will generate returns well into the hundreds of percent. However, given her current financial position, she will not be able to house hack quite yet. Her first step is to pinch her pennies and save that first $10,000 to $20,000 for the down payment.

Through blogs like Mr. Money Mustache, Mad Fientist, 1,500 Days to Freedom, BiggerPockets, and others, she discovered various tactics that allowed her to save an increasing amount of money. She moved into a less expensive rental apartment, stopped using her car as a primary method of transportation, and tried to eat as many meals as possible from home. The amount she saved each month increased to about $800 per month. From her research, Jessica understood that money sitting in a checking or savings account is utterly useless. You need to make your money work for you. For that reason, she invested her additional savings into index funds, a conglomeration of stocks that is used to track a market index (e.g., S&P 500 Index, and NASDAQ Composite Index). After eighteen months of saving, investing in index funds, and making the minimum payments on her student loans, this was her financial position:

Assets: $19,400 in index funds

Liabilities: $90,000 in student loans

Net worth: -$70,600

Equipped with all of the knowledge to purchase her first house hack, she is ready to start looking. Jessica knows the first step in finding a house hack is to find an agent and a lender. Through her local Real Estate Investors Association (REIA) and meetup groups, she was able to find a plethora of agents and lenders. She requested a time to meet and grab coffee one-on-one, evaluated each one, and ended up picking an agent and two lenders she would potentially choose. Jessica collected all of the relevant information and went through the pre-approval process with both lenders. Both pre-approvals came back showing that Jessica would be able to afford a house for $400,000 or less with a 5 percent down, owner-occupied conventional loan. One lender had her at a lower rate than the other, so she went with the lender with the lowest rate. Jessica relayed the news to her real estate agent, and they set her up with automatic MLS notifications so that whenever a property that met her criteria that was priced under $400,000 popped up, she would be the first to know.

With this information, Jessica had to make a decision as to what house-hacking strategy she would be willing to pursue. She understood the idea behind the house-hacking spectrum. The further she moved along to the right, the greater the lifestyle change and the greater the returns. Not willing to live in a trailer or rent out her own bedroom, she decided to go with the rent-by-room strategy.

**Least Profitable /
Smallest Lifestyle
Change**

← Airbnb ADU — Traditional — (Rent by Room) — Airbnb Bedroom — Trailer →

**Most Profitable / Biggest
Lifestyle Change**

Jessica looked for a single-family home that was within biking distance to where she works, has three bedrooms, two bathrooms, and at least 2,000 total square feet. She knew that it would be relatively easy to add a couple bedrooms and a bathroom to a property of that size with just three bedrooms and two bathrooms. This will not only add value to her property, but she will be able to ask much more for rent.

After a few weeks of scouring the MLS, Craigslist, and even driving around neighborhoods, she found a few properties that she liked. Her first few offers were rejected. Finally, she found one that was perfect. A three-bedroom, two-bathroom single-family residence listed for $340,000 that had 2,300 square feet, an unfinished basement, and only a seven-mile bike ride to work along a bike path. This checked all of the boxes! She submitted an offer at $350,000. Yes, she did it above listing price to increase her probability of having it accepted. Lo and behold. It worked! She put down $5,000 of earnest money and was officially under contract!

At this price, Jessica knew that her mortgage would be about $2,000 per month. She was confident that she could rent out each room for $700 per month. At first, she would have to spend $600 per month to meet her mortgage payment, which is still $400 less than the $1,0000 per month she was paying in rent. She understood that the true value would come in finishing the basement and adding the two bedrooms and bathroom. After taking a few months to work on this project in the basement, she will be able to charge $700 per month for those two bedrooms as well. Then, she will be generating in $2,800 in rental income on a $2,000 mortgage. After putting aside $400 in reserves and spending nothing to live, this is what her projected financial situation will look like when the house is fully rented.

Rental income: $2,800 per month

Mortgage: $2,000 per month

Reserves: $400 per month

Cash flow from property: $400

Monthly cash saved: $400 + $1,000 rent savings = ***$1,400 per month***

After doing this quick analysis, she was confident in the deal. Not only did she have the opportunity to save an extra $1,400 per month, she also knew that there was a lot of forced appreciation to be had with adding the bedrooms and the bathroom. Because appreciation of all types is speculative—you never know what the market is going to do—she decided not to have that factor into whether or not she wanted to go through with purchasing this deal.

Quickly after receiving the signed purchase and sale agreement, she immediately called her lender and sent them the property information so that they could begin the underwriting process. She called an inspector and scheduled the inspection for just a few days later. She walked through the property with the inspector. He pointed out a lot of things that *could* be fixed, but all in all, the property was sound, and there were no major renovations that were required to be done before the house was livable. With the inspection coming back clean, much of the work of acquiring the property had been completed. Now, she just needed to get the lender any paperwork as soon as possible so they could approve the loan and prevent any delays in closing.

Jessica is not one to sit around for weeks though. Especially given the fact that the largest investment of her life was at stake. She took the pictures from the listing and started advertising the rooms for rent on Craigslist and Facebook Marketplace. She was getting plenty of inquiries and set up an open house for the potential tenants on the first day she officially owned the property. After meeting everyone in person, asking questions, and giving more information to the potential tenants about the property and next steps, she had a great idea as to who she wanted her tenants to be for this property. She sent them an application. The application asked all of the necessary information including income, work references, landlord references, past addresses, the background check, the credit check, as well as answers to questions dealing with bankruptcy, smoking, and evictions.

Shortly after sending the applications out, Jessica had received all four back within a reasonable amount of time. Here is what they looked like:

	Tenant 1	Tenant 2	Tenant 3	Tenant 4
Background Check	Clear	Clear	DUI	Clear
Credit Score	595	640	730	750
Monthly Income	$4,000	$2,000	$5,000	$4,500
References	Great	Great	Great	Great
Eviction	None	None	None	None
Bankruptcy	None	None	None	None
Smoker	No	No	No	No

Given the information in the table above, which two tenants would you pick?

Remember, Jessica is going to charge $700 per room. In the real estate industry, it is standard to request that the tenants have at least three times their monthly rent in gross income. This can be a deal breaker, so tenant number two is out. Jessica sends tenant number two an email saying, *"I am sorry, but you do not meet my income requirements. Thank you for applying and good luck with everything!"*

That leaves her between tenants number one, three, and four to fill the two spots available. Tenant one seems great apart from the fact that they have a credit score that is just under the limit. After looking at the credit report, Jessica noticed that tenant one is not current on all of their debts and seems to be notorious for paying late. She thinks, if they are going to pay their lenders late, there is a high probability that he/she would also be paying her late. She decided to email tenant number one and says, "*I am sorry, but you do not meet my credit requirements. Thank you for applying and good luck with everything!*"

That leaves her with tenants numbers three and four to occupy the spaces. She sends them an email saying, "*Congratulations! You have been accepted to occupy the room at 123 Main Street in Denver, Colorado 80203. Your move-in date is June 1, 2019. Attached you will find a lease that outlines the terms we discussed. Please sign and send back to me along with your security deposit [add amount here] as soon as possible. Once I receive the security deposit, I will countersign the lease and send it back to you promptly. I look forward to seeing you on the first!*"

Let's fast forward to June 1, 2019. Jessica has a fully occupied three-bedroom, two-bathroom property. This is what her property situation looks like now:

Rental income: $1,400 per month

Mortgage: $2,000 per month

Reserves: $400 per month

Cash flow from property: -$1,000

Monthly cash saved: -$1,000 + $1,000 rent savings = **$0 per month**

At this point, Jessica is breaking even. She is paying the same amount toward her mortgage and reserves as she was previously paying for her own rent. However, she is now building equity through loan paydown and natural appreciation, which over time, will make her much wealthier. Jessica did not purchase this place to break even though. She wanted to fully eliminate her living expense. The only way to do this was to add additional bedrooms. The renovation project to add two bedrooms and a bathroom will cost her approximately $20,000, according to her estimates. Here is what her financial situation currently looks like after using her index funds to fund the down payment.

Assets: $5,000 in index funds

Property: $350,000

Total assets: $355,000

Liabilities: $90,000 in student loans

Mortgage: $332,500

Total liabilities: $422,500

Net worth: -$67,500

I am sure that you have heard of the quote, "You make money when you buy a deal in real estate." Well, that's funny, because this does not hold true in this situation. Her net worth is virtually the same before and after purchasing the property. That is because we are assuming that Jessica purchased the deal right at market value. This is rare. In many cases, you will buy a deal that is much less than market value. This means that you will have equity in the property at the time of purchase. For example, if you were to purchase a property that was worth $375,000 for just $350,000, you will have $25,000 of built in equity, which would be added to your net worth. Because it is difficult to assess the value of the property, and since Jessica has no intentions of selling, we will just assume that she purchased it at the exact value.

The other problem here is that Jessica has $5,000 in savings (or index funds) and needs $20,000 to do the renovation. Well that stinks. Jessica doesn't have enough. She will have to go another eighteen months to save up an additional $15,000 to complete the renovation. There's only one problem. Jessica is far too motivated to sit around and wait eighteen months before doing the renovation. She wants to be in a position to begin her next house hack in eighteen months. Waiting is not an option. Being risk-tolerant at her young age, she decided to open up a credit card for $15,000. The credit card was interest free for the first eighteen months and then the interest rate jumped up to a whopping 23 percent. She ran the numbers and calculated that she would easily be able to pay off the credit card with the additional rent coming in. Even if it does play to her downside scenario and it becomes close, she knows that she can always pick up some extra shifts at her job or walk dogs for additional income to pay it off before the interest rate balloons.

Jessica obtained the credit card, found a great contractor, and went through with the renovations. It cost her just under $15,000 for the full renovation. She went through a similar process as before to fill the two additional rooms. Each rented for $700 per month. Now, her monthly rental situation is exactly as she predicted:

Total rental income: $2,800 per month

Mortgage: $2,000 per month

Reserves: $400 per month

Cash flow from property: $400

Monthly cash saved: $400 + $1,000 rent savings = **$1,400 per month**

By doing the renovation, not only is Jessica making $1,400 more per month, but she also increased the value of her house. Whereas a three-bedroom, two-bathroom house was valued at $350,000 in her area, a five-bedroom, three-bathroom house was valued at $400,000. That is an added $50,000 of equity value by doing the renovation.

After four months, the property is fully settled. Jessica has executed on her plan. Now, we play the waiting game. She decided to carry on with her life just as she did before house hacking. She remains frugal and seeks out ways to generate additional income. She drives for Uber, walks dogs on the side, and even rents out her car on Turo. All of these things bring in a little over $1,000 per month that she can put aside to build up her reserve funds that she keeps in index funds and pay down her credit card debt before the high interest rates kick in. Here is what her financial situation now looks like:

Assets: $5,000 in index funds

Property: $400,000

Total assets: $405,000

Liabilities: $88,000 in student loans

Mortgage: $330,000

Credit card: $15,000

Total liabilities: $433,000

Net worth: -$28,000

Between the renovation project and making minimum payments on her student loans and mortgage, Jessica's net worth is now negative $28,000. Her net worth increased by $39,500 in just a few months during the renovation. After only putting a total of $17,500 for the down payment, she is looking at a NWROI of 226 percent!

Realizing how much wealth she has generated, and the fact that she now has $1,400 per month in passive income, it is clear to her that this is the fast lane toward financial independence. Right now, here is what her progress toward financial freedom looks like:

House #1 net income = $1,400 per month

Projected personal expenses = $2,000 per month

Let's say she house hacks again, but she wants to sacrifice a little bit of cash flow to get a place that needs less work. After year two, Jessica's financial position looks like this:

House #1 net income = $1,400 per month

House #2 net income = $1,000 per month

Total passive income = $2,400 per month

Projected personal expenses = $2,000 per month

Jessica is technically by strict definition, financially independent after only two years since her passive income exceeds her personal expenses. However, Jessica does not want her personal expenses to stay at $2,000 per month her whole life. Instead, she continues to house hack until she reaches a more sustainable $5,000 per month. Again, she purchases another house hack.

House #1 net income = $1,400 per month

House #2 net income = $1,000 per month

House #3 net income = $1,000 per month

Total passive income = $3,400 per month

Projected personal expenses = $5,000 per month

You can see how that over the course of five to seven years, it is very reasonable to achieve financial independence strictly through house hacking. After year five this is what Jessica's house hacking portfolio looks like:

House #1 net income = $1,400 per month

House #2 net income = $1,000 per month

House #3 net income = $1,000 per month

House #4 net income = $1,000 per month

House #5 net income = $1,000 per month

Total passive income = $5,400 per month

Projected personal expenses = $5,000 per month

She has reached her mark of financial independence and can now quit her day job and do whatever she wants with her life! The above equation is only taking into account the cash flowing portion of real estate investing. After you take into account appreciation, loan paydown, and individual tax benefits, there is a high probability that Jessica will be worth well over $1 million at this point if she continued to save and be frugal.

This story is not fiction. The only thing that is made up is the name, Jessica. I know many people who have house hacked their way to financial independence. They are no different from you and me. They did not come from a privileged background and most have little/no financial help from their parents. They are just hard-working individuals willing to put in the extra effort for five years to unlock their next fifty. By house hacking and doing so in the most aggressive way that pushes you to the edge of your comfort zone, you are setting yourself up for a lifetime of financial support. Financial freedom is within your reach. You can do it just one house hack at a time.

If you have progressed this far, you are now equipped with the knowledge of what it takes to get out there and start generating massive amounts of wealth and achieving financial independence through house hacking. As a wise man by the name of Dave Ramsey once said, "Live like no one else, so later you can *live like no one else.*"

You are now at a crossroad. The road that most Americans choose is simple and has been traveled time and time again. Purchase the new car, the new home, work forty hours a week, fifty weeks a year for forty years of your life. Save 10 percent of your income and retire a millionaire (if you're lucky) by the time you are 65 years old.

Or you can take the alternate road. The route less traveled. The fast lane toward financial independence. Be frugal. Save your money. House hack. House hack again. And again. And again! Keep doing this until you get to the point where you can physically no longer do it. If you do this for five years, the odds are extremely high that you retire with a net worth well over a million dollars well before you are 60, 50, or even 40 years old.

What road are you going to take? The choice is yours.

ACKNOWLEDGEMENTS

No book is ever written without the help of an army of people. Be it the physical publication or mental dedication it takes to write a book. For that reason, I would like to take a moment and thank a few of the people that have made this book possible.

First and foremost, I want to thank my mom, Louise Curelop; dad, Gary Curelop; and sister, Samantha Curelop, for the unconditional love and support throughout the years. Mom and Dad, you have put everything aside to ensure that Sammy and I live our best possible lives. For that, I am eternally grateful. You continue to inspire me every day. I love you. Keep pushing!

Thank you to my Uncle Jonathan. I am not sure that he even knows it, but he has been a huge inspiration in my life. Being a published author himself, he inspired me to want to write a book "someday." That day is here. Thank you. I love you!

To the gentlemen who started it all: Brandon Turner and Josh Dorkin. It is crazy to think that less than three years ago, I was sitting in my tiny San Francisco apartment watching you on BiggerPockets webinars, listening to podcasts, and reading your books. I would never have dreamed in a million years that Brandon would be writing the foreword to my book and that I could call both of you friends. You both changed my life. Thank you!

To Scott Trench, there is not a single person who plays as many roles as you do in my life: boss, friend, and mentor. Thank you for all of the inspiration, guidance, and advice during these past few years. I could not have done this without you.

Thank you to all of the fellow house hackers who took the time out of their busy schedules for the case studies at the end of each chapter.

Finally, I want to thank the team that made all of this happen. Special thanks to Katie Miller, who led this project from the start, with the help of Kaylee Pratt, Jarrod Jemison (baller cover design!), Wendy Dunning, Damon Banks, Katie Golownia, Katelin Hill, and the rest of the editorial team at BiggerPockets.

More from
BiggerPockets Publishing

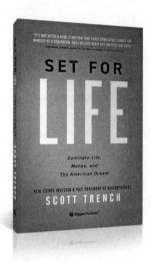

Set for Life: Dominate Life, Money, and the American Dream

Looking for a plan to achieve financial freedom in just five to ten years? *Set for Life* is a detailed fiscal plan targeted at the median-income earner starting with few or no assets. It will walk you through three stages of finance, guiding you to your first $25,000 in tangible net worth, then to your first $100,000, and then to financial freedom. *Set for Life* will teach you how to build a lifestyle, career, and investment portfolio capable of supporting financial freedom to let you live the life of your dreams.

The Book on Investing in Real Estate with No (and Low) Money Down

Lack of money holding you back from real estate success? It doesn't have to! In this groundbreaking book from Brandon Turner, author of *The Book on Rental Property Investing* and others, you'll discover numerous strategies investors can use to buy real estate using other people's money. You'll learn the top strategies that savvy investors are using to buy, rent, flip, or wholesale properties at scale!

If you enjoyed this book, we hope you'll take a moment to check out some of the other great material BiggerPockets offers. BiggerPockets is the real estate investing social network, marketplace, and information hub, designed to help make you a smarter real estate investor through podcasts, books, blog posts, videos, forums, and more. Sign up today—it's free! **Visit www.BiggerPockets.com.**

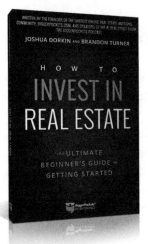

How to Invest in Real Estate

Two of the biggest names in the real estate world teamed up to write the most comprehensive manual ever written on getting started in the lucrative business of real estate investing. Joshua Dorkin and Brandon Turner give you an insider's look at the many different real estate niches and strategies so that you can find which one works best for you, your resources, and your goals.

The Book on Rental Property Investing

The Book on Rental Property Investing by Brandon Turner, a real estate investor and co-host of the *BiggerPockets Podcast*, contains nearly 400 pages of in-depth advice and strategies for building wealth through rental properties. You'll learn how to build an achievable plan, find incredible deals, pay for your rentals, and much more! If you've ever thought of using rental properties to build wealth or obtain financial freedom, this book is for you.

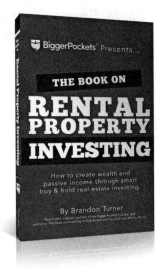

More from
BiggerPockets Publishing

The Book on Flipping Houses, Revised Edition

Written by active real estate investor and fix-and-flipper J Scott, this book contains more than 300 pages of step-by-step training, perfect for both the complete newbie and the seasoned pro looking to build a house-flipping business. Whatever your skill level, this book will teach you everything you need to know to build a profitable business and start living the life of your dreams.

The Book on Estimating Rehab Costs, Revised Edition

Learn detailed tips, tricks, and tactics to accurately budget nearly any house-flipping project from expert fix-and-flipper J Scott. Whether you are preparing to walk through your very first rehab project or you're an experienced home flipper, this handbook will be your guide to identifying renovation projects, creating a scope of work, and staying on budget to ensure a timely profit!

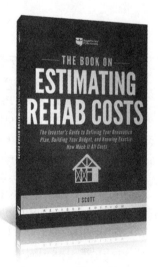

If you enjoyed this book, we hope you'll take a moment to check out some of the other great material BiggerPockets offers. BiggerPockets is the real estate investing social network, marketplace, and information hub, designed to help make you a smarter real estate investor through podcasts, books, blog posts, videos, forums, and more. Sign up today—it's free! **Visit www.BiggerPockets.com.**

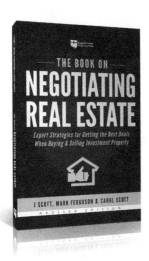

The Book on Negotiating Real Estate

When the real estate market gets hot, it's the investors who know the ins-and-outs of negotiating who will get the deal. J Scott, Mark Ferguson, and Carol Scott combine real-world experience and the science of negotiation in order to cover all aspects of the negotiation process and maximize your chances of reaching a profitable deal.

The Book on Tax Strategies for the Savvy Real Estate Investor

Taxes! Boring and irritating, right? Perhaps. But if you want to succeed in real estate, your tax strategy will play a huge role in how fast you grow. A great tax strategy can save you thousands of dollars a year. A bad strategy could land you in legal trouble. From Amanda Han's and Matthew MacFarland's *The Book on Tax Strategies for the Savvy Real Estate Investor* you'll find ways to deduct more, invest smarter, and pay far less to the IRS!

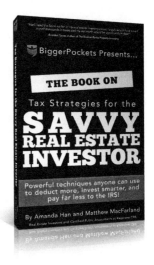

CONNECT WITH BIGGERPOCKETS

and Become Successful in Your Real Estate Business Today!

Facebook
/BiggerPockets

Instagram
@BiggerPockets

Twitter
@BiggerPockets

LinkedIn
/company/Bigger
Pockets

Website
BiggerPockets.com